EASTERN
8/16/72

W9-CKI-923

NORTHERN IRELAND: A Report on the Conflict

NORTHERN IRELAND:
A Report on the Conflict

by The London Sunday Times
Insight Team

 Random House · New York

First American Edition

Copyright © 1972 by Times Newspapers Ltd.
All rights reserved under International and Pan-American Copyright
Conventions. Published in the United States by Random House, Inc.,
New York. Originally published in Great Britain as ULSTER by
Penguin Books Ltd, Harmondsworth Middlesex, England, 1972.
ISBN: 0-394-48202-6
Library of Congress Catalog Card Number: 72-000065
Manufactured in the United States of America

Contents

THE NORTH OF IRELAND

There are nine Counties in the Province of Ulster. Six of these were partitioned in 1920 to form the area now governed by Stormont

ULSTER

DONEGAL

DERRY

Derry

ANTRIM

TYRONE

Belfast

FERMANAGH

ARMAGH

DOWN

MONAGHAN

CAVAN

CONNAUGHT

Galway

LEINSTER

Dublin

Limerick

MUNSTER

Waterford

Cork

Letterkenny

Donegal

Donegal

Ballyshannon

R. Erne

Fermanagh

Enniskillen

Clones

Cavan

Cavan

Lifford

R. Foyle

Strabane

Derry

Coleraine

Derry

Dungiven

Tyrone

Omagh

Dungannon

R. Blackwater

Armagh

Armagh

Monaghan

Monaghan

R.Bann

Toome

Antrim

Ballymena

Randalstown

Belfast

Portadown

R.Bann

Newry

Dundalk

Larne

Bangor

R. Lagan

Down

```
0   10   20   30   40   50
miles
```

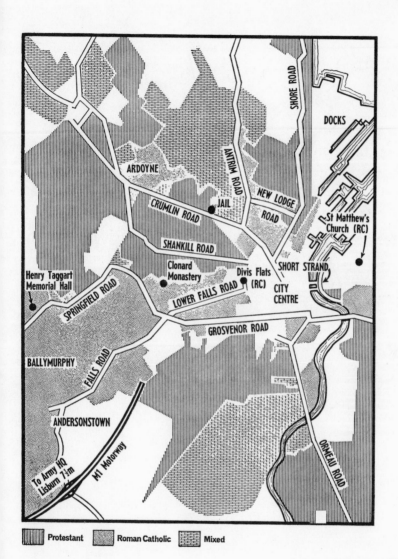

Protestant   **Roman Catholic**   **Mixed**

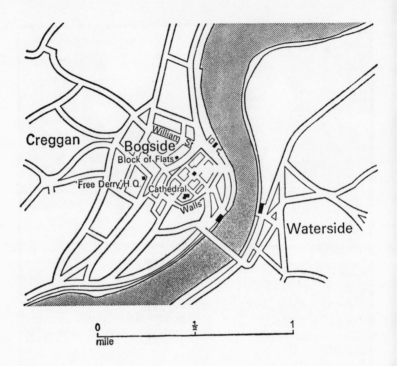

Creggan

Bogside

William St

Block of Flats

"Free Derry" H.Q.

Cathedral

Walls

Waterside

0   ½   1
mile

Foreword

This is a book of reporting. It is an attempt, by honest journalism, to get at the roots of the present tragedy in Ulster.

It is not a definitive history of Northern Ireland. It is not even a definitive history of the events the Insight team has focused upon. The Insight reporters have spent months talking to the main participants, but there remain areas of dispute, ambiguity, and ignorance. One serious problem for instance arises from the inability of the Provisional IRA leaders to agree what were their motives, plans or even resources at critical points. Another is that on the motives of men in public office at various times there are, inevitably, disputed recollections. Another is that Insight found Army records sometimes in conflict with other records and with the recollection of soldiers on the spot at the time (for instance in the 1970 Falls Road curfew). Most seriously of all, of course, the Insight team has had no access to Government papers.

But if history has to wait, Ulster cannot. Some sort of balance sheet, it seemed to us, must be drawn up, some judgements made and lessons pointed, if we are to prevent the apparently endless and cyclic repetition of old and

bloody miscalculations. Naturally there is a large element
of hindsight in an exercise like this and, if judgements are
now shown to be false, they were often at the time taken with
goodwill and prudence, and with the widest support of public
opinion. Least of all should any criticisms here of the use of
an army for police work be taken as detracting from the
soldiers' innumerable acts of individual courage and
forbearance.

Anyone who writes about Ulster inevitably invites an extreme reaction, so the circumstances of the effort must be set
out. The *Sunday Times* having, like the rest of Britain, forgotten about Ulster for a long time, began to take an interest
in 1966. We published then, during the editorship of Mr
C. D. Hamilton, an examination of discrimination entitled
'John Bull's Political Slum'. The suggestion in that article
that reform would never come without 'vigorous prodding
from Westminster' attracted deep Protestant fury. Our
interest, regrettably, tended then to follow events, but on 27
April 1969 at the end of a long analysis of the disintegrating
Civil Rights Campaign, Insight wrote:

> The monster of sectarian violence is well out of its cage. The
> issue now is no longer civil rights or even houses and jobs. The
> issue is now whether the state should exist and who should have
> the power, and how it should be defended; and this is an issue
> on which the wild men on both sides have sworn for 40 years,
> frequently in blood, that they will never back down.

In the aftermath of internment in 1971, and in the outrages which then followed, we realized that it was impossible
to report Ulster simply by reporting the latest shooting or
bombing, or allegation of ill-treatment by the military, or
the episodic twitches of political initiative. It was impossible
to judge what was happening in Ulster day to day if one
omitted a study of the origin of community conflict and the
way more recently the Catholics had been alienated.

That alienation is not, fairly, the entire story of Ulster, but it is one root of the crisis which was being overlooked in the daily focus on IRA violence. Two long articles were published on 14 and 21 November 1971, and provoked an enormous and typically extreme reaction. The newspaper was lauded for 'saving Ireland from insanity'; when in reality we could only have hoped to get a political debate started. Alternatively, the reporters were accused of 'doing the dirty work of the IRA'; when in reality they had undertaken an unpleasant task with vigour and skill. One was reminded, in the clamour for self-censorship, of H. L. Mencken's description of the kind of journalists censors would prefer: 'Reporters come in as newspaper men, trained to get the news, and eager to get it; they end as tin-horn statesmen, full of dark secrets and unable to write the truth if they tried.'

This book is a greatly expanded version of those two articles. The new material comes mainly in the sections on the origins and methods of discrimination, the growth of the Provisional IRA, the reform programme, the role of Whitehall and of successive British Governments, the aftermath of internment and the Compton report on allegations of brutality. We have tried to correct errors in the original articles and to revise judgements in the light of comments by participants. On occasion, this has proved difficult. The reason harks back to the first point of this foreword: this is a work of journalism, not of history.

If some of the criticisms that emerge are indeed informed by hindsight, we hope they may none the less have a lesson for the future; and it is in this modest hope that this book is presented.

Harold Evans

Editor, *Sunday Times*

London, January, 1972

Prelude
Full Circle

On 25 July 1953 three men backed an old van up to the hut housing the armoury of the Officers' Training Corps at Felsted public school in Essex. They cut open a rear window and from the racks inside took ninety-nine rifles, eight Bren light-machine guns, ten Sten sub-machine guns, a 2-inch light mortar, a Piat anti-tank gun and a Browning 0.3-inch machine gun. Then they drove off.

Their success was their undoing. The next morning as the van was waddling down a road in Bishop's Stortford, an observant policeman, Sergeant Halsey, noticed first that the vehicle was so overloaded that its tyres were flat. He then surmised, correctly, that its driver was lost. He finally saw that the van's rear windows were obscured by strips of paper. He stopped the vehicle to remonstrate at this contravention of the Highway Code, and to his surprise found himself the custodian of an IRA arms haul.

When in October the three occupants of the van were each sentenced to eight years' imprisonment, Mr Justice Streatfeild can hardly have imagined that he was making an unwitting contribution to the growth of what is known today in headlines throughout the world as the Provisional IRA.

11

For the leader of the raid was a happy-go-lucky thirty-one-year-old Dublin housepainter and friend of Brendan Behan named Cathal Goulding – today the Chief of Staff of the 'Official' IRA. His moonfaced accomplice was John Stephenson, a twenty-four-year-old English railway shunter and ex-RAF corporal. Under the Irish-ized version of his name, Sean Mac Stiofáin, he is today the military commander – technically, the head of their Army Council – of the 'Provisional' IRA. (The third man does not enter our story.)

Prison was a turning point for both men. Goulding, the more thoughtful, emerged from jail a potential new leader of a reformed IRA. Prison, on the contrary, transformed Stephenson into an embittered, obsessed figure – committed to the old violence.

The Felsted raid was not the first excursion in the early 1950s of an IRA re-activated after their disintegration during the war; in terms of personnel, though, it was the first of importance. The earliest raid was on an Army barracks in Derry on 5 June 1953. The last in the series of six – four of them failures – came in the early hours of 13 August 1955, when twelve men raided the depot of the Royal Electrical and Mechanical Engineers at Arborfield in Berkshire and removed five *tons* of arms. The fact that the getaway was bungled, and the police rapidly picked up three of the raiders and traced the arms to the Caledonian Road in north London, does not diminish the importance of the raid in the boost it gave to the IRA. Its leader, who was not captured, was a twenty-one-year-old trainee teacher named Rory Brady – today, as Ruairi O Bradaigh, head of the Provisional IRA's political wing.

But the Arborfield raid has now a more ironic significance. Brady led it brilliantly. One of the guards was cooking sausages when the IRA burst in; another was writing poetry. As people apparently tend to do in such situations, the poet thought the revolver pointed at him was a joke. The raiders had the trained response: the muzzle was pushed against the victim's teeth. The overpowering of the eighteen-man guard now has the greatest interest. According to an IRA man who was on the raid, the other soldiers were asleep. They were woken up in batches, and lined up against a wall – their feet some way from it, their legs spread, leaning by their fingertips. Most of them had been sleeping in their vests; their genitals were exposed. The sole pyjama-wearer was made to take off his pants. An awareness of the vulnerability of his most sensitive organs will distract a man from thoughts of escape.

As a technique of handling prisoners, it was ahead of its time. The IRA men had learned it from friends in the Irish Army. The Irish Army, in turn, had learned it from the British, whose methods with prisoners had been refined by the Korean War. Arborfield was the first occasion on which the British military saw their theoretical technique in operation; it worked.

When, sixteen years later, the report of the inquiry by Sir Edmund Compton confirmed in November 1971 the techniques of handling suspected Provisionals during interrogation – describing the spreadeagled posture, the fingertips, the awareness of physical weakness – did O Bradaigh or his colleagues remember Arborfield and reflect that, even in this, the history of Ulster had come full circle?

Chapter 1
Death of the IRA

So the story begins, as it ends, with the IRA – and the complexities of Ulster reduced to the simplicity of armed conflict. We began with the arms raids of the mid-1950s because they were the prelude to the last IRA campaign against Ulster. Formally, this dragged on from 1956 to 1962. Effectively, it was a disaster which petered out within weeks. In the wake of that, the Catholic community in the north threw up new – peaceful – leaders, new – peaceful – aspirations. For most of the 1960s it did seem as if Ulster could solve its problems quietly. Only when that hope died in 1969 was the IRA in the north reborn.

At that point, the arms raids we have just described became important once more. For the roots and structure of the *present* IRA campaign – especially the genesis of the split between the so-called 'Official' wing of the IRA and the Provisionals (definitions we shall explain later) – can be traced to those raids in the 1950s or their aftermath: the embittering effect of prison upon Stephenson, caught in the 1953 Felsted raid; the fact that Goulding, caught in the same raid, was out of circulation for most of the subsequent critical stage in the IRA's development; even the fact, useful in assessing the seriousness of the men involved, that the leader

15

of one raid is now a philosophy don in Canada, while the prime-mover of another is a lecturer in law at Dublin, and a near neighbour of the Irish Prime Minister, Jack Lynch (his wife used to baby-sit for Mrs Lynch).

The IRA campaign to which those raids were the prelude opened in earnest on 12 December 1956. About 150 men blew up targets in ten areas around the border that night: a BBC transmitter, a barracks, a Territorial Army building, a magistrates' court . . . It was an impressive opening shot. The IRA plan, known as 'Operation Harvest', was more ambitious still. It depended upon the fact that although Ulster's population is two-thirds Protestant, the province's 500,000 Catholics are not evenly distributed. Two of Ulster's six counties, Tyrone and Fermanagh, have Catholic majorities, while a third, Armagh, is almost evenly divided. Derry City is two-thirds Catholic, and Newry and the cathedral city of Armagh are also Catholic-dominated. These areas, the IRA leadership had planned, would be their strongholds. About twenty IRA 'organizers' had come up from the south, to set up local groups in these areas for sabotage and ambushes, and then to be conduits for plans and supplies from the south. The assumption, which the IRA never doubted, was that the local population would welcome them. They were mistaken.

Belfast, however, was not to be touched. The IRA commander there had been picked up by Ulster Special Branch earlier in 1956 with documents compromising much of the IRA in the city. But there was a strategic reason, too. Belfast is two-thirds Protestant, and the 114,000 Catholics huddle in enclaves set among the Protestant areas of the city – vulnerable to reprisal, almost impossible to defend. The most fragile of these ghettoes is the Short Strand-Mount Pottinger crescent cramped along the east bank of the River Lagan which divides Belfast. There, cut off by the river from retreat or reinforcement, 6,000 Catholics are hemmed in by 60,000 Protestants – an outpost of hostages, as the IRA saw them, for the conduct of Catholics in the western half of the city. Belfast, the IRA command decided in 1956, was safer left in peace. It is a judgement of great relevance to the whole of this history.

Despite the eight months of planning behind Operation Harvest, despite the promising bangs of 12 December 1956, the IRA campaign collapsed almost at once. Only days later, on 1 January 1957, an RUC (Royal Ulster Constabulary) man with a Bren gun turned an attack upon a police barracks in Fermanagh into a rout in which two of the attackers were shot dead and the remainder fled back over the border.

The Ulster Government promptly introduced internment. On 12 December 1956 the round-up of more than a hundred northern IRA men began. (By 1958, at the peak of internment, 187 were held.) The IRA had expected that. What they had not expected was the disaster which struck in the south. On 8 July 1957 the Dublin Government also introduced internment, and picked up sixty men – almost all the key figures in the IRA campaign. Internment in the south lasted for twenty months; in all, 206 men were held, the last being released on 11 March 1959. With the south hostile territory, the guerrillas lost their safe hinterland in which to train, prepare for operations, and re-group after them. More fundamental to what followed, however, were the divisions which racked the movement as a consequence of what happened in the internment camp.

Deprived of its leadership – and also of popular support – the campaign in the north foundered. One IRA assault illustrates both the bravery and the futility of the campaign. In a blinding snowstorm one night six lads rowed ten miles across Lough Foyle, on the north-west border of Ulster, to

17

plant a massive charge of gelignite in the British military camp at Ballykelly (a target chosen not because it was important but merely accessible). They were country boys from Cork and Kerry, who had never been near the border before. Their IRA training had consisted of a single instruction: 'Learn to row.' Professing a sudden and overpowering nautical urge, they had joined the Limerick Rowing Club, a posh Anglo-Irish establishment, and, to the amazement of friends more used to seeing them in bars, they had sculled furiously up and down the River Shannon.

They never got to Ballykelly. As they were about to land in their two rowing boats on the Ulster shore of Lough Foyle, flares and searchlights blazed from the camp. They prudently assumed that the attack was expected. Stumbling along in the snow, laden with gelignite, they tried to find another target – finally dumping the charge in the lee of a building which loomed so large in the storm that they reasoned it must be important. Then they set off for home, in only one rowing boat because the guard they had left on the shore had been restraining the second boat with the butt of his rifle. When he lifted it to challenge the returning warriors, the vessel promptly drifted away. It was a tight fit, and halfway back across the Lough they, predictably, lost an oar. But when it came, the massive explosion heartened them.

Back in the Republic, they tramped the hills for days, finally to be picked up by the Irish police and interned when in desperation they approached a farmhouse for food. Only then did they discover that they had demolished one of Ulster's ancient monuments, a Napoleonic Martello tower.

Most of the action was of that peculiarly stage-Irish nature – brave, amateur, comic, intermittently savage. Lord Brookeborough, the Ulster Prime Minister, aptly characterized the calibre of the campaign when he dismissed the

IRA as 'hooligans who raid this country'. A burst of activity over three days of July 1958 came after months of quiet; 1959 passed with only a couple of deaths; 1960 was almost wholly peaceful. The last man to be killed was Constable William Hunter, shot when a police patrol was ambushed at Jonesborough, Armagh, on 12 November 1961. Three months later, on 26 February 1962, the IRA called off the campaign. (It was no more than a recognition of reality: even the Ulster Government had not bothered to keep internment after April 1961.)

The *Irish Times* later summarized the campaign: 'Three hundred major incidents and several hundred minor ones, with damage estimated at several million pounds. [This is now amended to about £1.5 millions.] Six members of the Royal Ulster Constabulary were killed and nineteen wounded, according to Government sources. Eleven members of the Special Constabulary and two members of the British armed forces were wounded. According to the IRA, its own casualties were two killed in action and seven killed accidentally – most of them when bombs went off prematurely. On its own estimate, the IRA had been 'opposed by 5,000 regular British troops, 5,000 territorials, 3,000 RUC, 12,000 Specials, 1,500 specially trained commandoes, and sundry security and guard forces'. (The military presence altogether cost the British taxpayer around £10 millions.) It was, by present standards, a small-scale, homespun affair.

The reasons why the campaign failed – and the rather different reasons why the Unionist régime in Ulster believed it failed – are important to what followed. The Unionists credited their success to two factors: internment and 'the Specials', the Protestant militia known as the Ulster Special Constabulary or B Specials (so called because there were once A and C Specials too).

The role of the B Specials is a myth. We will examine later

19

the make-up and control, such as it was, of that peculiarly partisan force. But the image cherished by the Ulster Protestants of the B Special is that of a local stalwart whose grassroots knowledge of the Republicans in his area, plus of course his willingness to use the weaponry the State supplies him with, enables him to control the insurgent threat where more formal organizations, like the Royal Ulster Constabulary, fail. The truth is that the overwhelming burden of the 1956–62 campaign was borne by the RUC. The B Specials' main job was manning roadblocks – a marginal function, since the IRA tended to cross the border by unmarked tracks. 'The B Specials,' one soldier who has studied the records told us, 'were just a bloody nuisance.'

Internment was, however, an important factor, but for two reasons: one public, the other secret. The secret one was that the British Government lent to the RUC Special Branch a senior member of the Security Service, MI5. He got the files on IRA men into superlative order, so that the 1956–7 internment round-up really did net the IRA activities.

The public reason for the success was, of course, that Dublin had introduced internment – denying the IRA any escape route. But a cautious observer in Ulster might have wondered whether Dublin would ever be so obliging again. For on 11 June 1957 a man called Gerard Lawless was arrested as he was about to take ship for England and interned. Lawless objected that he was not an IRA man, which was literally true: he was one of a breakaway group. His case went to the Human Rights Commission of the Council of Europe. Lawless lost. But in the process the Commission gave a new ruling. The relevant treaty did say that a 'state of emergency' was sufficient reason for a State to violate human rights by such expedients as internment without trial. But the Commission decided that in future it had the power to pronounce on whether or not such a state of emergency did exist.

Reading this judgment in July 1961 the Ulster Government's law officers might have reflected that if, in any future campaign, the IRA had the wit to remain peaceful in the south, then the Dublin Government of the day – whatever its desire – would think very hard before introducing internment and risking a verdict of 'no justifiable emergency' in a second bout with the Human Rights Commission.

Whether this occurred to Ulster's then Minister of Home Affairs, Brian Faulkner, is debatable. All that mattered was that once more the Protestants had defeated the 'nationalist unrest', as they called the IRA campaign. It was an ironic description, for the real reason why the campaign failed was precisely the *lack* of nationalist unrest. Contrary to the IRA's own expectations, the northern Catholic population did not support the campaign. The IRA statement admitting defeat in 1962 acknowledged: 'Foremost among the factors motivating this course of action has been the attitude of the general public whose minds have deliberately been distracted from the supreme issue facing the Irish people – the unity and freedom of Ireland.' The statement was drafted by Rory Brady, leader of the 1955 Arborfield arms raid and, by 1962, IRA Chief of Staff.

Ulster, in other words, enjoyed at least the passive, tentative support of its Catholic minority. Whatever their views about the legitimacy of the Protestant Government and the injustices it visited upon them, the Catholics were not then ready to support its overthrow by violence. For the first time since its foundation, therefore, Ulster was, demonstrably, at some level a workable society.

The effect of this defeat upon the IRA was traumatic. Scapegoats for the failure of the campaign were sought; new

21

policies were sought; above all, new leaders. The excuse for much of the upheaval which followed in the movement was the course of events inside the Dublin Government's internment camp.

One of the peculiarities of the IRA is that so many of its leading members have been imprisoned or interned at critical phases of the movement's life that many of its rules, and much of its internal tensions, stem from what happened during these confinements. It is a rule, for example, that anyone 'put away' loses the IRA rank he held. Ranks 'inside' are decided by election among the detainees; the movement outside simply replaces the missing men.

When the Irish Government interned IRA leaders in July 1957 – exiling them in the traditional holding centre for IRA men, the military camp beside the Curragh racecourse, thirty miles out of Dublin – Tomas Mac Curtain, one of the three main planners of the campaign then starting in the north, was elected leader in the camp. He immediately laid down that escapes must not provoke a confrontation with the guards: previous confinements had convinced him that was pointless.

To the militants among the prisoners in the Curragh, already disgusted by the swift and humiliating failure of the campaign outside, the edict was final proof of the official leadership's cowardice. The first to escape were Rory Brady and another young teacher, David O'Connell – today the Adjutant-General of the Provisionals. But the real challenge to Mac Curtain's authority came when a group of militants staged a flamboyant mass escape, several of them being wounded in the attempt by gunfire from the guards. When the IRA campaign ended in 1962, the continuing row over the militants' 'mutiny' spread through the whole movement.

The petty dispute was the symbol of deeper strains. Even

22

before the 1956 campaign, there had been feuding within the IRA roughly along northern versus southern factional lines – the northerners being the more militant. Now, the movement was demoralized not merely by ignominious defeat but by the popular rejection which, more accurately than the Unionists, some of them discerned as its cause. But the IRA leadership drew conflicting conclusions about this. Some, like Rory Brady, thought merely that the population had deserted a losing cause; *next* time, they said, a better organized campaign would succeed. Others were well represented by John Stephenson: he had come out of prison a stubborn, embittered, obsessed man – having painfully learned fluent Irish in jail. Could he abandon his new-found cause now?

Personal tensions inevitably played a part, notably between Cathal Goulding and Rory Brady. Goulding was, with Stephenson, newly released from eight years in an English prison after the failure of the 1953 Felsted arms raid. Unlike Brady, the Chief of Staff, he bore no responsibility for the 1956–62 debacle. In 1963 the dispute ended in violence: the leader of Sinn Fein, the political wing of the IRA, was found shot in his garden in circumstances still unexplained. When the turmoil was over, the IRA had a new leadership: Goulding had replaced Brady as Chief of Staff, Tomas Mac Giolla was the new president of Sinn Fein, and a Marxist computer scientist called Roy Johnston had become the movement's 'education officer cum political commissar', a Dublin accountant called it.

Goulding is a remarkable man. He comes from a traditional Republican family and has a violent history: he was involved in his first IRA arms raid, in Dublin, at fifteen; and he has served a total of fifteen years in jail. Yet in a movement that treats its history – even its mistakes – with archaeological reverence, Goulding began to guide the IRA towards a new approach, more rational than the crude and

23

now discredited nationalism which had fuelled it for so long.
The Goulding–Mac Giolla–Johnston strategy was Marxism,
of a modish kind.

The analysis of Ulster which the new IRA began to produce was straightforward: the root of the problem was the
colonial relationship of Ulster to Britain. The economic
links between the ruling Unionists and the imperial power
were central. The religious issue was a device which – by
dividing the Protestant working man from his natural ally,
the Catholic worker – operated to the benefit of the ruling
élite. The remedy was to bring this vision home to the Ulster
masses by non-sectarian, non-violent means. What it boiled
down to, as one historian of the movement points out, was
that the 'physical force' party inside the IRA had lost.

From 1964 onwards, the IRA hierarchy began in the
north to concentrate upon political education, and in the
south upon such headline-catching operations as a 'fish-in', a
'housing action campaign', trade-union activism, and even –
a sentimental touch – a lobbying operation to preserve the
Georgian architecture of Dublin.

What appalled Goulding, a sensitive man, was the damage
which the fossilized nature of the movement was doing to
the young men in it. 'For them,' he told us later, 'the fight
had become an end in itself. They were not planning to
achieve the freedom of Ireland. They simply wanted to *fight*
for it.' To assuage these and other dissidents, Goulding tried
desperately to claim that his new IRA strategy was a legacy
of James Connolly, the Socialist philosopher so badly
wounded at the Dublin Post Office in the Easter 1916 uprising that the British firing squad had later to execute him
tied to a chair. Even this summary evocation of the hal-
lowed dead did not avail Goulding.

As the IRA leadership moved steadily leftwards through
the early 1960s, away from their simple historic dedication

to a thirty-two-county Republic achieved through violence, many old-time IRA men were bewildered by the change, and in Belfast the bewilderment was most acute. The IRA in that city are unique – as the planners of the 1956–62 campaign had recognized. For the *raison d'etre* of the movement there has always been primarily the defence of the Catholic ghettoes against armed attack by militant Protestants. (This was not fantasy: it happened in 1920 and 1935.) The ending of the partition in Ireland – however supreme it ranked in the IRA theology – has come second in Belfast. Now, under the dual impact of Goulding's new policies in Dublin, and the slow unwinding in the north of at least some of the old sectarian tensions, the old-style Belfast Republicans felt redundant. (They also felt resentful: over their heads, the new Dublin leadership gave power in Belfast to a couple of thrusting graduates of Trinity College, Dublin.)

The surprising thing, in a sense, is that so many old IRA men – like those in the Lower Falls ghetto in central Belfast – were willing to follow Dublin on its optimistically non-violent path towards a hazy Socialist revolution.

Gradually, the IRA in Belfast eroded. The process quickened in 1964 when the commander in the city, Billy McKee, was 'encouraged' by Dublin to give up the job – nominally after a dispute over the flourishing of the Republican tricolour on one occasion. After that, the old hands just drifted away. Their names read now like a roll-call of Provisionals: Joe Cahill (until recently the Provo leader in Belfast), Seamus Twomey (current Provo leader in the city), Billy Kelly (ex-commander of the Provos' Third Battalion in Belfast, now in the south). McKee himself was the Provos' first commander in Belfast; he is now in jail. A few old hands did stay in the movement: Sean MacNally (now Provo Quartermaster-General in Belfast); Francis Card (first

Provo propaganda chief, now jailed); Leo Martin (still at large). But they were isolated, and unhappy.

The younger political spirits, with slightly patronizing respect, called them 'the forties men', because they had been active in the IRA during the war, but interned so swiftly and successfully in 1956 that few had played any part then. Still, those, like Cahill, who dropped out in the sixties did not lose their nationalist faith. Many were supporters of the National Graves Association, which looks after the plot outside Belfast where most of the city's Republican dead are reputedly buried. Through Martin and MacNally, still in the movement, they also followed what was happening in the new-look IRA. And occasionally they met and reminisced about the old days.

Cahill was a foreman on a building site – he learned the trade in jail. Card, McKee and others were also in the building trade. Twomey became manager of a warehouse. The circulation of the *United Irishman*, (the newspaper of Sinn Fein, the IRA political wing) slumped from close on 100,000 in north and south to a mere 14,000. 'In August 1967,' Goulding recalls, 'we called a meeting of local leadership throughout the country to assess the strength of the movement. We discovered that we had no movement.' The IRA of legend – the trench-coats, the Thompson guns, the shots in the night – was virtually extinct.

Chapter 2
The State Revealed

The beginning of the subsequent story of Ulster is a fatal error by the ruling Protestants. It was to mistake the Civil Rights movement of the sixties for an attack on the State of Ulster itself. Thus, by choice of the ruling élite, the energy of the reformist impulse has been made to shake the foundations of society.

Every previous challenge to the authority of the rulers of Ulster had indeed involved an attack on the existence of their State. But by the mid-1960s Ulster was secure. As we have described – and as the Ulster Government was told at the time by its own police – the IRA no longer posed a violent threat: the Catholics of Ulster had discarded them. Surely now the time was ripe to begin dismantling the apparatus of total Protestant supremacy.

For Ulster was entering in the early sixties a period of at least partial social, economic and educational modernization. As this was procured more by virtue of the British economic connection than by any decision of the Unionist élite, though, it was perhaps not surprising that they ignored its most important consequence. (The Unionist Party had, for instance, bitterly opposed the introduction of the National Health Service in 1948.) It was left to Lord

Cameron, the Scottish judge who in 1969 was appointed through the offices of the Labour Government to inquire into the Ulster disturbances, to sum up the effects of this social advance: 'A much larger Catholic middle class has emerged, which is less ready to acquiesce in the acceptance of a situation of assumed (or established) inferiority and discrimination . . .' The weapons of this new class were not guns, but ones Protestant Ulster was perhaps less equipped to deal with.

This new Catholic middle class was close enough to its working-class origins – from which it had risen largely through the effects of the 1944 Butler Education Act – to see itself as a spokesman for working-class grievances. It contained able men, justly ambitious for office; naturally it developed a measure of theoretical radicalism among its student population. But the complaints it articulated in the mid sixties were moderate by any sensible standards. Again, in the words of the Cameron Report in September 1969:

We were impressed by the number of well-educated and responsible people who were or are in . . . the Civil Rights movement, and by the depth and extent of the investigations which they have made . . . to produce evidence to vouch their grievances and support their claims for remedy.

In a remarkable interview by a *Guardian* writer, Terry Coleman, published on 26 November 1971, Lord Brookeborough, Prime Minister of Ulster from 1943 to 1963, was asked about Protestant discrimination against Catholics in Ulster's second city, Derry. '"Well, that might be," he said, "I don't know about that one. I don't know the answer to that. I believe it came somewhere near the truth, but I never came up against it." ' Coleman persisted: 'But when he was Prime Minister he really *must* have known? – "No. I say, I never came up against it. I was told this was so. I never came up against it." '

County Fermanagh, the most south-westerly of Northern Ireland's six counties, has for many years had almost exactly equal numbers of Protestants and Catholics among its adult population. Yet in the late sixties the only local authority there, Fermanagh County Council – chaired for fifteen years by Lord Brookeborough till he became Prime Minister, and later by his son Captain John Brooke from 1961 on – had thirty-five Unionists, that is to say Protestants, among its members and only seventeen non-Unionists. The County Council itself employed 370 people: 332 of the posts, including all the top ones, were filled by Protestants. On the County Education Authority the most coveted jobs were the ones for school bus drivers, because of the long rests and long holidays. Of about seventy-five school bus drivers in Fermanagh, all but seven were Protestant.

It is fair to say that this extraordinary imbalance – symbolic of the whole of Ulster society – has genuinely complex roots. When the State was established in 1920, Catholics deliberately opted out of the system; even when they were offered State appointments they mostly refused them: teachers in State schools even went on strike for months. The entire mechanism of the State, therefore, was erected without the participation of the Catholic community. Imbalance was built into the system.

The charge against successive Unionist Governments is that, faced with this deeply divided community, they took steps which far from ameliorating the problem actually exacerbated it. They did this deliberately. While the founder of Ulster, Lord Carson, was genuinely non-sectarian, the inheritors of his legacy were avowedly anti-Catholic. In March 1925, the then Minister of Agriculture, Sir Edward Archdale, charged in Parliament with employing Catholics in his ministry, defended himself: 'I have 109 officials and so far as I know, four of them are Roman Catholics, three of whom were civil servants turned over to me, whom I had to take on when we began.'

On 12 July 1933 John Andrews, then Minister for Labour and later Prime Minister, said: 'Another allegation which is made against the Government which is untrue is that of the thirty-one porters at Stormont (the Ulster Parliament building) twenty-eight are Roman Catholic. I have investigated the matter and I have found that there are thirty Protestants and only one Roman Catholic – there only temporarily.'

Nor are such expressions unduly antique. At an Orange gathering on 17 July 1954, a rising young MP called Brian Faulkner said: 'There is no reason why Orangemen individually and collectively should not interest themselves in the economic welfare of the community. I mean by that statement, we should be anxious to find employment for our brethren.' Just in case the message had failed to get across, Faulkner proclaimed a year later: 'The Government must ask themselves whether it were safe to employ in Government service people who openly advocated treason.'

That was the explanation which Protestants offered themselves for the whole remarkable arrangement: Catholics were enemies of the State. If their higher birth-rate were not countered by these frank persuasions to emigrate, they would become a majority throughout the province and promptly vote it into the priest-ridden Catholic Republic to the south. Catholic bishops fed this fear by withholding the repeated protestations of loyalty which Protestants thought proper, and by insisting on a separate system of education for Catholic children.

And there are real grounds for Protestant anxiety at any prospect of incorporation into a united Ireland. The pervasive influence of the Roman Catholic church in political and social life there is underlined by Article 44 of Ireland's

30

1937 constitution, recognizing its 'special position'. (This has never been invoked in law – indeed, is believed to have no legal standing. Eamon de Valera, Prime Minister at the time, wrote it in to appease Church authorities who had been suspicious of him since his days as an extreme Republican during the Civil War of 1922–4.)

But Protestants are also offended by the Irish Republic's prohibition on divorce and the sale of contraceptives. And their fear of Church interference in political affairs is comprehensible in view of several postwar Southern Irish *causes célèbres*: the 1951 Mother and Child Scheme, for instance, when a plan for maternity care was thrown out at the Church's behest. Another controversy rages in the south at this moment over 'community schools': the Irish Government has virtually handed over control of much secondary education to the Church.

But active Protestant contempt for the Catholics in *Northern* Ireland goes back beyond any of the reasons currently advanced, beyond even the middle of the nineteenth century, when Macaulay – the historian of the Protestant ideal – found in the Ulster Protestants 'the faults which are ordinarily found in dominant castes and dominant sects'.

From his imperial service in India, Macaulay had plucked the right word: caste. It was an anxious sense of superiority which had its origins at the start of the seventeenth century, when Ulster – the last province of Catholic Ireland to be subdued by the newly-Protestant English crown – was settled by James I with spikily Protestant colonists, mainly Presbyterians from the Scottish borders. At the end of the same century this local Protestant hegemony was confirmed when James II, the only Catholic monarch that England has had since Mary Tudor, failed in a brief attempt to reinstate Catholic dominance. His army besieged Londonderry with-

31

Ulster

out success, and in 1690 he was finally defeated by William
of Orange at the Battle of the Boyne. Hence the magic of
those names for Protestants still. The fact that the Pope was
King Billy's ally in 1690 is not allowed to cloud that heroic
simplicity.

There is one instance of common cause in Ulster's history: at the end of the eighteenth century, Presbyterians and
Catholics – impartially oppressed by the Anglican land-
owners – joined together in a self-consciously non-sectarian
organization. The United Irishmen, to stage the abortive
1798 Rebellion under Wolfe Tone.

But mainly under the aegis of a newly formed Protestant
supremacist brotherhood called the Orange Order, this solidarity was broken. As Ulster drifted apart from the rest of
Ireland, so within Ulster the polarization of the two communities continued apace. Ulster's separateness from the
rest of Ireland was accentuated during the nineteenth century. The linen trade delivered the province from the worst
hardships of the mid-century potato famine; ship-building,
for the needs of the empire, made Belfast an industrial city
in an agricultural island – and laid out its acres of mean
streets for the shipyard workers.

When rising nationalism threatened a merger between the
two separated parts of Ireland, the Protestant Ulsterman's
answer, therefore, was Unionism: continued union with
Britain to forestall union with the Catholic south. It was not
a breach of this principle that Northern Ireland was
equipped in 1921 with a parliament of its own, distinct from
Westminster – 'a phoney wee parliament', as one of its present members once described it. The scheme was agreed
with Lloyd George, after years of painful argument, as a
means of letting the south go free without pulling the north
along with it. The south became a free state within the Commonwealth in 1922 and a republic in 1948.

32

And while the new parliament in the north, housed in vice-regal splendour at Stormont on the outskirts of Belfast, had initially little more formal power than a county council, the Protestants had so drawn the border of Ulster that they had a comfortable two-to-one majority over the Catholics inside it – and control of their own police and their own judiciary.

Those were the two great instruments of the Protestant supremacy: the gerrymander (the manipulation of boundaries so as to make sure that at any electoral level the Unionist cause comes out on top) and the control of law and order. Catholics tend to call it 'law and Orange Order', because the Orange Order in 1921 supplied most of the membership of the new Royal Ulster Constabulary (despite an early attempt to make a third of the force Catholic). It also supplied nearly all the membership of a part-time force, the B Specials. The two have been, in effect, the military arm of the Unionist party. Both forces carried arms, and had very little compunction about using them. The animating spirit of the B Specials was never conveyed better than by one of their own historians, Wallace Clark, recounting the words with which an early commander rallied his recruits at Magherafelt: 'I want men,' he cried, 'and the younger and wilder the better.' Nearly 300 people died violently in the first two years of the new state's existence.

Protestant law and order is further strengthened by a remarkable piece of legislation, the Civil Authorities (Special Powers) Act (Northern Ireland), 1922. It was annually renewed until 1933, when Stormont judged it more convenient to make it permanent. This is the measure for which the United Kingdom still has to apologize on behalf of Stormont by entering what is called a derogation from the obligations imposed by the European Convention for the Protection of Human Rights and Fundamental Freedoms. It permits indefinite internment without trial. It permits the authorities to suspend at will any and all of the basic liberties, from habeas corpus to the freedom of the press: they can arrest on suspicion, search people and buildings without warrant, restrict movement, reverse the onus of proof, and dispense if they wish with the holding of inquests on 'any dead bodies found in Northern Ireland'. (Until 1968, the Act also allowed punishment by whipping for a number of lesser offences concerned with explosives, firearms, arson and making menacing demands.) The application of these draconian powers is subject to fewer safeguards than the Emergency Powers Act which the British Parliament passed in 1939.

Nor has there been much risk of judicial pusillanimity in enforcing the Act. The first Lord Chief Justice of Ulster was a Catholic; thereafter the bench has been increasingly packed with Protestants. By 1970, out of seven judges of the High Court, three were former Unionist MPs at Stormont; a fourth was the son of a Unionist minister. The intimidation of juries is a weapon which both sides have tried to use; but control of the processes of law enforcement has made it a good deal more available to Protestants.

As the judges, so – until the late sixties – the boundary commissioners: at their Loyal Orange Lodges they quickly learned what was expected of them. The technique of the gerrymander is to draw constituency or ward boundaries in such a way that you spread your own support as thin as you dare over as many seats as possible, while you crowd your opponents' support into as few seats as possible. It was steadily applied in Ulster. That two-to-one Unionist majority on Fermanagh County Council was paralleled in the county's representation among the fifty MPs at Stormont: constituency boundaries were so drawn as to produce two narrowly held seats for the Unionists (Enniskillen and Lisnaskea) and one massively held one for the non-Unionists (South Fermanagh).

But the deftest, most dazzling gerrymander was the rigging of the Londonderry Borough Council. (The city's old name is Derry. The prefix was added by Protestant merchant colonists from the City of London in the early seventeenth century. Catholics have not accepted it yet.) In 1966 the city itself had 14,325 Catholic voters to 9,235 Protestant. But by corralling all the Catholics of the Bogside area into one huge Catholic ward, and contriving one small Protestant ward with the same number of councillors and one tiny one besides, it was found possible to produce a body with eight councillors on the Catholic side and twelve on the Protestant side.

Derry was one of a pattern. Dungannon, County Tyrone, with a population of 7,500, fifty-three per cent of which is Catholic, had in 1966 fourteen Protestants and seven Catholics on its council. Kilkeel, population 3,000, sixty per cent Catholic, has returned a Protestant dominated council ever since 1937 . . .

In case all this should not be enough, the Unionists had yet another device in service. The local government franchise was stacked in their favour. Businessmen – mainly Protestant – had extra votes; many of the Catholic poor had none. The business vote was abolished in Britain in 1948; in Northern Ireland, in the 1960s, limited companies were entitled to nominate up to six extra voters: these were a good deal more likely to be Protestant than Catholic. Further, 'resident and general occupiers' had the local government vote in the ordinary way; but sub-tenants, lodgers, servants, and children over twenty-one living at home did not. About 250,000 adults were thus disenfranchised for local government elections. The great bulk of them were Catholics.

To ordinary people – the working-class Catholics, say –

these things mattered for two main reasons: employment and housing. The expansion of local council activity after the Second World War made town halls and council offices a supplier of both. Employment was perhaps the less important. Tyrone County Council and Armagh Urban District Council, for example, followed the Fermanagh pattern of employment. So did Derry: there, in 1966, the heads of all City Council departments were Protestant. Of 177 salaried employees, 145 – earning £124,424 – were Protestant, and only thirty-two – earning £20,420 – were Catholic.

But the big employers of labour were privately run companies, and although Catholics regularly suspected anti-Catholic prejudice among foremen or personnel managers, it is a hard thing to prove. All that can be recorded is that of 10,000 workers in the Belfast shipyard – the biggest single source of employment in the city – just 400 are Catholic.

But, as well as their role as employers, local councils are also big providers of housing; and housing is crucial. There are several ways in which Protestant councils have discriminated against Catholics. One has been to put Protestants in better houses than Catholics, but charge the same rents. In Dungannon, for an identical rent, you got forty-two square feet of space less on the mainly Catholic Ballygawley Road estate than you got on the exclusively Protestant Cunningham's Lane estate. Another way has simply been to house more Protestants than Catholics. Of 1,589 houses built by Fermanagh County Council between the end of the Second World War and 1969, 1,021 went to Protestant families.

A third way – all three could be combined of course – was to refuse to house Catholics except in areas where other Catholics already lived. If there was no room, too bad. Derry before 1969 actually reduced its housing programme rather than let Catholics spill over the boundary of the

36

Catholic South Ward. Omagh and Dungannon were other councils which practised the system. It had an added beauty: it strengthened existing electoral arrangements; no Protestant wards were contaminated with Catholics: the whole system could continue as before. There seemed no reason why it should ever come to an end.

Arguably, the IRA itself bears some responsibility for the Unionists' unwillingness in the early 1960s to contemplate reforms in this ferocious mechanism of power. As one historian says:

> The main effect of the [IRA's] unsuccessful campaign [of 1956–62] was to strengthen Unionism by renewing, at a time when it might have begun to fade, the Ulster Protestant sense of being an embattled community, under siege from the forces of evil.

But whether, even with peace, this siege mentality would have abated to any politically significant degree must be doubtful.

For example, one controversy which mildly agitated Ulster at the start of the sixties was the suggestion that Catholics might be admitted to the Unionist party, and thus share some part of its monopoly of power. In the nature of things, they would hardly have been radical Catholics. At the first suggestion, however, Sir George Clark – today chairman of the Unionist party's central machinery of control, its Standing Committee – brought out the Reformation brimstone.

> I would draw your attention [he said] to the words 'civil and religious liberty'. This liberty we know is the liberty of the Protestant religion ... it is difficult to see how a Roman Catholic, with the vast difference in our religious outlook, could be either acceptable within the Unionist Party as a member or bring himself unconditionally to support its ideals. Furthermore to this, an Orangeman is pledged to resist by all lawful means the Ascendancy of the Church of Rome ...

37

The suggestion was knocked finally on the head by the Prime Minister, Lord Brookeborough – author of the dictum that 'there is only room for one political party in Ulster'. Those who were talking of admitting Catholics to that one party, he said, were 'charging against windmills and beating their heads against a wall on an issue which did not arise and probably will not arise'.

But there was one Unionist who did finally come to admit the need for reform, and publicly at that: Terence O'Neill, who succeeded Lord Brookeborough as Prime Minister in 1963. O'Neill was an Ulster aristocrat, descended from one of the ruling families among the seventeenth-century settlers, but with a less blinkered world view than some of his fellows. At the end of the Second World War he had tried to get a Westminster seat before he went into Stormont politics; and seven years at the Stormont Ministry of Finance between 1956 and 1963 had given him a useful insight into the realities of Northern Ireland's economic dependence on Westminster.

In Northern Ireland's terms he was, almost from the start of his premiership, an innovator; he aimed to create a political climate in which Catholics could give the constitution not just sullen acceptance but active support. Most of them found his sentiments worthy, even if patronizing; his way of urging Protestants to treat them better was to say blandly: 'If a Roman Catholic is jobless, and lives in the most ghastly hovel, he will rear eighteen children on National Assistance.'

But the wire mesh on the windows of his handsome pink-washed house in County Antrim was not there to keep out missiles from Catholics. O'Neill was an increasingly reluctant Orangeman and a startlingly maladroit party manager. He finally forfeited the trust of his Protestant followers on the morning in January 1965 when Sean Lemass, Prime

Minister of the Irish Republic and living symbol of the threat from the south, drove unannounced through the gates of Stormont. The visit had been secretly arranged. O'Neill knew that increased contact with the south had to come, just as Catholic emancipation had to come; but he could not persuade his party to agree. Their attitude is well summarized by a typical confrontation which occurred at a conference in London in 1965. Charles Brett, a Belfast lawyer (and a Protestant), called for 'immediate legislation to deal with discrimination in employment and housing'. John Taylor (now a Minister in the Faulkner Government) immediately repudiated the necessity for any such reforms. Religious discrimination, he declared, was being used as a 'political stratagem' by the Republicans.

O'Neill's inability to translate his desires into actual and concrete reform increased Catholic frustration. Powerful currents began to run through the community.

Chapter 3
Reform into Violence

Eamonn McCann, one of the few Socialist revolutionaries to have survived the sectarian passions of Ulster politics, was once asked by an English reporter of revolutionary sympathies what he was doing involving himself in a lot of merely 'reformist' demands like one-man-one-job and one-family-one-house. He replied: 'Because the transformation ... necessary to implement these reforms is a revolution.' It was the Protestant masters of Ulster who decided that it should be so.

The history of the reform movement in Ulster in the middle sixties is simply stated. At Ulster Cabinet level the reformers were labelled wholesale as Republicans and subversives. At unofficial levels, Protestants used violence against Civil Rights demonstrators with a confidence which plainly assumed that the State could not, or would not, seriously inhibit them. Underlying the scenes of violence of the past year is an earlier image: that of the Rev. Ian Paisley with his blackthorn stick, waiting in the streets of Armagh through the small hours of a November night in 1968 – while Protestants gathered to meet a Civil Rights march with billhooks, clubs, scythes and guns.

It did not begin like that. The most succinct summary of

how the reform programme did start comes in the study of Ulster *Governing without Consensus* by Richard Rose, professor of politics at Strathclyde University.

As is often the case, action was sparked by a particular case in a single locality – the housing of Catholics in Dungannon ... In 1963 Mrs Patricia McCluskey, wife of a doctor in the town, was incensed by the unwillingness of the Protestant-dominated council to move Catholics from very overcrowded housing to a group of empty postwar utility homes far superior to their existing accommodation. She organized a Homeless Citizens League in the town, and, after protests at Stormont as well as a direct action 'squat in', the Catholics were granted the tenancies they desired.

In January 1964, she and her husband, Dr Con McCluskey, founded the Campaign for Social Justice to collect and publicize information about cases of injustice in Northern Ireland.

The Campaign was intended to remain independent of party politics, but not to refuse cooperation with individual politicians with common interests. The other founders of the group were professional people relatively free from electoral ambitions and economic pressures. Its main effort was the preparation and distribution of leaflets and pamphlets attacking discrimination against Catholics in Northern Ireland. Recourse to the duplicating machine and the post made it unostentatious within Ulster. By the same token, it gave the McCluskeys access to a wide audience in Britain ...

But the violence endemic in the Protestant supremacy could not be contained by duplicating machines. The first challenge to O'Neill came not from the Republicans, nor even from pacific Catholics like the McCluskeys, but from one of its own nominal supporters, Ian Paisley.

Paisley became politically active in 1964 when he played a leading part in stirring up public agitation, during the election campaign, over the 'tricolour incident' – which, as we have already narrated, led to the deposing of Billy McKee as

41

leader of the IRA in Belfast. This was not Paisley's first appearance on the Ulster scene, though his reputation was still as a turbulent priest rather than as a formidable politician. His stock in trade was the public excoriation of Catholics. As a dissident Presbyterian preacher he had first come to the front in Belfast in 1956 when he claimed to have saved a fifteen-year-old Catholic girl from being mewed up in a nunnery against her will. Three years later, at a horse fair in his home town of Ballymena, he threw a bible at the head of a visiting ecumenical Methodist, Donald (now Lord) Soper.

Paisley's first political challenge came in 1965 when he accused O'Neill of betraying Unionism by entertaining at Stormont a 'Fenian Papist murderer' – a reference to the mild-mannered Irish Prime Minister, Sean Lemass, which astonished even many Unionists. Religion was Paisley's weapon.

As the religious climate in the world outside softened through the sixties, Paisley lambasted Protestant clerics who had ecumenical intercourse with the scarlet whore of Rome. He went to Rome himself in 1966 to protest against Archbishop Ramsey's visit to the Pope; a group who got in his way were later described as 'blaspheming, cursing, spitting, Roman scum'.

The unsolved question about Paisley was to what extent his interests were religious and to what extent political. His church (the Free Presbyterians) was his own foundation, and his doctorate was from Bob Jones University at Greenville, South Carolina. Yet he was no theological illiterate. His sermons were publishable, and regularly published. Indeed, with his vibrant voice, mountainous physique and computer-like command of scriptural reference, he could put on one of the most impressive homiletic turns in the kingdom. The massive brick church then being built for him on the Ravenhill Road in east Belfast was a monument to Paisley's drawing power in the pulpit.

For all that, his tone was steadily more political. 'O'Neill must go' was becoming one of his favourite texts. In his forays outside Northern Ireland, particularly to the United States, he harped much more on the dangers of Socialism than of Catholicism. The fact seemed to be that his aim was power, and his instrument was an adaptable eloquence. He knew how to talk to the Protestant working classes, just as – when he later became a member of the Westminster House of Commons – he showed that he knew how to talk to the Protestant ruling classes. And what the Protestant working classes in Belfast wanted to hear in 1966 was that uppity Catholics were to be kept down.

The religious and political violence welled to the surface in June 1966. On 6 June Paisley led a demonstration in Belfast. Its purpose was to protest at the 'Rome-ward trend' of the General Assembly of the Presbyterian Church. More important, however, was the fact that its route wound through Cromac Square. Since 1935, a year of terrible communal fighting, Cromac Square – which lies in a central Catholic area of Belfast just west of the river – had been territory forbidden to any Orange or 'loyalist' procession. To the Catholics, therefore, the decision of O'Neill's Minister of Home Affairs, Brian McConnell, to allow the procession was evidence of how worried O'Neill was by the rising tide of Orange feeling. (Their perception was correct. At his first meeting in May 1965 with the new Labour Prime Minister, Harold Wilson, O'Neill remarked his Special Branch had told him that while he could walk through the Catholic Falls Road area of Belfast without an escort, even with a full bodyguard they could give him no guarantee of security in the extremist Protestant areas.)

A riot followed in Cromac Square, but there were no

43

serious casualties. The march reached its objective, and Paisley's followers shrieked abuse at the Governor of Northern Ireland, Lord Erskine, and his wife.

Two weeks later, the darker underbelly of Ulster Protestant feeling was revealed. 'There is no evidence,' O'Neill said in Stormont on 23 June, 'that the militant Protestant organizations are contemplating the use of violence.' At 2 a.m. on the morning of 27 June a gang shot dead an eighteen-year-old Catholic barman and wounded his two companions as they were leaving the pub where he worked in Malvern Street, in central Belfast. Three men were later arrested. Their target had in fact been Leo Martin, one of the old-time IRA men still, as we have said, reluctantly in the movement; in his absence, the three shot the first targets to hand.

At their subsequent trial for murder in October one of them related, in detail, his involvement with a violent extremist Protestant group called the Ulster Volunteer Force. What he revealed was, to quote a subsequent Insight article, 'a nightmare world of casual violence, organized by trigger-happy hoodlums'. O'Neill, banning the UVF, called it 'a sordid conspiracy of criminals against an unprotected people'. The Orange Order evidently did not agree. All three, sentenced to life imprisonment, were members of the Prince Albert Loyal Orange Lodge No. 1892. On 12 July 1967, when in the course of its annual parade the lodge passed the gates of Crumlin Road jail in Belfast where the murderers were housed, the parade paused – to pay homage to the trio inside.

It was against this background that the middle-class Catholics took what was to prove a decisive step. They founded in 1967 the Northern Ireland Civil Rights Association. Almost unintentionally, they had discovered a means of tapping the growing Catholic resentment. The NICRA was modelled on the National Council for Civil Liberties in England, and for its first year of existence it behaved like its predecessor, the McCluskeys' Campaign for Social Justice, in dealing with individual complaints.

But in June 1968 a Catholic family was evicted from a council house in which they had been squatting at Caledon, a village of the Dungannon Rural District – home of the McCluskeys. On 13 June, a nineteen-year-old unmarried Protestant named Emily Beattie, secretary to a Unionist politician, was moved into the house. The case, which seemed a particularly gross one, was brilliantly publicized by Austin Currie, the local Nationalist (i.e. Catholic) member of the tiny opposition party at Stormont.

Currie suggested that the Civil Rights Association should stage a march over the four miles between the neighbouring towns of Coalisland and Dungannon, to protest against the inequities of local housing policy. With some reluctance, the CRA agreed, and it was announced for 24 August.

The immediate response from hard-line Unionists was that there would be violence if the march entered Market Square, Dungannon. Later, Lord Cameron inferred from their evidence that prominent local Unionists would have countenanced the organization of counter-demonstrations likely to lead to violence.

In the event, the march was a huge success – especially because it halted peacefully at a police barrier some distance away from Market Square. And to the astonishment of the organizers, 4,000 people turned up – including some radical students from Queen's University, Belfast – to hear Currie and a battery of speakers. The police, in the words of Miss Bernadette Devlin, were very good-natured.

'There was a hope among many participants that something new was taking place in Northern Ireland, in that here was a non-violent demonstration by people of many

differing political antecedents ... united on a common platform of reform.' The words are those not of a marcher, but
of Lord Cameron. One of the marchers, Mrs Betty Sinclair –
a veteran Communist, and secretary of the Belfast Trades
Council, who had played a big part in setting up NICRA –
put her feelings more directly: 'We had been looking for a
spark for years. At Dungannon we realized that we had
found it.' The meeting closed with the marchers singing,
under Mrs Sinclair's direction, 'We shall overcome.'

It took only one more demonstration – in Londonderry
on 5 October 1968 – to turn Civil Rights into a mass movement. And it was a mass movement which, according to the
well-publicized views of the then Minister of Home Affairs,
William Craig, was under the control of the Irish Republican Army.

Craig – 'that terrible plum pudding of a man', as one English Tory MP later described him to us – is an erect, busy,
choleric solicitor, Ulster educated, who had in fact by 1968
been in the Stormont Parliament for eight years and in the
Home Affairs ministry for two. A certain charm in personal
dealings, and a quiet effectiveness on public platforms, had
already begun to breed in him his sense that he was Ulster's
man of destiny; and if he was at first in doubt of the direction to ride off in, the climate of Protestant opinion increasingly showed him the way. So did his Larne constituents. In
Unionist politics, readoption at election times is not automatic; even sitting MPs have to bid for it, and in most divisions the only currency worth bidding in is Protestant
intransigence.

So Craig had for some time been more and more denunci-
atory of any concessions to Catholics at all. 'When you have
a Roman Catholic majority,' he said, 'you have a lesser standard of democracy': rule by the people was not much of an
idea if they were the wrong people. As for the Civil Rights

movement, he dismissed it as 'bogus and made up of people who see in unrest a chance to renew a campaign of violence'.

'We have investigated this matter with particular care,' wrote the Cameron Commission later; '... while there is evidence that members of the IRA are active in the organization, there is no sign that they are in any sense dominant or in a position to control or direct policy of the Civil Rights Association.'

The situation was admittedly subtle. The foundation of the Civil Rights Association took place at a public meeting in Belfast on 1 February 1967. But NICRA's real birthplace was a secret meeting six months earlier, at Maghera in August 1966, which Cathal Goulding, the Chief of Staff of the IRA, attended. Goulding's reaction to the plans for the movement was enthusiastic; the IRA's theoretician at that time, the Marxist Roy Johnston, was also keen to establish a Civil Rights movement in the north.

But Johnston wanted it to be controlled by the IRA. And on this point Cameron's judgement – that the IRA was active in the CRA, but not in control – is beyond serious dispute. The Maghera meeting, for instance, was attended by a couple of MPs who were anything but IRA men, and by scores of middle-class Catholics like the McCluskeys who, in a sense, posed a far stronger challenge to the IRA than did the Unionists – just as, in Britain, it is the Labour party and not the Conservatives who have drawn the teeth of the Communists.

Craig's accusations, therefore, had some validity. But they ignored every substantive point. First, not all Republicans are gunmen: the term can cover an IRA gelignite bomber or theoretical adherents of the Wolfe Tone Society and James Connolly Clubs. Secondly, Republicanism is one of the major streams in Irish political history: almost any

47

successful broad-based movement would take in people who
had been part of it. Indeed, an intelligent conservative perception would be to see that no moderate movement could
make any progress without beginning to take over the old
republican membership. Finally, optimistically, Goulding's
new policy for the IRA was to move away from the old
traditions of pious Gaelic violence and towards non-violent
Socialism – a trend which, as we have shown, caused many
of the movement's veterans to hang up their guns in disgust.

So far as Northern Ireland was concerned, the IRA concentrated on taking part peacefully in the open Civil Rights
Campaign. And at least among those members who stayed
with the new 'political' IRA, the policy stuck. The police
calculated that seventy of the stewards on the Dungannon
march were Republicans, and ten of them members of the
IRA – but on the other hand, there had been no display of
republican symbols, such as the Tricolour flag.

Cameron commented upon the fact that members of the
IRA who served as stewards in Civil Rights demonstrations
were 'efficient and exercised a high degree of discipline.
There is no evidence ... that such members either incited to
riot or took part in acts of violence.'

The leaders of the new-look IRA seemed to have an each-
way bet in the Civil Rights movement. If the reforms were
granted, so much to the good; they would share in the credit.
And the reforms would, presumably, result in greater freedom for the political expression of Republicanism. If, on
the contrary, reforms were savagely refused by the Unionist
Right, then there was a Machiavellian consideration: the
ruling party of Ulster would be split, and through the re-
sultant chaos the IRA would lead the people towards
Socialism.

The involvement of the IRA in the Civil Rights Campaign thus revealed more about the changing nature of the IRA than it did about the campaign. For if the IRA, instead of refusing as in the past to recognize the existence of Ulster, was now encouraging people to claim their full rights as citizens of it, only one conclusion – a correct one – could be drawn: the new-look IRA was prepared *de facto* to recognize partition and the separate existence of Northern Ireland.

That may be dismissed as hindsight. At this stage in the narrative, though, what is significant is that from any reasonable Ulster standpoint it should have been possible to see that a marching-and-talking IRA must be an improvement on a shooting-and-bombing IRA. And quite certainly it was a basic act of misgovernment to allow that there was anything revolutionary in the set of demands that Civil Rights finally adopted as its programme. These were:

1. One-man-one-vote in local elections.
2. The removal of gerrymandered boundaries.
3. Laws against discrimination by local government, and the provision of machinery to deal with complaints.
4. Allocation of public housing on a points system.
5. Repeal of the Special Powers Act.
6. Disbanding of the B Specials.

It was Lord Cameron's dry estimate that these reforms were not such as would 'in any sense endanger the stability of the Constitution'. To judge by his response, Craig, as Minister for Home Affairs, did not see things in that light. The confrontation came almost immediately after the success of the Dungannon march, when a similar demonstration was announced for 5 October in Londonderry.

Derry is an emotive symbol in the Ulster tragedy, a flashpoint of Catholic and Protestant history. In the siege of 1689

49

the Protestant citizens held the walls for 109 days against Catholic besiegers. Its recent history has been one of searing unemployment – one in five of the men out of work – and, as we have shown, the crudest Protestant manipulation of political power: a Catholic city where in the sixties a council house was in the gift of the Protestant mayor.

The request for the march came to the CRA from men well known to the Special Branch of the RUC. We quote from a police report filed to the Ulster Cabinet Office:

Matt O'Leary is a member of the Revolutionary Socialist Alliance and a self-confessed Communist. ... George Finbarr O'Doherty, unemployed, is a Republican known to the police for about six years ... John White is a member of the IRA ... Eamonn Melaugh is a known Republican who applied to join the IRA as far back as 1955 (and was not accepted) ... Eamonn McCann is a member of the Derry Labour Party, a Republican and believed to be a Communist ... He is closely associated with Gerry Lawless ...

The analyses were unsubtle. McCann, for example, has always tried to stop violence. What is not in doubt is that the idealistic Socialist students, the middle-class Civil Rights workers, had linked up with the men in trench-coats, the authentic grassroots of Catholic protest, faithfully following the new IRA line. Understandably, the Derry police regarded the local march committee with disfavour. Rather less reasonably, they followed Craig in equating the whole Civil Rights movement with republican extremism.

During September, the Civil Rights Association notified a march route to the police, one which crossed the river by the Craigavon Bridge and ended inside Derry's famous walls (whose gates the prentice lads slammed against the Catholic James II's army in 1689). Five days before the march was due, the General Committee of the Apprentice Boys of

Derry – who, of course, are substantial citizens these days –
informed the police that the 'annual' parade of persons at-
tending their Initiation Ceremony would be passing over
exactly the same route on the same day as the Civil Rights
march. The police concluded that violence was likely. On 3
October the Minister for Home Affairs issued an order banning marches in Londonderry.

The Apprentice Boys' initiation parade was cancelled
without demur. Cameron said later:

> We are satisfied ... that this proposed procession was not a
> genuine 'annual' event, and we regard the proposal to hold it at
> the precise time indicated as merely a threat to counter demon-
> strate by opponents of the Civil Rights march.

This seems to be unfair: some sort of 'initiation parade'
about this time of year by a branch of Apprentice Boys from
Liverpool was an annual event; and it does seem as if the
Liverpool Orangemen had planned to march that weekend,
for the mundane reason that it was the earliest occasion
upon which they could all get cheap off-season excursion
fares from Liverpool. But, certainly, Cameron is right in
thinking that, at the time, their march was regarded merely
as a Protestant counter-ploy. After a long and agonizing
meeting the local Civil Rights militants insisted on defying
the ministerial ban, and the national leadership reluctantly
acceded.

Originally, the prospects for the march had not been spectacular, because the local organizers did not carry great
weight in the Catholic community. But, as Cameron said

> ... the effect of the ministerial order was to transform the situ-
> ation. It guaranteed the attendance of a large number of
> citizens ... who actively resented what appeared to them to be
> totally unwarranted interference.

The events of 5 October were splashed on television sets

51

all over the world. Over 2,000 people gathered at the Water-side station, representing 'most of the elements in opposition to the Northern Ireland Government and the Unionist regime in Londonderry'. Mr Craig and the police, it seems, were prepared for violence. For the march immediately faced a police cordon, and the officer in charge warned that women and children should depart. The marchers tried to avoid the police by taking a different route, but when that route also was blocked they walked right up to the police. At this point, two Stormont Opposition MPs, Mr Gerry Fitt and Mr Eddy McAteer, were batoned.

Fitt, bespectacled, voluble and tireless, once a merchant seaman, was the only man in the British Isles to be a member of three elected assemblies: Belfast City Council, the Stormont Parliament and the Westminster Parliament. He had three Labour MPs from London with him that afternoon: they watched him led away to hospital. McAteer, a white-haired Nationalist, was the leader of the opposition at Stormont. The Cameron Commission found that Fitt's conduct that day was 'reckless and wholly irresponsible in a person occupying his public positions'. But, said Cameron, he and McAteer were batoned 'wholly without justification or excuse'.

The immobilized march now turned into a meeting, which after half an hour was asked by its leaders to disperse. What happened next is far from clear, but Cameron decided that there were certainly extremists present – not of the IRA – who wished to provoke violence, or anyway a reckless confrontation with the police.

Violence, certainly, was what they got. It appears that some of the Young Socialist Alliance from Belfast threw their placards and banners at the police. Some stones were also thrown, and 'many of the police having drawn their batons earlier, the County Inspector in charge ordered them to disperse the march ... the police broke ranks and used their batons indiscriminately ...'

It was hard for the crowd to disperse, because another body of police stood in their way. 'There is a body of evidence, which we accept, that these police also used their batons indiscriminately,' said Cameron. The police also used water cannons at close range. The effects were terrifying.

The physical injuries involved eleven policemen and seventy-seven civilians, mainly with bruises and lacerations to the head. The political results sprang from the shocking effect of televised police violence, and on Sunday, 6 October, a group of students from Queen's University, Belfast – some of whom had been at Derry – marched in protest to the home of William Craig. Cameron: 'Their reception by Mr Craig was hostile and calculated to incense already inflamed feelings. He so far forgot his position ... as to call the students generally "silly bloody fools".'

Everything was now ready for the next stage of escalation. The day after Craig's well-publicized display of intransigence, some 800 students decided on a protest march to Belfast City Hall. This immediately attracted a counter-demonstration led by Ian Paisley. Only at the price of halting the students' march and provoking a three-hour sit-down in the city centre could the police keep the two groups apart.

But since this restricted student march had been to protest against *previous* restrictions, the students were not unnaturally aggrieved. They began at the university a series of non-stop meetings. As one broke up on the evening of 9 October, they decided to meet yet again the next. John D. Murphy, a chemistry student turned printer, was asked to rush out a handbill announcing this. 'We will meet here ...' someone said. 'Who is we?' Murphy asked. 'Has this movement got a name?' Inevitably, there had been a lot of talk about democracy: 'How about Students for Democracy?' someone said. 'We want to appeal to other people, to workers,' was the reply. 'How about People's Democracy?' Murphy suggested. The name was accepted without a vote.

Next day's meeting decided, predictably, upon a march; but there was a snag. People's Democracy was, to put it politely, inchoate – without either officers, committee, procedure, or consistency. But police permission was needed for the march: someone had to sign the form. One of the more sober students warned that anyone who signed would be taken by police to be leader of the movement and might later face arrest. A young psychology student stepped forward. 'I've got nothing to lose. I'll sign,' she said. Bernadette Devlin, at twenty-one, was launched into politics.

The People's Democracy – Bernadette Devlin, a lecturer, Michael Farrell and a loose group of students and ex-students of Queen's – was no more a conspiracy of violence than was the Civil Rights Association (indeed, its members stayed under the CRA umbrella). It certainly contained extremists: Mr Liam Baxter, for instance, would no doubt accept such descriptions with pride; in 1969 he was offering the fashionable thought that 'our (PD's) aim must be to create a Socialist republic, something on the lines of Cuba.' (The presence of Mr Baxter has subsequently and absurdly been held to show that the true aim of Civil Rights was Fidelist revolution!) Cameron probably got PD's attitude to violence about right when he said that it was prepared to go further by sit-downs and disruption in bringing violence upon itself than other Civil Rights groups – 'calculated martyrdom', Cameron called the attitude.

But PD, to its credit, made one last effort to avert the clash which everyone could see was coming. One evening

around the middle of October, Bernadette Devlin went to
see Paisley at his home on Beersbridge Road in east Belfast.
In his austere front room, balancing cups of tea on their
knees, and frequently interrupted by Paisley's young children, Miss Devlin, Paisley and his wife Eileen endeavoured
to understand one another. The meeting was Miss Devlin's
idea, approved by her colleagues partly on the principle of
'know your enemy' but mainly to put to Paisley their case
that the Protestant and Catholic working classes had long-
term common interests and a short-term common aim: the
ending of the forty-year rule by gentlemen of the Unionist
party.

In personal terms, the trio got on well. Mrs Paisley chat-
ted about the kids. Miss Devlin was surprised, as people are,
to discover that the private Paisley is both a warmer man
and shows a far deeper intellectual grasp than his public
image. 'In a blinkered way he is quite bright,' Miss Devlin
later, patronizingly, reported to her friends. But in political
terms they got nowhere. Paisley agreed that there might be
injustices, conceded good grounds for Catholic resentment.
But in the end he said simply: 'I would rather be British
than just.'

Chapter 4
Spiralling to Disaster

Several streams of violence were now running in Northern Ireland. There was the violence of parts of the Royal Ulster Constabulary (the RUC, it should be remembered, was an over-stretched, if over-armed, force). There was the rhetorical violence of Paisley. There was the unofficial, sometimes conspiratorial physical violence of inflamed Protestants – fired perhaps by speeches, or perhaps assuming from Craig's behaviour that a Fenian rising was imminent. There was the potential violence of the old IRA men. There was, as we shall see, the special category of violence by off-duty members of the B special Constabulary.

The only man who could stem this tide was the Prime Minister, Terence O'Neill. But he was still struggling to stitch together a Cabinet consensus which would enable him at last to deliver tangible reforms to the Catholic population. His problem was not only the attitude of his Home Affairs Minister, William Craig. O'Neill's private suspicion was that his Minister for Commerce, Brian Faulkner – an old enemy – was calculating the best moment to withdraw support. Yet still the violence grew.

That is the theme of those last nine months before the disaster of August 1969 – nine months which may yet turn out to have been the last gasp of an independent Ulster. As the Protestant violence grew, so did the grassroot Unionist pressures on O'Neill not to accede to the Catholic demands. This political pressure was, of course, couched in the name of law and order – a cynicism which in turn fanned the violence lurking within the Catholic community.

Events still centred on the city of Derry, sick with unemployment and communal tension, as indeed they were to do again and again until Derry became the immediate cause of British involvement. In the furious aftermath of the 5 October beatings the Derry Citizens' Action Committee was formed, pulling together various earlier 'ad hoc' groups: its dominant figure was a thirty-one-year-old local businessman and ex-teacher called John Hume.

Hume's short, dark-haired figure was already familiar at gatherings in defence of local Catholic interests. Indeed, if any man can be called the exemplar of the new Catholics of Ulster, whose civic passions – far more than the atavistic violence of the IRA – fuelled the Civil Rights movement, then that man is John Hume. The eldest of seven Derry children, whose father was unemployed for twenty years, Hume knew poverty. He trained for the priesthood, became a teacher, and finally went, successfully, into the salmon smoking business. He had been active in organizing a credit union and a housing association, and in demanding (without success) that the new university planned for Northern Ireland should be established in Londonderry. Within a few months he was to replace McAteer as Stormont MP for the Catholic area of the city.

The sixteen-man Action Committee which Hume dominated was 'middle-aged, middle-class and middle-of-the-road' said Eamonn McCann, departing from the Derry scene. It was certainly not violent. But if its members wanted to control the violence latent in the city, they had to take

57

action. They decided to mount a series of protests against the behaviour of the police and the partisan structure of Derry Corporation. On 13 November Craig announced a one-month ban on all processions within Derry Walls. O'Neill was horrified. So was Craig's police chief, the Inspector General of the RUC, Sir Albert Kennedy. He was on holiday – and resigned as soon as he returned.

Three days after Craig's ban, on 16 November, an enormous Catholic and Civil Rights procession, 15,000 strong, marched over Craigavon Bridge and into Derry. The day has since been proclaimed as a triumph of non-violence – and it is true that Hume, with considerable bravery, prevented a riot. The police barricades protecting the forbidden territory of the city centre were swept aside, and the police – evidently anticipating this – then directed the marchers along the base of the city walls. Volleys of stones, bottles, bricks and flour showered down from the Protestant, Union Jack-waving crowds above. At this, the marchers began to break through the police barricades, and their sheer weight of numbers prevailed. Ten thousand people stormed the open space in the heart of Derry known as the Diamond to hold a public meeting. (The violence was not all on one side. At least two RUC black marias were badly damaged by the marchers.) But the speakers saw this as a great day for the non-violent Civil Rights movement. Many of the police, aware of what might have happened, privately agreed. The Unionists had mustered more police than ever before – and they had been beaten. Stormont, the speeches ran, must now grant reforms.

All this had been watched with rising alarm by the Wilson Government in London. Westminster had become used to the notion that the best thing to do with Northern Ireland was to pay the bills and let Stormont get on with it. But the violence in Derry of 5 October, seen on television screens throughout Britain, projected Northern Ireland into British politics for the first time in a generation. On 4 November, O'Neill spent five hours with Harold Wilson and James Callaghan, Home Secretary for the past year. Next day Wilson told the Commons that if O'Neill or his ideals were overthrown, the British Government would need to consider a 'very fundamental reappraisal' of its relations with Northern Ireland. Thus fortified against his own backbenchers, O'Neill hurried ahead with a package of planned reforms: on 22 November he made it public.

It contained five reforms – meeting, in intention, the main points of Catholic grievance articulated at that time. The O'Neill Government undertook to see that local councils allotted their houses on a basis of need and in accordance with a clear 'points' system. It agreed to consider the need for grievance investigation machinery, and to bring in a bill to appoint an Ombudsman. It announced the replacement of the gerrymandered Londonderry Borough Council by a Development Commission. It indicated an intention to reform local government by the end of 1971, and with it the franchise. And it announced that those parts of the Special Powers Act which were in conflict with international obligations would be withdrawn 'as soon as the Northern Ireland Government considered this could be done without undue hazard'.

The first points, in fact, although formally carried through within a year, turned out to make little difference; the last two were still unachieved three years later. The only visible gain for Catholics was the Derry Commission. That was in place within three months, and did much to calm the streets of Derry – for a time.

The effect on Protestant opinion was otherwise, as was shown at Armagh and Dungannon. A Civil Rights march had been announced for 30 November in Armagh. Once the route was slightly modified, the local police had no objection to the march plans; known Republicans were heavily involved, but the police did not expect them to be provocative. However, the Armagh RUC found themselves confronted with Ian Paisley, who informed them that the Government had quite lost control in Derry, and that if they did not stop the Armagh march he intended to do the job himself.

Minatory posters appeared on Armagh's walls, bearing the initials of the Ulster Constitution Defence Committee (UCDC): that is to say, the controlling mechanism of the Ulster Protestant Volunteers (UPV), whose members pledge that 'when the authorities act contrary to the Constitution, the body will take whatever steps it thinks fit to expose such unconstitutional acts.' The arbiters of unconstitutional behaviour appeared to be Paisley, chairman of the UCDC, and Major Ronald Bunting, commandant of the UPV. Bunting is a Belfast mathematics lecturer who once – such are the complexities of Ulster politics – campaigned for Gerry Fitt. But if Bunting was mildly Socialist, he was also fervently Protestant. (His son, on the contrary, was a hardened Civil Rights worker. The generation gap can go no wider.)

During the week before the march, red-painted notices were shoved through letter-boxes in Armagh:

ULSTER'S DEFENDERS
A Friendly Warning
Board up your windows
Remove all women and children
from the CITY on SATURDAY,
30th November
O'Neill must go

James McCarroll, the heavy-weight Belfast building contractor who was vice-chairman of the Ulster Constitutional Defence Committee, was later asked by Insight to define his movement's requirements. 'The Orange Lodges go for quantity. We go for quality,' he said. And how would he define quality? 'Determination.' He was equally frank about the UPV's origins and power. Its motivations, he said, were the same as those behind the Ulster Volunteer Force – which O'Neill had banned in 1966 after the Malvern Street murders. According to McCarroll, the UPV's power was such that it met in Orange Lodges – though the UPV officials were rarely the same as the lodge officers – and even took it upon itself to discipline errant supporters.

Around 1 a.m. on 30 November Paisley and Bunting arrived in Armagh with a convoy of about thirty cars, which were parked around Thomas Street on the route of the march. For the rest of the night about 130 people stayed with them, walking about and talking in small groups. Approached by the police, Paisley said he intended to hold a religious meeting.

At 8 a.m. the police placed road-blocks around the town and began to search incoming cars. They found two revolvers, and 220 other weapons, such as pipes hammered into points. The groups standing in Scotch Street and Thomas Street were now seen to be carrying sticks and large pieces of timber. Paisley carried a blackthorn stick and Major Bunting a black walking stick.

The police, 350 strong, did not care to break up the Paisleyite crowd – now swollen to 1,000 – because individually any armed members might be even harder to control. There was no option but to ask the unarmed Civil Rights march to stop. And it did. The stewards, many of them IRA men, had 'rough work', though, enforcing this order in the 5,000 crowd. Trouble was thus averted, except for the ITV cameraman struck down by a Protestant with

61

a leaded stick. But the fact remained that a lawful march had been prevented by the threat of violence.

In Dungannon, where Major Bunting had been involved, to quote Cameron, in a 'violent and irresponsible' counter-demonstration to break up a People's Democracy meeting in a local cafe on 23 November, there was worse trouble on 4 December. Protestant extremists, including off-duty B Specials, gathered to counter a Civil Rights meeting in the Parochial Hall. There was stone-throwing, from both sides; and a member of the Protestant crowd fired a revolver shot at a press photographer, which narrowly missed.

The right wing of the Unionist fringe was already affronted by the failure of the Catholics to respond with sufficient humility to the O'Neill reform package. On 11 December the Prime Minister went further by dismissing William Craig from the Ministry of Home Affairs. It was a vain gesture: Craig had already made his decisive contributions to the Civil Rights campaign; all O'Neill achieved by his dismissal now was to evoke still deeper hostility from the Right. But the previous day O'Neill had made an emotional appeal on television: 'What kind of Ulster do you want? A happy and respected province . . . or a place continually torn apart by riots and demonstrations, and regarded by the rest of Britain as a political outcast? . . .' There was enormous public response in his support, and the Civil Rights bodies agreed to give him time; they called a truce over Christmas.

It was at this delicate moment that the most militant left-wing elements in the People's Democracy decided to stage a three-day 'long-march' seventy-five miles across Ulster from Belfast to Londonderry. The Civil Rights Association were against it, so were the Derry Citizens' Action Committee. With the O'Neill package and the Craig dismissal already achieved, it was a dangerous exercise in gloating.

According to some leaders of the People's Democracy, the march – through Protestant strongholds – would not have been completed if the ferocity it met with at the end could have been anticipated. But that may have been only one of many views in the amorphous body of the PD. The character of the outfit was frankly conveyed by Bernadette Devlin:

We are totally unorganized and totally without any form of discipline ... I'd say there are hardly two of us who really agree.

And while the PD leaders liked to think of themselves as non-communist Marxists, pursuing the idea of inter-denominational workers' revolution, one of them observed some time after the march: 'Everyone applauds loudly when one says in a speech that we are not sectarian, that we are fighting for the rights of all Irish workers, but really that's because they see this as a new way of getting at the Protestants.'

Because a march right across the province would, in crossing strong Protestant areas, entail physical risk, it appealed to the militancy of the PD leaders – a quality in which they held themselves superior to the 'bourgeois' leadership of Civil Rights at large. That the march might heighten the sectarian passions which they wished to dissolve was discounted or ignored. Again, Bernadette Devlin's comments were thoughtful:

People outside Northern Ireland fail to appreciate the confusion that exists here; nobody knows what they want ... and the sectarian problem prevents some people from even discussing these problems.

For all their supposed intellectual originality – original, at least, in Ulster – the PD were still in the same ideological trap as everyone else.

The march began on New Year's morning, 1969, peacefully and comically, with eighty participants. Their progress, inevitably, was haunted by Major Bunting, who started off skittishly pretending to 'lead' the march with a Union Jack; he dropped out of the procession, his timing inviting ribald remarks, at the entrance to the Bellevue Zoo.

One anarchist had turned up, but nobody would help him carry his banner. A Republican Club contingent was asked not to carry the Republican flag; in the end anarchist and Republicans compromised. They would carry their poles but the banners would be furled.

The carnival atmosphere could not last. Both sides began to prepare. On the night of 2–3 January the marchers – by now about 200 – were persuaded by 'friends' to spend the night in the Gaelic Hall of the Catholic village of Brack-aghreilly, near the town of Maghera. It was an isolated village, but with one advantage: it was strategically placed at a crossroads, with good views in all directions. Shortly after dark, fifty armed men set up roadblocks at the approaches to the village. They were the local company of the IRA. The company commander had been told of an impending attack upon the marchers and, acting on his own initiative, he persuaded the leaders to halt in the safety of the village.

Most of the marchers did not know this. One student went out of the hall in the middle of the night and was caught literally with his pants down when a man thrust a double-barrelled shotgun into his back. 'Who are you?' the stranger asked. 'A student PD' the frightened young man replied. 'Sorry,' said the stranger, 'I was just checking.' At first light, the armed men melted away. Michael Farrell, one of the ablest though most militant of the PD leaders, warned the marchers that there might be trouble. Anyone who could not sincerely continue on the basis of non-violence should drop out, he said. Some of the local IRA men ditched their guns, and joined the march unarmed.

But the IRA intelligence had not been quite accurate. The night of Brackaghreilly, a Protestant mob of about 1,000 contented itself with sweeping through Maghera smashing the windows of shops and houses with stones, sticks and bottles. The ambush was planned farther up the road – at the next bridge, Burntollet.

On 3 January Paisley saw Captain Long, the new Minister for Home Affairs in succession to Craig, and tried to persuade him to ban the last stage of the march. He had no success. That night, while the PD marchers rested under guard in Claudy, eight miles outside Derry, Paisley held a religious meeting in the Derry Guildhall. Outside, in Guildhall Square, a riot broke out, and the windows of the Guildhall were smashed. Major Bunting told the audience to prepare for the defence of the women and children: chairs and banisters were broken up to make clubs, and Paisley supporters debouched the hall in defensive formation. Outside, a considerable fight took place, and Major Bunting's car was burnt out.

Bunting informed both the Protestant audience and the media that it was a 'Civil Rights mob' which had endangered women and children. This was not so: John Hume, another MP, and Eamonn McCann had desperately – and at some physical risk – tried to quell the crowd. And the Cameron Commission later found that the Guildhall riot had nothing to do with any Civil Rights organization. It was random and largely drunken sectarian hooliganism, sparked by the mere fact of Paisley's presence. But Bunting also told the Protestants that as many people as possible should be at Brackfield Church next morning, near Burntollet Bridge.

More detailed planning was going on, meanwhile, at the Orange Lodge at Killaloo, two miles back along the marchers' road to Burntollet. The meeting was under the general direction of a local farmer with whom Bunting later spent the night. A third meeting was in progress at a pub, the Beaufort Arms, in Claudy. After that meeting broke up, at 3 a.m. on the morning of 4 January, a member of a large local family drove to the quarry where he worked about a mile from Burntollet. With the help of men from a row of cottages near by, he loaded up with sackfuls of stones, then drove to Burntollet Bridge and emptied the sacks in piles spaced at twelve-foot intervals along the hillside sloping down to the approach road.

By 8.30 a.m. that morning, 4 January, the men of Derry had assembled. They came equipped with iron bars and nail-studded coshes, and they sported white arm-bands as a means of identification in the mêlée to come. While a hand-ful scattered to cover alternative routes, about 200 gathered in ambush on the hillside. From eye-witness accounts and the mass of press photographs taken in the hours that fol-lowed, about 100 of these 200 men were subsequently identified as being members of the Ulster Special Con-stabulary – the B Specials.

About 11.00 a.m., 500 marchers arrived at Burntollet Bridge, led by an escort of eighty policemen. The ambush commenced. 'A curtain of bricks and boulders and bottles,' as Bernadette Devlin later put it, rained down on the march-ers. The men in waiting burst through the hedge with their weapons. The narrow lane became, in the old sense of the word, a shambles. Screaming Civil Rights demonstrators fled into the river, to be stoned from the bank, or on to the fields, where they were beaten senseless. (There was nearly a murder; the recollection of one marcher is that a girl, felled by a stone, had to be dragged unconscious from the river and revived.)

Both the police and the marchers were taken aback by the ferocity of the attack, and indeed the affair probably ex-ceeded any coherent Protestant intentions. Bunting – apparently finding that sectarian passions, once raised, are not easily controlled – seems to have tried to halt the bloodshed. Yet the belief, implanted by him, that the Derry riots of the night before had been fomented by Civil Rights workers probably inflamed the mob in the first place. There was no chance that the police could protect the unarmed marchers against assault. They had watched the gathering of the ambush with staggering complacency, chatting with the B Specials as they assembled with their cudgels. Perhaps, as Cameron later said, the mob grew too fast for them to disperse. Certainly, once it attacked, the police fought to protect the head of the march. But they could do nothing about the main body. Nor, of course, could they control the political consequences of the violence – which were disastrous.

If it was the aim of the PD marchers – by means of what Cameron called a 'calculated martyrdom' – to demonstrate a commitment to violence among substantial numbers of Protestants, they succeeded better than all but their hardiest spirits can have desired. Also, in Catholic mythology, Burntollet demonstrated a complaisance by the police towards Protestant violence. And if that was, as Cameron found, an unfair judgement, the police behaviour in Derry on that night, 4–5 January, and on several nights thereafter was enough to justify some, if not all, of the mythology.

As the Catholics of Derry now tell it, there has been for years a simple, frightening pattern about police reactions to trouble in the city. Disorder breaks out – sometimes, as on 4 January 1969, the result of Protestant provocation. Immediately afterwards, the police mount a punitive expedition against the Bogside, the Catholic 'ghetto' area.

That is a wild exaggeration. Individual policemen were accepted in the Bogside much as they are anywhere. Eamonn McCann recalls as a child his exasperated parents telling him: 'If you don't behave, I'll give you to Constable

67

So-and-So' – the sort of mock-threat used only when the child knows quite well that the policeman is not an ogre at all. But by January 1969 that confidence had been swept away. Under the Craig régime, the RUC had closed down the only police station within the enclave, and 'law and order' had long consisted of occasional armed patrols in Land-Rovers. And whatever the truth about other occasions, something very like a police assault on the Bogside must have happened the night after the Protestant attacks on the PD marchers.

It should be said that the first reaction of the Bogsiders that night was to start building barricades in their streets, a task in which they were encouraged by some of the PD people. This, which they themselves called 'protection', could be counted as a provocation to the forces of the law. It did not warrant the RUC response.

'We have to record with regret,' said the Cameron Commission,

that our investigations have led us to the unhesitating conclusion that on the night of 4–5 January a number of policemen were guilty of misconduct which involved assault and battery, malicious damage to property, to streets, in the predominantly Catholic Bogside area giving reasonable cause for apprehension of personal injury among other innocent inhabitants, and the use of provocative sectarian and political slogans . . .

This was a cool, legal description of a night in which groups of burly RUC men roamed through the Bogside, crashing from time to time into the tiny terrace houses and even into a department store, dealing out arbitrary 'punishment' with their batons. After that weekend, 163 people were treated in hospital. The Commission thought that even though the police were overstretched and exhausted, there could be 'no acceptable justification or excuse' for this 'unfortunate and temporary breakdown in discipline'.

But O'Neill's very announcement of the Cameron Commission, on 15 January, to examine 'the causes and nature of the violence and civil disturbance in Northern Ireland' was itself now to become part of the drama. The appointment was used as *casus belli* for the campaign which brought O'Neill down.

Some people surmise that had Brian Faulkner, the present Prime Minister, himself succeeded to the Premiership in March 1963 instead of O'Neill, then his power-base on the Unionist Right might have been used to make successful reform where O'Neill was found to fail. What is beyond surmise is that, as events turned out early in 1969, the effect of that power was to destroy O'Neill's last chance.

Faulkner, as Deputy Prime Minister and Minister of Commerce, was not only the ablest man in O'Neill's Cabinet; he was also, with Craig's departure, O'Neill's most important surviving link with the Unionist grassroots. On 23 January, eight days after Cameron's appointment, he resigned from the Cabinet, citing as his reason the lack of 'strong government'. Weakness, in Faulkner's view, was being shown by appointing a Commission to investigate the disturbances of the Civil Rights campaign: he had always been 'unhappy' about the idea. Then, while claiming to be in favour of reform, Faulkner deployed a classic reactionary defence: he affected to object to the manner, not the matter, of reform – meanwhile stating the reformist case in a manner guaranteed to mean its rejection.

The Ulster Government, he said, must choose between two quite different courses. *Either* it must gain Unionist party approval for a 'change of policy', including immediate universal suffrage in local elections, *or* it must set out simply to resist 'the pressures being brought to bear'.

O'Neill's reply was bitterly contemptuous even by the standards of Ulster's inbred politics. In view of the supposed strength of Faulkner's view on the Commission, O'Neill found it 'rather surprising . . . that you did not offer to resign when the Cabinet reached its decision . . .'

'I will remind you,' he went on, 'that . . . after the events of 5 October in Londonderry . . . it was you who were one of the principal protagonists of the view that there ought to be no change under what you described as "duress".' It was true, said O'Neill, that when the Commission was mooted, Faulkner had proposed instead that the party be asked outright to approve one-man-one-vote. But as Faulkner himself had said earlier that the franchise could not be changed in the short term, and knew 'full well' that the party would refuse, then the suggestion was 'disingenuous'.

'You also tell me that you "have remained" through what you term "successive crises". I am bound to say that if, instead of passively "remaining" you had on occasion given me that loyalty and support which a Prime Minister has a right to expect from his deputy, some of these so-called "crises" might never have arisen.'

By the beginning of February 1969 – after more resignations, and with a group of backbenchers in open revolt – O'Neill had one move left to make. He called a General Election for February 24. It was a gamble predicated on the hope that he might find among the electors the 'middle ground' support which was insufficiently available among his fellow politicians.

It is hard to recall, now that the Falls Road and the Ardoyne are IRA fortresses, that in February 1969, O'Neill, the Unionist Premier, could go into those districts and be greeted by friendly crowds. And it is worth remembering that, in strict terms, O'Neill won the election. That is, he and the Unionists who supported or tolerated his policies formed a simple majority in the new Parliament. It is, finally, worth recalling that – for all the talk of the current

Faulkner Government being the 'democratic' choice –
O'Neill's election, two Prime Ministers ago, is the last Ulster
has seen.

But to resurrect his full authority, O'Neill needed to inflict
exemplary punishment on his opponents. He did not do so.
Many Unionist constituency parties split into pro-O'Neill
and anti-O'Neill factions, each fielding a candidate. In only
two cases were established anti-O'Neill members upset by
O'Neill supporters. Out of thirty-one contested Unionist
seats, eleven were won on specifically anti-O'Neill platforms, while others were ambiguous. The anti-O'Neill vic-
tors included some of the most important Protestant
spokesmen (William Craig, Desmond Boal, Joe Burns)
together with Brian Faulkner and several of his present
Government (Captain John Brooke, John Taylor, Harry
West). 'Wee Johnnie' McQuade, a wizened docker who
outdoes Paisley in intransigence if not in coherence, increased his majority; O'Neill, who had never had to defend
a seat, came within 1,414 votes of losing to Paisley.
Although, in the aftermath of these elections, attention
naturally focused upon this weakening of O'Neill's position,
another election two months later seems, in retrospect,
equally important. On 17 April 1969, at a by-election
for the Westminster seat of Mid-Ulster, Bernadette Devlin
was elected. The personality of Miss Devlin herself created
most stir at the time. And the optimists of Ulster were
cheered by the fact that her election was made possible by
the unification, for the first time, of the Opposition's splin-
tered political forces.

The real significance seems, with hindsight, altogether
darker. For that unity was achieved by the secret intervention of the IRA. But it was to prove the last occasion
upon which Cathal Goulding and his new-style left-wing
IRA were able to control the more primitive forces in the

Catholic community of the north. After this, as the situation declined through the summer, the old traditionalists of the Republican movement – the men who had dropped out through the sixties – drifted back into view. One more historic element in the violence of Ulster re-asserted itself.

The Mid-Ulster constituency has a natural Catholic majority; in the fifties the voters there twice elected to Westminster a Republican called Tom Mitchell, at the time serving ten years in Crumlin jail for his part in the 1954 IRA arms raid on the Omagh Army barracks. But even had he been able to take his seat, Mitchell would not have done so. He was then an 'abstentionist' Republican, holding to the traditional IRA line that as Westminster and its puppet, Stormont, should have no power anywhere in Ireland, the correct policy was to boycott all British institutions such as Parliament and the courts. Hence, the ostentatiously unoccupied Parliamentary seat.

But, in Mitchell's absence, the Catholics of Mid-Ulster were split. Some followed him along the hard 'abstentionist' line. Others – among them the new Catholic middle-class strongly represented in the Civil Rights movement and People's Democracy – increasingly favoured a 'nationalist' approach: that is, an attitude which encompassed the re-unification of Ireland, but by peaceful and constitutional means. (The debate between the two schools – the old and the new – is, usefully, a very rough parallel of the factions within the IRA.) But while this argument divided the Catholics of Mid-Ulster, the Unionists narrowly won the seat.

When the death of the incumbent Unionist precipitated the April 1969 by-election, the Catholics looked like splitting once more. The traditional Republicans wanted a lawyer called Kevin Agnew, who did not conceal his sympathies with the IRA's political wing, Sinn Fein. The others, the

72

'Nationalist' school, had their own contender. Neither looked like yielding to the other; yet if the non-Unionist vote was split, the Unionists would undoubtedly hold the seat. A group of Republicans came up with the name of a compromise candidate: Bernadette Devlin.

Miss Devlin was twenty-one and five feet tall. She had first gone up to Queen's University, Belfast, in October 1965; but her studies (Celtic, then psychology) had been a good deal interrupted. In particular her mother's death early in 1967 – her father had died more than ten years before – made her spend a good deal of time looking after younger brothers and sisters in the family house at Cookstown, County Tyrone, which is in Mid-Ulster.

Besides the fact that she was a local girl, her advantage in Irish political terms was that she had no record. Republicans and Nationalists could both vote for her in hope. She was in fact both a Republican and a Nationalist, but she was a Socialist before she was either. Her first steps in politics had been along the road from Coalisland to Dungannon in August 1968 – the first Civil Rights march. She had added to her campaign medals at Derry in October; then she had been to the front in forming People's Democracy at Queen's, and at Burntollet in January; after which she had fought a vigorous campaign against James Chichester-Clark in the Stormont general election in South Derry – 'real, primitive, Paisleyite country', she called it. It was her first experience of conventional politics, and she showed herself a hardworking candidate and a rousing speaker.

On 1 April, the IRA took a hand in the Mid-Ulster byelection. At 11.30 that evening, in a house in the upland village of Pomeroy, the Republican executive of Mid-Ulster met. Present as 'advisers' were Tom Mitchell – his sentence had expired in 1961 – and Tomas Mac Giolla, the president of Sinn Fein. Both had driven that day from Dublin. Their advice was clear: the Republicans should not field a candidate against Bernadette Devlin.

At the final selection meeting the next day, 2 April, Agnew and the other contender withdrew. And two weeks later, on 17 April, after a barn-storming campaign, Bernadette Devlin – 'the pan-Papist candidate' as the PD wits dubbed her – won Mid-Ulster. The Catholics were united: the poll was 91·5 per cent.

At the time it seemed to the reformers a heartening victory. To the old sweats of the IRA, however, it signified a great betrayal. Cathal Goulding and the Dublin leadership of the IRA were, after all, heretics – prepared *de facto* to recognize British rule in Ulster. In Belfast, where these old-timers were concentrated, resentment against Goulding's Dublin leadership intensified ominously.

To the Protestants, as well, Miss Devlin's election was a portent – demonstrating what Catholics, united, could now achieve. (And her campaign rhetoric had been unrestrained.) The most immediate result of Bernadette Devlin's victory, therefore, was to polarize the communities still further – and the factions within them. Forty-eight hours after the by-election, in this tense atmosphere, the struggling O'Neill was pinched by one more turn of the screw. Derry was once again the scene of an incident with powerful symbolic effects: the Samuel Devenney affair.

The North Derry Civil Rights Association proposed to stage a march on 19 April which would start at Burntollet Bridge and enter the city. Fears that Protestant reaction would be violent caused the Ministry of Home Affairs to ban the march. After a long meeting with the Minister the CRA officials agreed to respect the ban. But on the 19th there was a spontaneous sit-down by Civil Rights supporters inside the Derry walls. Near by, there was a gathering of Paisleyites who had been out to Burntollet just in case the march did take place. Stone-throwing between the two groups began, and developed into a riot.

The police response was to drive the Catholics back into the Bogside, and the result was a battle which lasted until midnight. (One policeman in difficulties fired two shots, which he said were sent up into the air.) Although the events of the 19th were outside Cameron's terms of reference, the Commission still reported that 'we were presented with a considerable body of evidence to establish further grave acts of misconduct among members of the RUC ... these should be vigorously probed and investigated'.

Among the victims were the Devenney family. According to the subsequent inquest records, at 9 p.m. on the 19th, Samuel Devenney, a man of forty-three with a weak heart and a record of TB, was at home with his wife and five children, aged between five and eighteen. Near by, some Bogside teenagers were stoning a group of RUC men. Six police Land-Rovers came round the corner, and the youths dashed into the nearest open doorway, which chanced to be the Devenneys' in William Street. Just what happened to them is uncertain, but somehow they got away – probably by rushing straight through the house while the Devenney children tried vainly to stop them.

The policemen then burst into the house, and fell upon the Devenney family with batons and boots. Later, Catherine Devenney, aged sixteen, described in evidence the scene in the tiny front room:

> She said her sister Anne was screaming that the witness (i.e. Catherine) was a girl and lay across her and asked the police not to touch her as she was only out of hospital and the policeman said, 'I don't give a fuck where she's out of.' Witness sat on the floor with her knees up to protect her stomach because she had had an operation. Her brother was crying . . .

Samuel Devenney was taken to hospital with a badly-cut

scalp, and within hours he and his family had become symbolic martyrs for the whole of the Bogside.

His subsequent death – which was never linked by medical evidence to the police assault – and the consequences of the delayed, abortive inquest belong later in the narrative. But the vital fact should be noted here that the officers who made the assault were never brought to justice. And the reason why the matter could never be 'probed and investigated' as Cameron recommended was more significant than the brutality of the event itself.

On the night Samuel Devenney was beaten, the senior officers of the RUC in Derry were not in control of what was happening in Bogside. Police from other forces had poured into the city; nobody knew where they had come from, or where they had been deployed. At the station nearest to the action, the desk log was not kept properly: in any normal force, the culprits might have been traced from the duty rosters, but in Derry that night those basic documents were not kept. Records are one essential attribute of a police force which is restrained by law, but in Derry on the night of 19 April 1969, large sections of the RUC had turned into a sectarian mob. The forces of law and order themselves had surrendered to lawlessness, and to borrow the language of a famous American inquiry, the Devenney family were victims of a police riot.

Yet the beatings which the RUC had handed out in Derry did not slake the increasing right-wing Unionist demands for 'strong government'. Indeed, the case for strength appeared to become incontrovertible, for bomb explosions now became part of the political brew.

The first Catholic-inspired explosions in the recent history of Ulster came around 10.20 p.m. on 20 April 1969, when the first of eleven petrol bombs burst in Belfast sub-post offices. Nobody was ever charged with them, but Ulster ministers have since consistently said that the IRA was to blame. This is not so. Insight discovered – and wrote the week afterwards – who had caused them: a tiny gang of hot-headed teenagers from the Falls Road Catholic ghetto, styling themselves the Belfast Housing Action Group (some were young relatives of members of PD). One of the youths was injured rescuing an old couple trapped above one of the post offices he had set alight.

The reason why they flung the bombs was the first demonstration of the mechanism that was to operate in Belfast, more lethally, in the final catastrophe a few months later. On 20 April, the riots in Derry, during which the Devenney family was savaged, were still in progress. Late on the evening of the 20th, a series of desperate phone calls came to Belfast Civil Rights workers from the beleaguered Bogsiders. Could Belfast, they pleaded, do something – anything – to relieve the pressure of police reinforcements into Derry?

It is a measure of the way in which events were forcing people, as they saw it, towards steadily more radical steps, that some members of the Belfast Civil Rights executive – meeting in the Wellington Park Hotel, near the university – considered lying down on the runways of the city's airport. The executive, though, settled merely for holding immediate protest rallies wherever they could. But Frank Gogarty, the Belfast dentist who was then CRA chairman, and Michael Farrell, the PD leader who was on the CRA executive, had been in Derry as observers, and they produced a tape-recording of one of the Devenney children recounting her family's experiences, which they played despite protests that it was an atrocity story which could only inflame feelings.

The critics were right; second-hand reports of this horrifying tape roused the subsequent protest rallies. The last meeting ended around 10 p.m. that evening, 20 April. Twenty minutes later, the first petrol bomb exploded. The

Falls Road youths, who had been at the meeting, had simply stolen a car and milk bottles, and made the petrol bombs as they drove along. Thus, the desire to 'take the pressure off Derry' had bred in Belfast a desperate violence. It was the shape of things to come.

But other, more calculated, and far more expert saboteurs were already at work. In the early hours of 30 March, £500,000 worth of damage had been done when an electricity supply sub-station at Castlereagh in east Belfast was blown up. Now, in the early hours of 20 April, an electricity grid pylon at Kilmore was blown – not so expertly: the saboteurs blew equal lengths from all four legs and the pylon remained upright. That night, 20–21 April, a few hours after the amateurish petrol bombings, the outlet from the Silent Valley reservoir, supplying three quarters of Belfast's water supply, was expertly wrecked. In the week that followed, a systematic and successful campaign to dislocate water supplies to the city seemed to be under way.

'IRA PLAN BEHIND THE BLASTS SAYS RUC' ran the *Belfast Telegraph* headline. The story quoted police sources as saying that 'it can now be taken that these incidents were caused by people working to an IRA plan ... a "terrorist blueprint" '.

The bombs alone, of course, did not bring O'Neill down, but they were weighty final straws. On 13 April, O'Neill's Minister of Agriculture, Major James Chichester-Clark, resigned – on the grounds that, in the circumstances, he disagreed with the timing of O'Neill's proposed reforms. On 28 April the Premier resigned, saying that what was impossible for him 'may be – I do not know – easier for someone else'. He was, in the words of the *Daily Telegraph*, 'the one politician willing to lead this province of 1,500,000 people out of the dark shadow of religious strife'. Two other, less sensible, comments on his fall may be worth recording, one denying the reality of any 'dark shadow' and the other revelling in their opacity.

Bernadette Devlin, on this occasion, thought it was all capitalist nonsense to talk about religious strife, and distilled the PD view into the starkest naïvety it has yet achieved: 'Ulster's problem is *not* a Catholic-Protestant problem.' Paisley, exulting over the fall of a 'traitor', said: 'We see this as the hand of God.'

The Almighty's hand, however, had received some assistance on this occasion. At the time, the view that the Silent Valley bombs were IRA work could not be effectively discounted, and even today the history of the episode is clouded. (There are still persistent rumours, for instance, that disgruntled right-wing members of Ulster's security services were involved. And the role of several influential adherents of the Free Presbyterian Church is unclear.) But after the British intervention, and after Sir Arthur Young had taken over the Royal Ulster Constabulary, Samuel Stevenson and several other men were placed on trial for the Silent Valley explosions. Stevenson was self-styled 'Chief of Staff' of the Ulster Volunteer Force, the shadowy Protestant equivalent of the IRA proscribed by O'Neill in 1966. Stevenson pleaded guilty, and gave evidence against the others, who pleaded not guilty.

Stevenson had a criminal record. His fellow-prisoners were acquitted. (The atmosphere of the trial was marred by the fact that towards its end a bomb went off outside the jury rooms.) But it is still reasonable to take Stevenson's own plea and conviction as evidence that it was Protestants who first turned to the use of gelignite in this particular cycle of Ulster politics. As O'Neill resigned, in April 1969, his last message to the Prime Minister at Westminster, Harold Wilson, was to warn him of the dangers of right-wing extremism.

Chapter 5
Preparations for a Showdown

Ulster's constitution is the Government of Ireland Act, 1920, one section of which says that

Notwithstanding the establishment of the Parliament of Northern Ireland ... the supreme authority of the Parliament of the United Kingdom shall remain unaffected and undiminished over all persons, matters and things (in Northern Ireland).

If there was one thing which united Labour and Tory at Westminster through the sixties, it was a desire to leave that section gathering dust as long as possible.

During all the Civil Rights campaign's long exposure of Ulster injustice, any parliamentary question at Westminster was turned aside on the grounds that 'by convention' the 'internal affairs' of Northern Ireland should not be discussed. During the 1964 election, Harold Wilson saw Sir Alec Douglas-Home, about to appear on a TV programme beamed at Northern Ireland, tear off his own tie and put on one which bore the Red Hand of Ulster. Wilson was amazed at even so trifling and symbolic a breach of this tradition of separateness. 'Any politician who wants to get involved with Ulster,' he muttered, 'ought to have his head examined.'

It was an attitude which suited O'Neill. Labour's Home Secretary for two years from the end of 1965 was Roy Jenkins; he was heard to remark later: 'Whenever I met Terence, I used to say: "Shall I come over?" And he would say: "What a good idea, but perhaps not just at the present." After a couple of times, I got the message.' In five years, the only Labour minister to visit Ulster was Wilson's first Home Secretary, Sir Frank Soskice – for an afternoon.

Nor did O'Neill come to see the Labour ministers much. Between 1964 and his resignation, he had four face-to-face discussions with Wilson and three with the Home Secretary. Certainly, Labour pressed for reforms in Ulster. (Jenkins, particularly, was sensitive to Labour's backbench Ulster lobby, led by a young Manchester MP called Paul Rose. Rose, in turn, was close to the McCluskeys, the Dungannon doctor and his wife who had begun the Civil Rights movement in Ulster in 1964.) But this desire for reform was tempered by an equally earnest wish on Wilson's part to preserve O'Neill.

The moment when it first crossed Wilson's mind that these aims might be incompatible can be dated precisely: it was at a lunch between himself, Jenkins and O'Neill on 5 August 1966. This was just a month after the riot in Belfast following Paisley's first big public demonstration, and just a week after the Malvern Street murders – the shooting of the Belfast barman which led O'Neill to proscribe a Protestant extremist group, the Ulster Volunteer Force. At the lunch, O'Neill was a worried man. He asked for 'a period of consolidation' to stem 'a dangerous tide of reaction' before he tried to push through further reforms. Wilson and Jenkins agreed. But the intractability of the situation is indicated by the fact that, although O'Neill had by 1966 brought a measure of economic progress to Ulster, he had – certainly in Catholic eyes – done virtually nothing towards civic

81

reform. All he had done was to meet the Irish Premier, Sean Lemass. A survey in 1966 showed, for instance, that of 102 members of Ulster's statutory committees and boards, nine were Catholic – yet this was an area of discrimination which O'Neill had supposedly remedied.

Even then, however, O'Neill foresaw where reform might lead. That lunch in August 1966 was the first time that the possibility of British troops having to keep the peace in Northern Ireland was raised. The legal situation was delicate: any policeman of sufficient rank, in Britain a Chief Constable, can, in theory, call troops 'to aid the civil power' if he faces a breakdown in law and order which the available police cannot control. Britain had a garrison force in Northern Ireland, about 2,500 troops. The procedure – so far as anyone at the time hazily understood it – would be for the head of the Royal Ulster Constabulary, the Inspector General, to make his request to the General Officer Commanding the Ulster garrison. But at their August 1966 lunch, Wilson, Callaghan and O'Neill agreed that, in fact, the decision would be government-to-government – the Inspector General consulting Ulster's Minister of Home Affairs, and the Stormont Cabinet Office then having to liaise with the Home Office in Whitehall.

In 1971 Wilson defended O'Neill's 'period of consolidation' throughout 1967, though he did not mention the military consideration. 'It was the right decision,' he said. 'But more time, the most precious commodity in the explosive northern situation, was being inevitably lost.' It was indeed. But it is doubtful if Wilson, in 1966, realized how 'explosive' the situation was. For until October 1968 – more than two *years* after that lunch with O'Neill and the first talk of military intervention – Whitehall had no civil servant devoting full-time attention to Ulster. Westminster's watch on the affairs of the province was handled by the General

Department of the Home Office, where it ranked somewhere alongside the control of London taxis.

The first bloody confrontation between Civil Rights marchers and police in Derry on 5 October 1968 – the violence of which erupted on every television screen in Britain – thus came as a shock to Whitehall. Their reaction was scarcely excessive. The new Home Secretary, James Callaghan, who had taken over from Jenkins the previous November, put one civil servant on Ulster affairs full-time – the same assistant secretary who had been handling the province part-time for years. Across the road, in the Ministry of Defence, the reaction was more foreboding.

The job of commanding the Ulster garrison had always been a pleasant task, allocated as the last posting before retirement – 'a good place for hunting', one of the Defence staff said. But in the autumn of 1968 the then Ulster commander had less than a year to serve; the Ministry's search for a replacement suddenly assumed a bleak importance. The 1966 lunch looked prophetic: the new man could face trouble. The civil servants set about finding a soldier with three qualifications: he should be at least a Lieutenant-General, the rank necessary to command the Ulster Force; he should know the Irish; and he should have experience of politically tricky situations. By the end of the year, they had found him. At that point, their preparations for trouble came to a halt.

Nor did the political thinking get much further. In the wake of the 5 October 1968 riots, Wilson and Callaghan saw O'Neill in Wilson's room at the House of Commons on 4 November. It was a bruising meeting, for O'Neill had prudently brought with him his severest critics: William Craig, his Minister of Home Affairs, and Brian Faulkner, his Minister of Commerce. 'Harold can be rough without realizing it,' one of Wilson's staff said later. Wilson and Callaghan

83

ended the meeting confident that no doubt remained in the dissidents' minds about Britain's commitment to reform. At a deeper level, however, the meeting was the first revelation of the characteristic Westminster policy on Ulster ever since: reversing Theodore Roosevelt's dictum to walk softly and carry a big stick, British politicians stamp around the topic of Ulster but carry no stick at all.

For although Wilson proceeded to support O'Neill's reforms with a statement in the House of Commons that if he were overthrown a 'very fundamental reappraisal' would follow in Westminster, no steps were actually taken against that contingency. Ministers continued to cheer themselves with the thought that O'Neill would somehow survive. One of Labour's most senior Ministers reflected recently: 'If anyone had told me that we would let O'Neill fall to be replaced by someone further to the right, and that he in turn would be replaced from the right – well, I would not have believed it.'

As O'Neill struggled to survive the failure of his election strategy in February 1969, it became steadily plainer that the British Government was, after all, going to get involved. On 21 April, twenty-four hours after the sabotage of the Silent Valley reservoir outside Belfast, troops of the Ulster garrison were called out – alongside a contingent of B Specials – to guard power stations, reservoirs and other utilities throughout the province.

For the first time, the question of what became known in Whitehall as 'the implications' was raised with Stormont. Wilson had, of course, hinted at this in 1966; but the Stormont civil servants took that 'reappraisal' for the window-dressing it was. Now, with British troops actually on guard, Whitehall raised the question in earnest. It seems to have been done at civil-servant level between the Home Office and the Stormont Cabinet Office. It was, so far as we can tell, confined to politely menacing phrases about 'having to consider the implications of such intervention'. But Stormont civil servants took it seriously. One of the threads in the months that followed was Ulster's fear of the 'implications'. Whitehall, on the other hand, did not take its own words seriously.

It seems reasonable, for instance, to look for evidence that some major debate began at this point inside the British Government – perhaps the drawing-up of contingency plans – to implement the threats now brandished at Stormont. None of this took place. When, shortly after O'Neill's collapse in April 1969, the Westminster and Stormont MP Gerry Fitt appealed to the Home Secretary, Callaghan, to intervene in Ulster before it was too late, he was politely rebuffed. On the other tack, the Unionist M.P.s at Westminster – led by the new Ulster Prime Minister's brother, Robin Chichester-Clark – tried to pressure their Conservative colleagues into a firmly pro-Unionist stand. The shadow Home Secretary, Quintin Hogg, flatly rejected this. Westminster, it seemed, still had faith in Stormont.

Terence O'Neill's calibre had been that of a decently competent Westminster Tory, which is what he set out to be before he became king fish in the more limited Stormont pool. He was succeeded by an honourable, but politically simpler man, forty-six-year-old James Chichester-Clark – later Lord Moyola, a name he took from his estate in County Derry. Besides sharing O'Neill's Eton-and-Irish-Guards background – he had retired in the rank of major – Chichester-Clark was O'Neill's cousin. He was also the man who administered the final blow to O'Neill's administration: when Chichester-Clark resigned his cabinet post as Minister of Agriculture on 23 April in protest against O'Neill's determination to implement the promise of a fairer local government franchise ('one man, one vote'), O'Neill's credit with the Unionist parliamentary party could stand no more. It was the only piece of political cunning Chichester-Clark ever displayed.

Conceivably relations with Westminster would have been better subsequently had Brian Faulkner, the 'professional', won. (Several Labour ex-ministers now think so, anyway.) But the contest illustrated the effect of personality in Ulster politics. O'Neill voted for his cousin against Faulkner, who was the only other candidate; and Faulkner lost the election in the parliamentary party by seventeen votes to sixteen. ('One man one vote did it,' said the main headline in the Belfast *News Letter* next day.) O'Neill's reasoning had little to do with family loyalty or reasons of state: 'Jimmy had only been trying to bring me down for six weeks. Brian had been trying for six years. Childish, isn't it?' A few days later Chichester-Clark, now Prime Minister, duly accepted the inevitability of one man, one vote: it became law that autumn, though there was little prospect of any local government elections to use it in.

Chichester-Clark, the tall, big-boned gentleman sheep-farmer, looked out of place in the little Commons chamber or at press conferences. On television he was ill at ease. This did not damage him; indeed, it conveyed accurately the impression that he was a decent, simple man, a little out of his depth, but prepared to do what he could for all sides. He also had the advantage over Faulkner that he had taken few public positions on the question of Catholic emancipation: he was a man without a past. All this gave him an unusual opportunity. For a while he had the ear of both communities. Brian Faulkner, keeping his own counsel, set stoutly to work at the Ministry of Development on housing rules and local government reform. Chichester-Clark might have persuaded the bulk of Catholics that reform was becoming a reality; he might have persuaded the bulk of Protestants that reform was inevitable and right. But he had the faults of his virtues: plain men are not persuaders. The opportunity went by.

The authority of O'Neill's government had been destroyed during the long winter of repression of marches and demonstrations designed to advertise the grievances of the minority. The authority of the new government now faced the summer season of Orange marches, designed to exalt the supremacy of the majority. More than one newspaper speculated that British military force would soon have to come into play, and it was scarcely difficult to anticipate the dangers. The complacency of both Stormont and Westminster was unabated. But the Dublin Government could not wait; and the old hands of the IRA in the north would not . . .

This is not the point in the narrative at which to discuss the role that the Irish Government in Dublin played in the crisis. Its most important contribution was not for some months to come. But this point in the story does mark the beginning of Dublin's involvement. And it entwines with the first stirrings of the group now known in headlines throughout the world as the 'Provisionals'.

As the violence grew in Ulster through 1968 and 1969 resentment between the Dublin-based official command of the IRA and its northern cohorts grew in parallel. Among sections of the Irish Government, there was equal concern. Several members of the Irish Cabinet and an important section of the ruling party, Fianna Fail, come from northern families. While the Irish Prime Minister, Jack Lynch, was treading a cautious path, these 'northerners' naturally felt strongly that they could not long remain mere spectators. Foremost among Lynch's critics was his Minister of Agriculture, Neil Blaney, a vociferous Republican whose family hailed from Donegal, the Irish county facing across

Ulster's western border into Londonderry. After the aban-donment of the 1956–62 IRA campaign, Blaney had con-tinued to condemn the partition of Ireland. His was a lonely voice, as the IRA's emphasis changed to the exposure of social grievances in the south, and support of the bur-geoning Civil Rights movement in the north.

The savagery at Burntollet Bridge on 4 January 1969 – when the 'long march' of People's Democracy was set upon by a Protestant mob – persuaded many of the Fianna Fail 'northerners' that they had to act. On a day in February, a man claiming to be an emissary from political figures in the south approached the commander of the IRA in South Derry – the area around the city itself – and put to him a startling proposition.

The emissary claimed that a handful of sympathizers – a dozen or so Fianna Fail M.P.s were mentioned – thought that the time had come when the Catholics in the north should prudently prepare for self-defence against possible Protestant attack. The Fianna Fail men were prepared to underwrite the cost of the preparations. The obvious attrac-tions of this offer were somewhat offset by what the emissary demanded in return. The operation in the north, he said, should be run by an IRA command in Belfast – *separate* from the command in Dublin.

The Derry IRA commander went by the book. A detailed report of the meeting was sent back to Cathal Goulding, the IRA Chief of Staff in Dublin. (The IRA in Dublin kept remarkably detailed records of all these meetings and dis-cussions; these – amplified by some of the participants – are the sources for what follows.) Goulding decided to play along with the emissary. It seemed a safe enough course. He might represent those he claimed to do, and even if the ap-proach was quite unofficial, the IRA might get cash. But the insistence upon a northern IRA command separated from the south raised a more intriguing question. Was the approach, perhaps, a manoeuvre by the Lynch Government to provide support in the north, while making sure that the south saw no repetition of the 1956–62 fiasco?

Events in the north disrupted this leisurely conspiracy. Essentially, the old hands in the northern IRA were fed up with Dublin. Their criticisms articulated around two points. They disapproved of the IRA's support of Bernadette Devlin in the Mid-Ulster by-election in April 1969; and they felt defenceless.

The Devlin decision followed logically from Goulding's declaration in 1968 that the movement was now for socialism and against violence. But it also implicitly recognized the legitimacy of Stormont – an acceptance which the Dublin hierarchy later publicly acknowledged. This was heresy to the Belfast traditionalists.

The dispute centred, however, on the gut issue of self-defence. The IRA in Belfast is, as we have said, a different animal from the IRA elsewhere in Ireland, for the cold-blooded reason that the Catholic enclaves of the city – particularly the Short Strand in east Belfast – are particularly exposed to swift Protestant reprisal. Previous IRA campaigns thus prudently avoided the city, and the IRA men there have always seen themselves as the community's defenders against this potential Protestant attack – with the idea of a thirty-two-county Republic a secondary objective. But the IRA in Belfast had no weapons in 1969. To subsidize the Sinn Fein newspaper, the *United Irishman*, the Dublin hierarchy had sold its arms in 1968 to the Free Wales Army – who promptly lost most of them to Scotland Yard Special Branch.

A few IRA men in Belfast, mainly the old hands, had kept their personal armouries. Francis Card – one of those who had stayed, unhappily, in the new-look IRA after the

1964 upheavals in Belfast – had three pistols hidden under his bath. Others took precautions: in the summer of 1969, Leo Martin paid £8 for a Smith & Wesson revolver, a holster and some ammunition. But any re-arming was on that minuscule scale. As news of the emissary's offer of help from the south seeped through the movement, it seemed especially tempting to men facing what they foresaw as a pogrom of Catholics in Belfast.

It was four months before the next feelers from the south. On this occasion, the emissary – who again claimed to be speaking for political figures in the south – was a rich Dublin businessman. In June 1969 he arranged a meeting with IRA men from north and south in Donegal, over the border from Londonderry. At the last minute, the meeting was transferred to Leinster House, the Dail or Parliament building in Dublin, and then again changed to one of the best hotels in Dublin, the Shelbourne. There, in a private room facing out across St Stephen's Green, the February proposition was repeated to a group of senior IRA men. Among them was not only the Chief of Staff, Goulding, but also the IRA's Director of Intelligence, a man who now called himself Sean Mac Stiofáin. As John Stephenson, the twenty-four-year-old railway shunter-driver, he had been jailed with Goulding for their part in the 1953 Felsted arms raid which began this narrative.

Cautiously, the IRA leaders decided to postpone a decision, although with the Orange marches now only weeks away in Ulster the temptation was acute. After the meeting, the argument inside the IRA leadership was fierce.

Neither emissary revealed exactly where the money would come from. But at the Shelbourne Hotel meeting, and probably at the February meeting as well, there were members of the organization *Taca*. Taca – it means 'defence' in Irish – is the fund-raising club of the ruling Irish party, Fianna Fail. For a decade it had been holding £100-a-plate dinners in Dublin to boost party funds. If Taca members were the source, the IRA men thought, there would be no problem about the cash. Another point was clear from the presence of the Taca men: whoever the emissaries represented, the plan they put forward must command wide support within the Fianna Fail party.

Yet the Irish Prime Minister, Jack Lynch, had given no indication of support. That was not surprising – he faced a general election. But when Lynch announced his new Cabinet on 2 July 1969 – having defeated the Opposition parties by seventy-four seats to sixty-six – the IRA leaders expected to glean some indication of his future policy towards the north from the prominence he gave to the 'northerners' among his ministers. But Lynch once again did a balancing act: it was impossible to deduce anything.

While the Dublin leadership pondered this delicate dilemma, the oldest of the Belfast old-guard took a hand. On 4 July the remains of two IRA men, Peter Barnes and James McCormack, were flown back to Dublin from Birmingham. Both men had been hanged for their part in planting a bomb which killed five people in the centre of Coventry in August 1939. For two days, in the Franciscan church beside the River Liffey in Dublin, the two bodies lay in state. On 6 July they were buried in the plot reserved for Republicans at Mullingar Cemetery, in County Westmeath. An IRA guard of honour sporting black berets, battledress and six revolvers fired a volley over their graves – the police ignoring this illegal act.

It was a deeply atavistic occasion and, in his funeral oration over the graves, one of the IRA's most legendary characters, Jimmy Steele, took advantage of the fact. Steele, sixty-two years old and a baker's roundsman, was one of the rocks of the Belfast IRA – a veteran not only of the

1950s campaign but of the Civil War as well. He was honest, close-mouthed and honourable, a man who had literally devoted his life to the IRA: in twenty-five years of marriage, he and his wife had taken one week's holiday. He commanded a passionate respect within not merely the IRA but the whole Catholic community of the north. (He died the next year, and 20,000 people came to his funeral in Belfast.)

When Steele devoted his oration, therefore, to an attack upon the IRA's new look, and what he identified as 'alien influences' within the movement, he instantly gave focus and respectability to the discontent simmering in the north at Dublin's apparent passivity in the face of the mounting Protestant violence. When the Dublin hierarchy reacted by dismissing Steele, there was open talk in Belfast of the need for a coup to overthrow Goulding.

The men in the north wanted arms. Yet Goulding and the Dublin hierarchy were unwilling to do what was necessary to get them: make a deal with the men of Fianna Fail and Taca. On top of that, Dublin would not even send north the few arms it did have. A group in the Belfast IRA wrote Goulding a scornful note: 'At least send us the six revolvers you used at the funeral of Barnes and McCormack.' They never came.

Into this ferment walked an Irish intelligence officer, Captain James Kelly. Kelly comes from Baileyboro in Cavan, one of the counties bordering Northern Ireland; and he is a staunch Republican. In the first days of August 1969 he was 'taking a holiday' in the north – staying for a time with an MP for one of the Catholic areas of Belfast, Paddy Kennedy – and he contacted representatives of the Catholic communities in Belfast and Derry. Inevitably, these included IRA men; they pressed upon Kelly their requirements: money, guns and ammunition. Kelly seems to have seen Derry as more threatening than Belfast. The RUC's incursions in April, the death of Samuel Devenney, and the prevailing Protestant mood, had made the Bogsiders apprehensive. Kelly left the north convinced that Derry needed help from Dublin.

Captain Kelly's trip does seem to have been genuinely unofficial; he proceeded to report, unofficially, that the organization of the IRA in the north was under-manned, under-equipped and totally without finance – while the Catholic communities, he thought, faced a real prospect of bloodshed. He urged help. By the time that Kelly's report reached the desk of his immediate superior, Colonel Michael Hefferon, head of Irish Army Intelligence, this prospect had been transformed into a near-certainty.

Decisions had been taken in Whitehall and Stormont that were to lead irrevocably to violence. The Stormont Cabinet had agreed to let the 12 August marches in Londonderry go ahead. It would be hard to say who was more appalled, Captain Kelly or the new British military commander in Northern Ireland.

Chapter 6
The Bluff that Failed

Lisburn, the headquarters of the Army garrison in Northern Ireland, is on the outskirts of a small country town of that name, less than ten miles by motorway from Belfast. The headquarters – actually called Thiepval Barracks, though nobody refers to it as that – stands in a pleasant wooded estate amid rolling country, worlds away from the gritty Belfast slums. Nevertheless, when Lieutenant-General Sir Ian Freeland arrived to take up his new command as GOC Northern Ireland on 9 July 1969 he knew at once there would be trouble. 'There was a smell in the air,' he said later.

Freeland had been chosen for the Ulster job by Easter 1968 – over a year before – and confirmed by the selection process set in train at the Ministry of Defence after the riots of 5 October 1968. He fulfilled the Ministry's three criteria. He was a Lieutenant-General: before going to Lisburn he had been Deputy Chief of the General Staff. (He was its last incumbent: the Defence Secretary Dennis Healey axed the job as one of his economies after Freeland had held it for nine months.) He could be held to know the Irish: in Cyprus at the start of the insurgency in 1954–6, he had commanded a battalion of the Royal Inniskilling Fusiliers.

And he had survived in politically treacherous terrain: apart
from Cyprus, he had commanded forces in East Africa in
1963–4 while Kenya, Uganda and Tanzania were all in the
first throes of independence; and he had put down the unrest
which followed in all three armies.

With his silver hair and athletic figure – he had played
cricket and golf for the Army – Freeland looked the very
model of a modern General, and sounded one too with
quiet, crisp manner.

Professionally he was ambitious and confident; but personally he was a shy man and hard to know. 'The more I
talk to him, the less I know him,' Chichester-Clark once
said. This reserve was an obstacle. 'With other people, you
could have an argument, say "Don't be a bloody fool," and
there would be no hard feelings afterwards; but Freeland
would have frozen,' another of his Ulster colleagues
said.

There is no lack of people now, both in Ulster and Whitehall, to explain that Freeland was not 'the right man for the
job' – whoever that paragon might have been. It should be
said at the start, therefore, that he had two virtues rare in
Ulster. He was not afraid to make decisions and stick by
them. And he never tried to pretend the problems
away.

Since one of the themes of what follows is the destructive
effect of a military presence in a civilian community, it is
paradoxical that, in the summer of 1969, a *stronger* Army
presence might have improved matters. For, inevitably, the
influence of Freeland's predecessor had waned as retirement
approached. On 10 July the day after his arrival, Freeland
went to the Prime Minister's office in Stormont Castle to
meet Chichester-Clark. Anthony Peacocke, head of the
Royal Ulster Constabulary, was there. (Peacocke had been
next in line as Inspector General of the RUC after Kennedy

95

resigned following Craig's ban on Civil Rights marches. An urbane, silver-haired man, Peacocke was nearing retirement after long service to the force. His brother is the Protestant bishop of Derry and Raphoe.)

Freeland was alarmed by their complacency. The first big Orange parades, the Boyne celebrations in Derry, were just forty-eight hours away. Violence had been mounting for the past three weeks: rival crowds, savage speeches, sporadic punch-ups. Yet Chichester-Clark and Peacocke were unworried. There would be no trouble. Orange marches, they said, never caused trouble.

(This is an enduring myth in Ulster. Orange parades actually have a history of attracting disorders which is, in the nature of things, much longer than the Civil Rights movement. In 1920, the City of Belfast faced damage claims of a million pounds after the parades. In 1935, two people were shot dead and forty injured. In 1953 an entire village, Castlewellan, population 819, was bound over to keep the peace for a year.)

Facing this annual flashpoint in 1969, neither Freeland nor any other senior soldier seems to have been exactly enthusiastic about the chances that a military presence could restore communal peace to Ulster. The one thing they were sure of, however, was that the inadequate military presence they had would be disastrous. Freeland had 2,500 soldiers in the province, half of them tied up guarding public utilities after the April bombs. Still, Ulster ranked, in Ministry of Defence reckoning, behind the Far East, the Rhine Army and the Strategic Reserve in the queue for reinforcements. 'Why won't they realize we are on the brink of civil war?' Freeland said to one of his staff in July.

On 12 July the Orangemen marched in twenty places throughout Ulster. One of them was Derry. It was now a city of seething neurosis. The sequence of winter outrages had

afflicted a city whose already serious unemployment had
been worsened by the closure of a railway line and several
factories – and by the belief of both Protestant and Catholic
communities that the industrial development policy of the
Stormont Government was discriminating against Derry in
favour of the Protestant half of the province east of the
River Bann. The Protestant marches were thus all the more
provocative, the Catholic resentment all the more savage.
But while Derry was to cause the deepest crisis, the total
polarization of the communities was visible elsewhere too.
In Belfast that 12 July the first ominous signs came, ironically, around a block of flats called Unity Walk.

Unity Walk is an isolated Catholic citadel at the mouth of
the Protestant stronghold of Shankill Road. This Catholic
presence at the entrance to the city's major loyalist ghetto –
the legacy, as its name suggests, of an optimistic piece of
town-planning – had long been an irritant. Even before
breakfast on 12 July, Orange bands coming down the
Shankill Road dallied at Unity Walk for ostentatious sectarian fanfares. Despite protests from residents the bands
were not moved on; some police were afterwards alleged to
have said that the Twelfth was the Orangeman's day and
if the residents didn't like it they could go down south.

In the evening, as the bands were returning, trouble flared.
Unity Walk's residents were on the forecourt of the flats,
and missiles were exchanged with the bands' followers. A
boy taking part in the parade with his father was hit by a
bottle and quite badly hurt. The RUC occupied the balconies and forecourt of the flats, but apparently did little –
possibly, could do little – to break up the Orange crowd.
The affair was trivial, but the residents took it as evidence
of police partiality. More important was the belief it in-
stilled in Protestant minds that the Orange parade had been
'attacked' from the flats.

If the Unity Walk incident was misinterpreted by both sides, there could be no mistaking what happened in Dungiven, a town thirty miles south-east of Derry with a population of 1,500, eighty-five per cent Catholic. There was, not surprisingly, no tradition or demand for Orange parades there until the middle fifties, when the cry was raised by a Mr William Douglas – who later contested the Unionist party nomination in the Stormont constituency, South Derry, against James Chichester-Clark in 1969. (In 1960, Brian Faulkner, then Minister of Home Affairs, travelled across the country from Belfast to take part in the Dungiven march.)

Feelings ran high in Dungiven in 1969. Local people had been hurt in the Burntollet ambush of January, and a few local Orange extremists were thought to have taken part – and, more recently, to have broken up a nearby Civil Rights meeting. But the first of the three 1969 Orange marches went off with only minor disturbances, despite the refusal of the organizers to re-route it. The second, on 28 June, was also peaceful, though the Orangemen tore down banners hung across their route bearing such inscriptions as 'We allow you to walk, do you?' Local anger gave way on 12 July. The Orange Lodge marched through the town in the morning, and when a crowd sat down to block the road the local police were none too gentle in clearing the way. Windows in the newly-built Orange Hall were broken, and that evening there were attempts to burn the building – prevented mainly by the exertions of local priests.

Perhaps the Dungiven police, with reinforcements from Derry, could have kept the peace. But there were no reinforcements to be had. Derry itself was the scene of a pitched battle. By later standards the Derry riot of 12–13 July was not spectacular: forty petrol bombs thrown, sixteen police and twenty-two civilians hurt. But by the morning of 13 July the police were scarcely able to keep the two communities apart, and throughout the province their exhaustion was evident. (In a force of 3,200 men, the RUC had suffered 800 casualties by the end of the summer.)

On the evening of 12 July the Minister of Home Affairs, Robert Porter, consulted with Freeland's Chief of Staff, Brigadier Tony Dyball. Porter was a gentle, academic lawyer who had been pitchforked into the job early that year. (He is now back in private practice as Sir Robert Porter. His friends call him Beezer.) 12 July was Porter's baptism of fire, and Dyball agreed to his request: a contingent of British troops transferred from Lisburn across to a naval base called Sea Eagle outside Derry on 'stand-by' to move into the city.

They were not needed. Instead, at lunchtime on 13 July, Porter met the Inspector General of the RUC, Peacocke, and one of the commanders of the B Special police reserves. Peacocke suggested, and Porter agreed, that the B Specials should be mobilized for riot duty. In the light of what happened, it was a desperate decision.

The recruiting procedure for the B Specials was simple. Virtually anyone who was Protestant, of age, and without a criminal record could join. (There was no formal prohibition of Catholics, and a few had once served in the force. But by 1969 they had long departed.) Once accepted, the B Special was given a police uniform and a rifle – or even an automatic weapon – which he took home. His training consisted almost wholly of drill, and forty-eight hours of weapons practice in his first year. Such police luxuries as criminal law did not figure. Nor did riot control. The B Specials, in fact, were a Protestant militia, designed as a border protection force, and by 1969 as inflamed as the rest of the Protestant community by what they saw as the imminent threat of a Catholic uprising. Now they were to be

99

unleashed in the cities and towns of Ulster – in a role for which they were so ill-prepared that when, at Porter's insistence, they were armed not with their weapons but with batons, not enough could be found to go round.

Once again, Dungiven was a portent of the crisis to come. Around 4 p.m. on 13 July, after a day of trouble, the local Protestants appealed to Porter to allow their contingent of B Specials to be mobilized. Porter agreed – partly because he knew that, if he did not, a gang of Protestant vigilantes was already assembling in a nearby farmhouse with the intention of enforcing their own law and order that night.

On the evening of the 13th, to protect the Orange Hall from a second arson attempt, the local police gathered inside it. To the Catholics, of course, this was symbolic of an alliance between the police and the Orange Order. Two police tenders bringing in reserves were burnt and more attempts were made to burn the hall. The police baton-charged the crowd. Among those injured was a seventy-year-old farmer, who died of his injuries the next day.

The B Specials, meanwhile, had been deployed to another part of Dungiven, near a dance-hall full of young people – in the nature of things mostly Catholics. When the crowd emerged from the dance-hall and threw stones and bottles at the B Specials, they replied with a fusillade of shots from a Sterling sub-machine gun, three rifles and two revolvers. Nobody was hurt. But Porter's explicit instructions had been that the B Specials should *not* be armed. Dungiven was the first terrifying example of the authorities' inability to control the very forces which Stormont was now nominally enlisting to preserve law and order.

Three days later, the British Government began to prepare. On 16 July, a rising young minister, Roy Hattersley, was summoned to the Prime Minister's room at the House of Commons. Wilson explained that he had planned a

Government reshuffle in September, but the Defence Secretary, Denis Healey, had to go into hospital. Would Hattersley therefore leave the Department of Employment and Productivity at once, and go to Defence as Healey's deputy? His first task would be to make ready for the possible use of British troops in Ulster.

The obvious step, after the disturbances of 12 July, was to ban all further parades in the province. It could hardly be said to be undemocratic after the bans imposed on Civil Rights marches, and it was clear that the RUC's capacity to maintain order was now vestigial.

Both Wilson and Healey favoured a ban. But Ulster was firstly the responsibility of the Home Secretary, James Callaghan; and Callaghan was a figure no one could ignore. With Wilson himself, he was the only surviving minister who had also been a minister under Attlee twenty years before, and he was still not sixty. Politically he had enormous durability: even after his comparative ill-success at the Treasury, when three years of 'we will never devalue' talk had ended in the enforced November 1967 devaluation three years late, he remained the rival of whom Wilson was most wary.

One of Callaghan's Cabinet colleagues later remarked that Ulster had been 'Jim's Roman Spring'. 'We sent him to the Home Office for a *rest* – legislation on minors, that sort of thing,' he said gloomily. 'Then Ulster happened. Jim was rejuvenated.' And with his solid, slightly stooping frame and his rueful smile, Callaghan was indeed as well equipped as any British minister is ever likely to be to deal with Ireland. At least he was a hard man to fault. He was a southern Englishman who sat at Westminster for a Welsh seat, which could be taken to mean that he understood small-nation nationalism without necessarily underwriting it. In the Navy during the Second World War he had been a lower-deck

101

man: some Tories still called him 'the Stoker'. Yet his sympathies were not so firmly with the underdog as to weaken his regard for law and order: for nine years he had been parliamentary consultant to the British Police Federations.

Callaghan now took advice from the Ulster Home Affairs minister, Porter, who informed him that the RUC had neither the resources nor the resolution to impose a parade ban. In the Home Office, the advice of Callaghan's civil servants was that there was a fair chance of the parades passing off peacefully. Most conclusively, Callaghan talked to Chichester-Clark, and reported that the Ulster premier would fall from power if he had to cancel the Orange marches still to come. Reluctantly, the Cabinet agreed to the marches. It was to become a familiar mechanism: a British government agreeing to follow a policy which it did not favour, but which was thought necessary to protect an Ulster premier from his 'supporters'. The alternatives were to accept a new premier – probably Brian Faulkner – who would almost certainly be more resistant to change than Chichester-Clark, or to impose direct rule.

Both courses were rejected. The group that reached this momentous decision was the most powerful of all Labour's cabinet committees – and one supposedly so secret that Wilson insisted it be known merely by a number. Everyone promptly forgot which number it was: by default, the 'Northern Ireland Cabinet Committee' was born. Its composition was obvious enough: Wilson, Callaghan, Healey, the Chancellor Roy Jenkins, the Foreign Secretary Michael Stewart, the government's senior legal adviser Lord Gardiner – plus the Social Services minister, Richard Crossman, 'because he kept making a nuisance of himself'. So far as we can tell, the committee was only formed in July. Its attitude was set fairly firmly from the start.

Callaghan made no claim to be an historian, but he 'knew enough about 1912', he said. He was thinking not merely of the fact that in the years before the First World War when Asquith was pushing through Parliament his plans for Irish home rule (i.e. a united Ireland with semi-independence), the Conservatives under Bonar Law actively supported Ulster Protestant resistance. Callaghan could to some extent meet that this time by keeping the Tories informed and involved; and as shadow Home Secretary, Quintin Hogg (later, as Lord Chancellor, Lord Hailsham once more) was very guarded in what he said – and disliked by his party's Ulster Unionist contingent as a result. But Callaghan also knew that during Asquith's Ulster crisis there had been serious doubts about the loyalty of the Army and the civil service. Callaghan's principal fear about direct rule was that the Northern Ireland civil service, the indispensable local agents of Westminster, would refuse to cooperate. The Cabinet Committee therefore seems to have presumed that direct rule would mean military rule.

On this basis, through the middle weeks of July, the planning staff at the Ministry of Defence examined the likely consequences of committing British troops to Ulster. They constructed, on one account, nine 'scenarios' of future events. All were bleak. One ended in civil war between north and south. All prophesied an unstoppable escalation in the numbers of troops committed.

The exercise was received lightly in Whitehall. 'Soldiers forecasting doom, as usual,' was one comment. But the study came to the conclusion that direct rule run through the military would – if the Protestants resisted – require 20,000–30,000 troops. 'Impossible,' said Healey, struggling with BAOR and the Far East. 'In practice,' one minister recalled, 'our policy therefore amounted to doing anything which would avoid direct rule.'

Yet the assumption about a dissident Orange civil service was a measure of the utter ignorance about Ulster which still reigned supreme in Whitehall. If Callaghan had gone there, he would have discovered that the Northern Ireland civil service at Stormont was – considering its origins – a remarkably competent, constitutional and liberal-minded body of people. (The official discrimination of which Catholics complained came chiefly at the local level.) All but a very few of the Stormont bureaucracy would in fact have actively welcomed a change of masters.

Oddly, some of Whitehall's most senior civil servants knew this quite well in 1969, and now pour scorn on the idea that direct rule would perforce have been a military operation. 'That,' one said loftily, 'was a fantasy confined to the colonels of the Ministry of Defence.' The Home Office – working with the Treasury and the Stormont Cabinet Office – had compiled a list of key Ulster jobs that should be filled from London under direct rule. No more than a handful were involved; the Whitehall replacements had been selected. Their function was to improve the Ulster bureaucracy and, even more, to inject a cadre used to the ways of British ministers, rather than to circumvent likely insurrection.

There were other arguments against direct rule. Crossman produced ingenious reasons why no troops should be sent at all. He made the point that since the long-term solution in Ulster must entail both communities learning to live together, then anything which staved off that day – such as the insertion of British troops as a buffer between the two sides – was counter-productive. His colleagues agreed, but asked if they were to ignore immediate bloodshed. Nor could anyone agree what direct rule meant: should Ulster become a colony with a Governor and a Council; or should it be absorbed into Westminster like, say, the Isle of Wight?

But the deepest reason against direct rule seems to have

been a plain dread of getting their feet as deep as that in the Irish bog. Jenkins, Asquith's biographer, lectured the Cabinet on the lessons of Irish history. 'If there is one thing I have learnt,' he said, 'it is that the English cannot run Ireland.' The notion that direct rule could be a step on the way to Irish reunification, ending British involvement for good, was not then current; reunification was to remain a dirty word for another two years. (Though Jenkins privately favoured it in 1969.) Even peace-keeping moves had a dangerous air of permanence. Callaghan recalled Cyprus: 'It was damned easy to get Makarios to the Seychelles,' he said, 'but damned hard to get him back.'

Much of the Cabinet Committee's discussions towards the end of July turned on a technical question. Assuming that the troops were to go in, on what legal basis could they do so? The Attorney General, Sir Elwyn Jones, cobbled up a rapid answer which raised as few issues of principle as possible. The soldiers should go in as 'common law constables'. Every citizen of the British Isles is of course a common law constable and has a duty to go to the aid of the civil power if asked – for instance, if a policeman calls on him to help stop a street fight. Soldiers are in law no different. But in practice they have, as soldiers under the Crown, much more force at their disposal than ordinary citizens. Callaghan pointed out that Jones's solution thus begged several questions. Notably few citizens, after all, are in a position to shoot their fellow men. What would happen to a soldier who did? At this point the doctrine of 'equivalent force' was wheeled out. Roughly, it would be in order for a soldier to shoot someone *if* they had been preparing to do something equally drastic to him. It was a solution that was to cause the Army endless problems.

For instance, the Catholics cannot understand why the Army continues to insist in the face of all the evidence that certain men were carrying weapons when shot. Why not admit error sometimes, in order to increase credibility next time? The answer is that for the Army to admit error may be to accuse one of its own men of manslaughter or murder. And this 'minimum solution', as Sir Elwyn's expedient was called, evaded precisely the point the Labour Cabinet should have been debating: the nature of the 'civil power' the soldiers were to aid. The problem was not faced. On 30–31 July 1969 the Labour Cabinet held a two-day meeting to wrap up business before the summer holidays. Wilson and Callaghan were given authority to provide Chichester-Clark with troops if he asked for them. The 'strings' would be worked out later.

Stormont, of course, did not know that. Throughout the first two weeks of August 1969, the policy of the British Government was to blackmail Stormont into doing what Westminster wanted (cancel the parades) by means of the bluff that Westminster had decided on direct rule if the troops went in – when, in fact, it had decided precisely the reverse.

On 2 August the Junior Orangemen marched down the Shankill – once more, past Unity Walk flats, scene of the 13 July trouble. Once more, the residents turned out to protest. When, after a few stones had been thrown, the BBC's local news bulletin at 12.55 flashed the 'news' that the marchers had been attacked at Unity Walk, it was inevitable that there would be a confrontation on the return of the parade that evening.

Early in the afternoon, a Protestant crowd, led by the Chairman of the Shankill Defence Association, Mr John McKeague, rushed towards the flats demanding the arrest of a Republican leader, Jim Sullivan, who was seen in the courtyard. The presence of Sullivan was for many Protestants proof of a Republican plot justifying the attacks to come. From 4.30 p.m. an enormous hostile Shankill crowd gathered behind Unity Walk. The waving of a tricolour at the window of one flat provoked a massive attack. All the windows down one side of the block were smashed. The police, short of men, had to devote their energies to preventing an invasion of the flats by the returning Orange parade. Then they baton-charged the stone-throwing Protestant crowd and drove them up the Shankill.

It was too late. The Unity Walk flats complex occupies a large area, and to forestall a Protestant invasion through a side-entrance a police unit drove into an outer courtyard of the flats themselves. But just as they arrived, so did a section of the Protestant mob. To the besieged residents, it seemed that the police were leading the Protestant onslaught. Rioting broke out between the police and the inhabitants. When another police unit, guarding another entrance to the flats, rushed to the assistance of their colleagues, the Protestants invaded there too. Which confirmed the residents' fears. To the police, however, the incident looked very different: they thought they had been ambushed by the residents.

They reacted violently. A former British soldier, Emmanuel O'Rourke, who had just arrived home from work, was batoned unconscious and then dragged across ground littered with broken glass. And an elderly illiterate, a Mr Corry, was batoned on the head, suffering three fractures of the skull and five separate areas of brain damage. He was dragged unconscious and bleeding into a Land-Rover – but not taken to the nearby Mater Hospital. Instead he was driven to Tennent Street Police Station. Mr Corry later died. (The policeman who took him to the station was himself later killed – by Protestants.)

When serious rioting broke out on the Shankill Road on the next day, Sunday 3 August – beginning when a mob again attempted to march on Unity Walk flats – the police just managed to hold off the crowd. But they were by now exhausted.

Around 3 p.m. that afternoon, the Belfast Police Commissioner, Harold Wolseley, told the Home Affairs Minister, Robert Porter, that he feared the police might not be able to cope much longer. The machinery for calling in the troops should be set in motion. At a Stormont Cabinet meeting at 4 p.m. Porter got permission to obtain clearance in advance from Whitehall so that troops could go in at once if and when they were needed. Porter has since insisted that this was purely a 'contingency request': he was, he has said, worried because 3 August was a Sunday, and he thought there might be delay in London. Wolseley and his deputy were not certain that they would need troops – they were merely 'apprehensive' as the reports of the Shankill rioting continued to flow into their headquarters Operations Room.

Without knowing what London's answer would be, Freeland sent a precautionary contingent into Belfast. For a few hours, about sixty men of the Second Queen's, plus a tactical HQ unit, were actually stationed at the city police headquarters in east Belfast, waiting to go into action. There are differing accounts of what happened next. Freeland himself was certainly unhappy at the prospect of their going in. Labour's legal 'minimum solution' entailed that all the civil power's resources must be exhausted before the troops could legally go to its aid. Freeland now told Porter that he did not think this point had been reached, because in the more unruffled areas of the province the RUC were still working an eight-hour day, five days a week: they could try harder. And the police reserves had not yet been called into action in Belfast.

But that meant the B Specials. And to call the B Specials into Belfast was the one move the Catholics were certain not to forgive or forget. Whose decision was it that this must be done before troops could go in? Freeland has since said that, unhappily, the B Specials were just another police reserve who legally had to be used. After troops had been on 'stand-by' at the Sea Eagle base outside Derry on 12–13 July, Freeland's Chief of Staff, Brigadier Dyball, had said as much to Porter. The Army had no power over them.

But a senior Labour minister now says that when Porter's request came to London it was Wilson and Callaghan who that evening decided that the B Specials must first go into Belfast – and that their decision was communicated to Freeland by the new Army minister, Roy Hattersley.

Troops were withdrawn from the police headquarters. The 3 August message log of 39 Brigade (the Ulster force) gives as the reason: NO QUESTION OF COMMITTING TROOPS UNTIL ALL METHODS EXHAUSTED BY THE POLICE. But there was more to the decision than that. For just before the troops withdrew, while Commissioner Wolseley stood talking to them in the courtyard of his headquarters, he was approached by the Secretary to the Stormont Cabinet, Harold Black – who warned him, very quietly, of the possible constitutional consequences for Northern Ireland if he went ahead and put them on the streets.

Harold Black had been Secretary to the Northern Ireland Cabinet since 1965. He was knighted in 1970 – largely for his work during the August 1969 crisis – and he is everyone's idea of a civil servant: neat, bespectacled, demure. A Belfast man, he was little known outside Stormont, yet he was one of the most influential men in Northern Ireland. Prime Ministers might come and go at Stormont Castle, but the man in the next-door office was still Harold Black. And in the manoeuvres of August 1969 between Stormont and Westminster, all the strings ran through his hands.

It was Black who, on 3 August, channelled Stormont's

109

'contingency request' to Whitehall – and it was Black who got back what the Home Affairs Minister, Porter, later called 'a dusty answer'. Wilson and Callaghan, desperate to stave off military involvement, bluffed Black with dire warnings of the 'implications'. They had reckoned without Irish cunning. On the instructions of his Prime Minister, Chichester-Clark, Black promptly *withdrew* his request. Wilson and Callaghan had forgotten that, in the last resort, Freeland – under the Manual of Military Law – would *have* to go to the aid of the civil power if the request came in the right form. As Porter later blandly recounted: 'It was withdrawn on the basis that the GOC should not be in any way inhibited by getting a negative response to the Government discussion and it was left then that he should rely entirely upon his common law power . . .'

Nevertheless, Stormont was deeply worried. Two days later, after a bout of tense telephone calls, Harold Black flew to London on Tuesday 5 August to see the Permanent Secretary at the Home Office, Sir Philip Allen. (The two of them constituted the liaison machinery between their two governments.) Allen repeated what Wilson and Callaghan had said.

Just to underline the point, the political correspondent of the *Financial Times* carried a story next day, 6 August:

British troops would be used to restore law and order in Ulster only if the Northern Ireland Government first agreed to surrender its political authority to Westminster.

The source for this, according to one civil servant, was 'Harold, huffing and puffing about not being a rubber stamp for Stormont'. The same source recalls the mood: 'It wasn't so much Machiavellian as "God, I hope they don't call our bluff".' It was, in retrospect, a characteristic Wilson manoeuvre.

Equally inevitably, Chichester-Clark did call the bluff. He and Porter had an angry showdown with Callaghan at the Home Office on Friday 8 August. Porter, the lawyer, maintained that under the common law, calling in troops was entirely a 'law and order' matter for the civil power without political implications. Chichester-Clark, wilier, said that if Labour wanted to prop up the 'civil power' without committing troops, why not let the RUC have more CS riot-control gas with fewer restrictions on its use, plus Army scout helicopters in aid of the police? (The Ministry of Defence had been against any idea of the RUC having CS, but had caved in a few days earlier when, to their horror, they discovered that the RUC already had CN. CS is technically a smoke; but the Ministry view was that CN was a gas as defined, and forbidden, by the Geneva Convention. To remove the CN, the Ministry had to provide CS.)

Chichester-Clark's suggestion of bolstering the civil power appealed to Wilson, with whom Callaghan consulted, and he got a freer hand with CS. Only a Ministry of Defence veto prevented him from getting helicopters. But on the central political issue, Callaghan was adamant. The Unionists could not just borrow the British Army. Callaghan, one admiring civil servant said later, was 'explaining the facts of life to a man who, if he had the necessary intelligence, would have grasped them for himself some time ago'. As Chichester-Clark drove off – in such a hurry to escape waiting demonstrators that he left Porter behind on the Whitehall pavement – the Unionist view of the encounter was necessarily simpler. 'Jimmy more or less told Callaghan to stuff it,' said his brother Robin, the Westminster MP.

But Chichester-Clark had won from Callaghan what his colleagues considered a crucial concession. Callaghan now said merely that '*extended* use of troops' (our italics) would involve constitutional repercussions. A swift 'peace-keeping

111

operation' would not. The bluff had been called. On Monday morning, 11 August, Chichester-Clark and his Cabinet ratified an earlier decision to let the Apprentice Boys parade through Derry the next day. It was, as things turned out, an insane decision.

Certainly, they had had ample warning of the likely consequences. On 25 July a delegation from the Bogside – shopkeepers and other solid citizens – had come to Porter to appeal for a ban. Over the next week, he had tried to persuade the Apprentice Boys to re-route their march. When they rejected his plea, Porter was so worried that he considered banning *all* parades. On 14 August John Hume, the Civil Rights Social Democrat MP who knew the Bogside best, appealed to him to stop the march and what he called 'the frightening prospect' of its likely aftermath; so did the two senior members of the Derry Development Commission appointed by O'Neill to run the city. On 7 August Chichester-Clark saw the Apprentice Boys' leaders and appealed for a voluntary ban. They rejected the idea. At a meeting just afterwards, Porter consulted the police: the Inspector General, Peacocke, and his deputy, and the officers in charge of Derry. They were against a ban – because they did not think that the troublemakers among the Apprentice Boys would observe it.

On this basis of surrender, the Stormont Cabinet decided on 11 August to allow the parade. Whitehall was unruffled. In the first days of August, with General Freeland pleading for reinforcements, the Ministry of Defence actually reduced the number of troops in Northern Ireland. The First Battalion, the Light Infantry, was sent to Kenya on a routine training exercise. Its replacement – in the week of the marches – was the First Battalion, the Royal Regiment of Wales, which was only three quarters the size.

Chapter 7
Insurrection

The week of 12–16 August 1969 was when the British public came face to face with the fact that there is a part of Britain where politics can kill. The physical savagery on the streets was brilliantly conveyed at the time by television and newspapers. What was harder to distinguish, let alone convey, in this bloodstained jumble of events, was the actual sequence which precipitated British power into Ulster.

For Northern Ireland, those five days were a watershed, not only because the British Government and its Army became inextricably and fatally involved, but because the clock was set back fifty years, finally disintegrating O'Neill's brittle reconciliations. The events have since entered the folk histories of both Protestants and Catholics. The Catholics, especially of Belfast, now see August 1969 as an attempted Protestant pogrom. The Protestants had their suspicions confirmed that the Civil Rights struggle was merely a 'front' for traditional IRA insurrection.

What follows in the next two chapters is, so far as we know, the first attempt to confront both mythologies. To do so it is necessary to examine in some detail what actually did happen on the streets of Ulster. The evidence is gleaned mainly from the voluminous transcripts of the hearings of

113

the tribunal set up under Mr Justice Scarman to report upon these events. We, of course, are writing before it has done so. Our interpretation is necessarily subject to Scarman's correction. But we have had the advantage of amplifying some of Scarman's evidence by talking to various participants whom he did not see, particularly in Whitehall and Westminster.

Our conclusions can be simply stated. There was an element of pogrom in the Protestant 'attack' on some Catholic streets in the Falls area of Belfast. There was, too, IRA influence in the disturbances. But the Protestant 'attack' was largely provoked by the Catholics, and was for the most part unplanned, uncoordinated and concerned with self-defence. The IRA, as later convulsions within the movement were to reveal, was largely an irrelevance. The B Special police reserves, who in Catholic mythology swept like an avenging Protestant horde through the Catholic communities of Belfast, did indeed misbehave there and elsewhere – but mainly from fear, muddle, and a total lack of proper training, for none of which can they properly be blamed. The behaviour of the RUC, on the other hand, was horrifying.

The Apprentice Boys' parade around the old city walls of Derry each 12 August is a matter of solid Protestant citizens celebrating their continued enjoyment of something which they hold to be required for their survival: political hegemony over their Catholic fellow-citizens. On 12 August 1969 the parade took its normal form: 15,000 men in dark suits, sashes and bowler hats (the Orange 'uniform') marching along the walls which enclose the old Protestant town and look down upon the impoverished Catholic Bogside. They were accompanied by bands and banners, and they sang 'The Boyne' and other blood-curdling anti-Catholic songs. As they went, various members of the parade threw

114

pennies down into the Bogside – an area of about one in four male unemployment.

That day's parade was no more 'provocative' than those of previous years. Indeed, it was a model of order and well-stewarded discipline. To discuss it in degrees of provocation, however, is to imply that it is like a students' demonstration in England – a basically pacific event which on occasion may be taken over by wild spirits. The point of the Apprentice Boys' parade is that it is an annual political experiment of the most empirical kind. If the Catholics take the insult lying down, all is well. If they do not, then it is necessary to make them lie down. In August 1969, after nearly ten months of intense political excitement, the Bogsiders were not prepared to lie down.

The Bogside was cordoned by police. But around 2.30 p.m., as the parade was passing one of the entrances to the ghetto, stones, bottles and marbles were thrown and catapulted at the marchers. There seems to have been no plan to attack the parade – more than half of it had gone by – and few of the marchers were hit. But the Catholic community's own stewards on duty in the Bogside failed to control the hooligans responsible, so the police became involved.

Violence was implicit in the situation. The moment it broke out it assumed a pattern which by definition the police could not contain for it began at the junction of the ghetto and the centre of the city: as the Bogside drew up its battle line, the police – outside the ghetto – were inevitably on the Protestant side of the line.

When the trouble broke, the Catholics retreated a little way from the entrances to the Bogside, and men began to drag barricades across the streets. On the flat roofs of blocks of flats, crates full of petrol bombs had already been stacked up by the children. As the RUC drew up on the perimeter of the Bogside, behind them in the old city gathered gangs of

Protestant youths, anxious to follow the police into the Bogside and teach the Catholics a lesson.

Around 7.15 p.m. on the evening of 12 August the police attempted to penetrate the Bogside. It transformed the disturbance from being an incident engaging a handful of police and a few youths into a war between the residents of the Bogside and the RUC. It represented an attack which the residents had feared and for which they had prepared ever since the police incursions of 4 January and 5 April – on the last of which Samuel Devenney and his family had been beaten. And the police behaviour was reminiscent of those two previous 'raids'. They were shouting 'IRA scum' and 'Fenian bastards' as they began their charge, and they batoned several bystanders, including a uniformed first-aid man.

As the police – vastly reinforced from other parts of the province – stormed the first barricade, the crowd withdrew behind another and more formidable one, deeper inside the Bogside. When the police continued their advance, they were showered with petrol bombs from the flat roof of a ten-storey block of flats on Rossville Street, the tactical key to the Bogside. The clothes of one policeman were set on fire: the RUC retreated.

That entire charge was against orders from Derry police headquarters. When representatives from the Bogside appealed to the headquarters, the police were ordered back to their original position – on the periphery of the ghetto. So began the three-day siege of the Bogside.

It was to prepare for this that almost a month earlier, on 20 July, the Derry Citizens' Action Committee – the 'middle-aged, middle class, and middle of the road' body dominated by the MP, John Hume – had been superseded in the Bogside by a new grouping, the Derry Citizens' Defence Association, the DCDA. Hume's group had two representatives on the DCDA, but it was dominated by people not renowned for their moderation – such as the senior local Republican, Sean Keenan (currently interned).

That was anathema to the Protestants, of course, but it was inevitable in the Bogside – and sensible if the organization was to have the authority to keep the peace. It is a measure of the degree to which Stormont's authority to govern had collapsed even before the bloody events of this week, that the critical function of policing the Bogside had been abdicated by the legally-constituted forces of the law. It was left entirely in the hands of this Catholic vigilante group, the DCDA, to keep the peace.

That is what the police, not the friendliest of observers, thought the DCDA genuinely wanted. The Home Affairs minister, Porter, has since testified that while police reports coming to him spoke of the DCDA members' persuasions, 'I had nothing before me to indicate that any of the people on that committee were prepared to encourage or embrace violence.' The DCDA had even met amicably with representatives of the Apprentice Boys at the beginning of August, both promising to provide effective stewarding on the day of the parade. The Apprentice Boys kept their side of the bargain; the DCDA did not keep theirs.

One Leonard Green, who had no previous experience, was appointed DCDA chief steward – in preference to a man who had stewarded previous demonstrations. Green was given a list of about 350 people who had previously acted as stewards for the supplanted Derry Citizens' Action Committee; he did not inquire how many, if any, would be available on 12 August. Lists of other willing stewards were compiled; Green says that he never got them. (He did issue a general invitation to such people to come to a meeting in a hall some way outside the Bogside on the eve of the parade and to report again on the 12th at some unspecified time.)

Green said later that he had detailed people to 'keep an eye' on potential flashpoints and summon stewards if trouble arose. Even this broke down: the stewards' headquarters was in a hall so remote as to be useless; its only communications links were a public call-box outside or a private telephone 100 yards down the road. Alternatively, one of the stewards would pedal up to the hall on his bicycle. Not that there were enough stewards, anyway. When one of those appointed by Green visited the HQ on his bicycle at 2.00 p.m. on the afternoon of the march, there were only about twenty-five stewards there. When he called back an hour later they had all gone. Green himself was asleep in his bed.

When it came to the 'defence' of the Bogside in the event of attack, however, the Derry Citizens' Defence Association showed a professionalism markedly at odds with the amateurishness of its arrangements to preserve the peace. While the stewards relied on bicycles to keep the peace, for instance, those in the DCDA preparing for battle had obtained two-way radios – 'to report', as one DCDA man said later, 'on the actions along the fronts'. In the three weeks before the march the DCDA made elaborate defensive preparations. They set up three first-aid stations inside the Bogside to be manned by doctors and ambulancemen of the Knights of Malta. They established a communications system with the two-way walkie-talkie radios. They installed two powerful radio transmitters. They formed their own fire brigade. They even organized the evacuation of the old and ill from sensitive or dangerous areas.

The DCDA also made prior arrangements for the erection of barricades in coordinated positions throughout the Bogside. The main job of Green, the 'stewarding organizer', was in fact and in his own words, 'immediately hostilities commenced, to go round the areas and ensure that bar-

118

ricades were erected all round the Bogside area to prevent the police, or whoever were attacking us, from getting in round the back'. Volunteers for barricade and patrol duties were, unlike the stewards, properly organized.

Other preparations were 'free-lance'. Heaps of stones were piled at strategic points on the periphery of the Bogside; petrol bombs were prepared; barricades were erected on the night of the 11th; and milk bottles from the week-end – normally returned on Monday, the 11th, and Tuesday, the 12th – were hoarded. (The dairy lost 43,000.)

The Bogside, in other words, was spoiling for a showdown with the police on 12 August. Perhaps some Catholics saw the preparations as reasonable precautions against a likely repetition of previous actions. Samuel Devenney, beaten in the last police punitive expedition, had finally died on 17 July. The DCDA was set up three days later. Once such preparations are made, however, they almost inevitably generate a momentum which ensures that they will not be unnecessary. That is what happened in Derry on 12 August.

As the police advanced to the first barricade – determined to put down what they correctly saw as a major defiance of law and order – the DCDA's elaborate administrative plans went into operation. The field hospitals opened – the police assault on the barricade produced many casualties. The communications system worked; the barricades were manned; patrolling of the area commenced. So long as the twenty to thirty teenagers on the roof of the Rossville Street flats could be supplied with petrol bombs – which they were by relays of children – the Bogside was impregnable to the police. It was insurrection. 'Free Derry' was born.

That Tuesday night, the 12th, and throughout the two days which followed, the violence assumed an almost ritualized form. RUC constables, armed with batons and riot

119

shields, made charge after charge into the Bogside streets. They were repelled by coordinated petrol bomb attacks from the roofs of the multi-storey flats. (Hundreds of gallons of petrol had been stolen from a local post office depot.) Buildings in the area were fired; some burned for three days.

Around midnight, after the policeman in charge had telephoned Porter, CS was used in the Bogside – for the first time in the United Kingdom. (As the days went by, the use of CS became more and more indiscriminate, but the police had no other possible weapon except stones.) Again, the DCDA was organized: wet handkerchiefs were used as masks; vaseline was available to soothe irritated eyes and skin; wet blankets were thrown over the CS canisters as they fell. Within twelve hours the DCDA had produced leaflets on how to counteract CS.

The mood in the Bogside – 'Free Derry' its residents now called it – was euphoric. Republican tricolours flew from the roofs of the high flats beside the emblem of the 1916 uprising, the Starry Plough – the ultimate act of defiance. The prediction of one local Nationalist Party leader that these days 'could raise the curtain on the last terrible act of the age-old Irish drama' seemed the sober truth. Bernadette Devlin was there; as one observer said later: 'She really seemed to feel that the revolution had come ... She was sure there was nothing left for the British Government to do but to suspend the Constitution and chuck out the police.'

But Stormont hung on grimly – while its supporters in London bargained for better terms from the Wilson Government. At his meeting with Chichester-Clark and Porter on 8 August the Home Secretary, Callaghan, had distinguished between a brief military exercise and a protracted involvement. Chichester-Clark's brother Robin, the West-

minster MP, now tried to do better. He telephoned the
deputy leader of the Tory party, Reginald Maudling.

Maudling was unhappy at launching himself into the
Ulster conflict, but Callaghan's shadow, Hogg, was climbing
in Lucerne – and Edward Heath was aboard his yacht, be-
calmed in the middle of a race round the Isle of Wight. (This
gave Callaghan the best line of the crisis. When, towards the
end of the week, one of his advisers raised the question of
the recall of Parliament, Callaghan said: 'I haven't heard
anything from the Leader of the Opposition about that' –
adding thoughtfully: 'By the way, did Ted *ever* win that
race?')

On the morning of the parade, Tuesday 12 August,
Maudling requested an interview with the Home Secretary.
Callaghan would not budge from his Sussex retreat. Maudling had to see his deputy, Lord Stonham. And Stonham
spelled out what Callaghan had hinted at: the longer the
troops had to stay, the greater the political involvement. In
other words, if Stormont could clear up the mess quickly,
they could indeed borrow the British Army. At lunch the
next day, Wednesday 13 August, Maudling put the solution
to his party's two senior Unionists: Robin Chichester-Clark,
and Captain Lawrence 'Willy' Orr – one the new Ulster
Premier's brother, and Orr the leader of the Orange Order,
the 'Grand Master of the Grand Orange Council of the
World'. Maudling's efforts were the best Stormont could
hope for.

By that Wednesday 13th lunchtime – the second day of
the siege of the Bogside – Westminster knew that troops
were inevitable. The Ulster commander, General Freeland,
had a senior officer in civilian clothes on the streets of
Derry; he reported that the police could not possibly contain
the Bogside for more than thirty-six hours. And when they
retreated, he said, there would be considerable blood-letting

between the communities. Quietly, Freeland sent 300 troops across to the Sea Eagle naval base outside Derry. And waited.

As Stormont hung on for better political terms, however, worse was to come on the streets. That Wednesday saw the first of the communal conflict that Freeland's officer feared. A gang of Protestants who had marched through the centre of the city came up to the periphery of the Bogside, and rioting broke out with the Catholics. Quelling it, the police demonstrated rank partiality towards the Protestant crowd – understandably, in view of the hammering they had been getting from the Catholics over the last twenty-four hours.

It was an ominous preamble. For the threat of inter-communal rioting centred on one street, Long-Tower Street, which led out of the Bogside and into the Protestant Fountain Street area. At their 11 August meeting which permitted the Orange marches, the Stormont Cabinet had also decided to allow mobilization of the B Specials at the discretion of the local police. Ministers were worried, though, at how un-trained the B Specials were for crowd control and riot duty. In Derry, on the evening of the 12th – after the wind changed and CS clouds began to blow over Protestant streets as well – a B Special patrol was mobilized around Fountain Street. For the first two days they seemed to exer-cise a restraining influence on the Protestants in the area. But on Thursday, the 14th, a second B Special patrol was mobilized there. The events which followed were to be the final trigger of British military involvement.

While 'Free Derry' was celebrating its 'victory' through-out the 13th and 14th – and the police massed, impotent, on the fringes of the ghetto – the spill-over of the revolt else-where in the province was disastrous. For in response to appeals from the Bogside, Civil Rights leaders called mass meetings in several towns; inevitably, they led to violence.

Dungiven, still tense after the behaviour of the B Specials there on 12 July (which we described in the last chapter), was one of the first to react. On 13 August mobs assembled on the street and attacked the police station, to be driven away with warning shots. The Courthouse and the Orange Hall were then burnt down.

The cathedral city of Armagh was next. The implications of what happened there were frightening. A Civil Rights meeting was held in the town on the evening of Thursday 14 August; trouble broke out afterwards. The police intervened and the Catholic crowd was driven up Cathedral Road – the two mobs continuing to stone each other over the heads of the police. Because of the disturbance, the B Specials were called in. Without the knowledge of his seniors, a junior RUC man then ordered a platoon of the Specials (from a nearby village, Tynan) to follow him in their cars to Cathedral Road – at the rear of the Catholic crowd.

On the way, fatally, he and the Specials lost each other. When the Specials arrived, therefore, they were leaderless and faced by a Catholic mob furious at what they saw as an attempted ambush. To defend themselves they had only their guns – four revolvers, two Sterling sub-machine guns, and eleven rifles. They used them. Thirteen of the seventeen members of the platoon opened fire, with 24 shots. One Catholic, John Gallagher, was killed by a high-velocity bullet in the back. Another was hit in the left buttock. A third was hit in the leg. Nearby houses and a road sign were also hit.

The Tynan platoon were appalled by what had happened and later made a clumsy effort to cover up their part in this shooting. The reason why the luckless platoon only had these lethal weapons – and not the riot sticks which were what the Ulster Cabinet had envisaged – lays bare the fatal weakness of a one-party system in which the political process and the forces of armed supremacy are intimately linked.

The District Commandant of the B Specials in Armagh was also a powerful figure in the local Unionist party. When the senior RUC man on the spot was later asked, at the Scarman tribunal, why he had not removed the B Specials' arms, he replied: 'I do not consider it to be open to me to direct them.' He was pressed: 'Could you not insist that it would really be too dangerous and unfair to the men to put them on the streets with side-arms and without batons or shields or helmets?' The unhappy man blurted out the truth: 'I think that would be completely ignoring the unique position which these men had in Government circles.'

It was precisely the effects of this untrained and ill-equipped militia, outside anyone's control, that precipitated the final conflagration in Derry. By the morning of Thursday the 14th, after more than forty-eight hours of rioting, the police and the Bogsiders had fought each other to a standstill. It was at that point that a unit of the B Specials stationed on the city walls overlooking the Bogside began to throw stones on the Catholics below. The reason was simple: the B Specials were having stones flung at them, and they had neither helmets nor shields to protect themselves. Retaliation was their only defence.

So began the communal confrontation which the RUC in Derry had feared for months past. Rioting broke out between Protestants and Catholics in the Long-Tower Street/Fountain Street area. The police – depleted by casualties, exhausted by the previous forty-eight hours – were overwhelmed. When another unit of the B Specials had to be deployed in the Fountain Street area to relieve them, some B Specials joined in the rioting and in the burning of Catholic homes.

124

At 1.30 that afternoon, Thursday the 14th, as the Home Affairs minister, Robert Porter, was eating in the dining-room at Stormont, the RUC Inspector General, Peacocke, telephoned to ask for military help. Shortly after 2 p.m., in the Prime Minister's room there, Porter, Peacocke, the Army Chief of Staff, Brigadier Dyball – with, at intervals, Chichester-Clark himself, Brian Faulkner and another minister – decided to give in. They had to leave the Parliament building and walk the 300 yards or so to the Cabinet office where there was a scrambler telephone. Chichester-Clark made his request to Downing Street at 3 p.m. At 4.30 p.m., Wilson and Callaghan sent back their agreement. (Had Chichester-Clark not asked by 5 p.m., in fact, Wilson and Callaghan had been planning to order him to do so.) To observe the legal formalities, a letter from the police chief, Peacocke, was delivered to the GOC, General Freeland. He, of course, knew already.

At 5 p.m., lorries of men from the First Battalion, the Prince of Wales' Own – those who had been on 'stand-by' at Sea Eagle base outside the city – rumbled over Craigavon Bridge across the River Foyle and into the heart of Derry. It was Thursday, 14 August 1969. The troops, said a spokesman in Whitehall, would be back in barracks by the weekend. But the catastrophe of Belfast was still to come.

Chapter 8
The Truth about the 'Pogrom'

In Derry a Catholic victory was always possible, for the Catholics have a local majority and easy access to the border with the Republic. In Belfast, on the other hand, the Catholics are outnumbered and hemmed into their ghettoes: traditionally, the Belfast Catholics have seen themselves as hostages for the good behaviour of their co-religionists elsewhere. On the night of Thursday 14 August 1969 a few hours after British troops had moved into Derry, that traditional mechanism went into action in Belfast.

The events in Belfast are now known in Catholic mythology as 'the pogrom'. This is a misreading of history as severe as any Protestant rubbish about 1688. The Scarman tribunal transcripts not only disclose nothing remotely akin to the Turkish massacre of the Armenians. They do not even support the idea that there was a Protestant plot to attack the Catholics – except late in the rioting, and even then in supposed self-defence. Nor is there much evidence that the B Specials were any less irrelevant to what happened than was the IRA.

What the Scarman transcripts do horrifyingly disclose is that the RUC on the night of 14–15 August used firearms with such freedom as to disqualify it from being called a police force. And while there can be no doubting the ferocity of the violence which reached its apex in Belfast on the night of 14–15 August – before it was extinguished, ten civilians had been killed, and 145 civilians and four policemen wounded by gunfire – the bloodshed was altogether more random than accepted accounts have suggested. The ultimate tragedy of Belfast is that, given better standards of policing that night, bloodshed need never have happened on the scale it did.

Rioting, burning or shooting took place in three separate areas of the city – Divis Street, Crumlin Road, and Clonard. Each riot was precipitated by different forces. Each, once begun, fanned the flames of the others. We propose to examine in detail the first and finally the most savage of those riots: Divis Street.

The geography of the area was critical to what happened. The heartlands of the Protestant and Catholic ghettoes in Belfast lie along two roads that run parallel to one another westward from the city centre. The northern one is the Shankill Road (Protestant); the southern one is the Falls Road (Catholic). Divis Street is an extension of the Falls Road, actually running into the city centre. Those two roads – the Shankill, and the Falls plus Divis – are joined by seven narrow streets which run north–south. Four of these – rows of low, crammed terrace houses – are mixed: Catholics live at the southern Falls end, Protestants live at the northern Shankill end. There the catastrophe of 14–15 August began.

It all started the day before, on the evening of 13 August, with a Civil Rights meeting in the courtyard of Divis Flats – a high-rise block on the south, or Catholic, side of Divis Street. The meeting was called by the Civil Rights Association after appeals from Derry to 'take the heat off the Bogside', and to protest about police behaviour there. Only

127

200 people turned up. It was peaceful, orderly and was said afterwards to have had a 'calming effect'. But the meeting decided to hand in a protest about the alleged brutality of the police in Derry to their local police headquarters. This was in Springfield Road, which lies westwards of the flats along the Falls Road. So along the Falls the crowd somewhat noisily marched.

As the lawyer for the Falls Road residents commented to the Scarman tribunal: 'If the petition had been received . . . (at Springfield Road) . . . the probabilities are that the whole incident would have fizzled out there and then.' But although the RUC District Inspector, named Cushley, was in the station, he refused to accept the protest because 'it was not the proper place'. The local headquarters had been transferred temporarily to the Hastings Street station–which was right back down by Divis Street. Cushley promptly departed for Hastings Street, to be ready to receive the protest. While this bureaucratic nicety was sorted out, however, the crowd had been standing around outside the Springfield Road station for about fifteen minutes. As their irritation grew, a few windows were smashed. But as the crowd set off back down the Falls Road to the Hastings Street station, they were, although disgruntled, still more or less peacefully inclined. Just as they arrived, however, a group of teenagers broke away and began to stone the police station. A few who lived near by produced petrol bombs, which were also thrown. No damage was done.

But, amazingly, District Inspector Cushley *ordered out the police armoured cars*. The fact that a police force anywhere in the United Kingdom should have armoured cars at all seems startling. But the Royal Ulster Constabulary were not only policemen; they were also a para-military force, whose duties included guarding the border. And it was for border duties that O'Neill's hard-line Minister of Home

Affairs, William Craig – the man who had dubbed the Civil Rights movement a cloak for IRA subversion – had in 1967 ordered a squadron of armoured cars from the Belfast shipyards. The Dublin Government thought this almost certainly contravened a treaty between Britain and the Republic of Ireland – and that, as we shall see later, had serious consequences.

What mattered on the night of 13 August, however, was that these armoured cars, known as Shorlands, were widely supposed still to be on the border. Certainly, Craig's successor as Minister of Home Affairs, Robert Porter, had no idea they had been brought to Belfast – and would not have approved if he had known. Now, three or four of them roared out from the courtyard behind Hastings Street police station. The crowd, forgetting in its terror all thoughts of an orderly petition, scattered as the Shorlands confronted them. And they scattered into two of the 'mixed' streets running northward up to the Protestant Shankill.

Relations between the communities on the two streets had been good for decades. The communal rioting of the early 1920s was almost forgotten. But tensions had been mounting there for months – mainly because of the Civil Rights campaign, but inevitably heightened in the previous forty-eight hours by the news from Derry. Now, seeing the Catholic crowd approaching, the Protestants thought an attack was coming. They realized almost immediately that this was not so – but the seed had been planted.

Meanwhile the great mass of the Catholic crowd had headed the half-mile back up the Falls Road to Springfield Road police station once more. This time, outraged by the police decision to loose armoured cars upon them, they attacked it in grim earnest with stones and petrol bombs. The first shot rang out. Allegedly as a warning, the RUC fired from the station. Two youths were injured – the forensic

129

evidence suggested by direct hits rather than ricochets. A couple of people in the crowd had guns, and they fired back. A policeman on the station roof opened up with a rifle. There were no casualties.

Why did the RUC over-react so violently in Belfast that night? Partly because they were an exhausted and depleted force after a summer of rioting. Partly because they were deeply, and properly, frightened by the violence they could see welling up in both communities – being mainly Protestant, they were of course more frightened of potential Catholic violence. But mainly the RUC over-reacted, so far as we can see, because by Wednesday 13 August every man in the RUC was filled with stories of the insurrection in Derry – *and was expecting the same to happen among the Catholics in Belfast*. According to the RUC Deputy Commissioner in Belfast, Sam Bradley, intelligence sources said that the IRA had plans to pick off selected officers with sniper fire. (In fact, it was not until October 1969 that the first RUC man was killed – by a Protestant gunman.) A few minutes after Cushley ordered out the armoured cars from Hastings Street station, an incident further up the Falls Road seemed to the RUC to confirm their fears.

One RUC armoured vehicle parked for only a couple of minutes in Leeson Street – a militant Republican stronghold running south off the Falls Road which the police had not really patrolled for a year past. It was stoned before the RUC man inside, realizing his imprudence, could drive off. When the RUC men got out of the vehicle and, sensibly, tried to clear the crowd with batons, they were shot at. And a hand grenade was thrown. Amazingly, nobody was hurt. Equally surprisingly, the disturbance then petered out – most possibly because the crowd themselves were abashed by this violence. But the Leeson Street incident finally seems to have convinced the RUC in Belfast that they were facing

130

an armed Catholic uprising. And the Belfast police commissioner Harold Wolseley reported to Porter later on that evening, 13 August, that the IRA were playing a leading part. That conviction dictated the disastrous police response over the next forty-eight hours.

The Shorland armoured cars had now been brought on to the streets of Belfast – unarmed. But a second and literally fatal decision had also been taken. On the morning of Wednesday, 13 August – that is, before trouble had broken out in Belfast – Anthony Peacocke, head of the RUC, had consulted with Harold Wolseley, the Commissioner for Belfast, and with Wolseley's deputy, Sam Bradley. An immediate order had been placed for eight more Shorlands. This decision was certainly Peacocke's, as evidence before the Scarman tribunal shows. But the decision was also taken at or shortly after that meeting to allow the existing Shorlands to mount their usual weapons, 0.30 calibre Browning machine-guns.

Bradley told the tribunal that he and Wolseley recommended to Peacocke that the guns – normally kept for border skirmishes – should be fitted. Peacocke said he could not remember being asked to take such a decision; the evidence of the Home Affairs Minister, Porter, as to Peacocke's later reactions supports this. Whoever gave the order, what matters is that the machine-guns were fitted and several, inevitably inexperienced, crews were assembled to man them.

The Browning 0.30-inch medium machine-gun has a range of almost two-and-a-half miles, and fires six to eight high-velocity bullets every second. It can only fire bursts, never single shots. It was for many years the American Army's standard machine-gun. This sophisticated weapon of war was now to be used for riot control in the huddled streets of Belfast.

As if this firepower were not enough, the B Specials now

appeared. At 3 p.m. the next day, Thursday 14 August, the B Specials were mobilized throughout the province. That was a Cabinet decision. But the Cabinet were thinking of B Specials with batons. In Belfast, however, they went on the streets carrying their arms. Who decreed that is, once more, uncertain. There is some evidence that it was neither the Inspector-General, Peacocke, nor the Belfast Commissioner, Wolseley. But by the 14th the city was so tense that it seems possible that nobody decided it.

The scene was set for the tragedy which followed.

From early in the evening of the 14th, the tension was evident in the 'mixed' streets running between the Falls Road and the Shankill Road – particularly in the two, Dover Street and Percy Street, up which the crowd scattered by the armoured cars had fled the night before. Knots of people gathered in doorways. About 8.30 p.m. a company of B Specials came up to the northern, Shankill, end of the streets. Their orders were sensible: to prevent anyone other than residents from entering the streets at the Protestant end. After an hour or so, though, the B Specials had so mingled with the Protestants of the two streets as to form one crowd. Peacefully, though with a certain menace, they all drifted south down the streets towards the Catholic, Falls Road, end where a riot was now in progress.

What had happened was that, when the Catholics of the Falls heard of the mobilization of the B Specials – it was broadcast as a news flash at 3 p.m. on the 14th – they reacted with real fear. The armoured cars roaring along Divis Street–Falls Road the night before had left the Catholics panic-stricken at the force the RUC were evidently prepared to use. Now, they thought the B Specials, the police reserve, were being mobilized as assault troops. Barricades went up at strategic points along the Falls Road. Hundreds of petrol bombs were prepared.

In this atmosphere of tension, a large crowd assembled in the Divis Street end of the Falls Road, hard by Hastings Street police station. Predictably, a few teenagers attacked the place with stones and petrol bombs. Equally predictably, the police again over-reacted. Once more, the armoured cars – this time, armed – were ordered on to the streets. They drove up and down Divis Street – as before, scattering the Catholic crowd up into the 'mixed' streets running north. Two of those streets were, of course, Percy Street and Dover Street – down which a murmuring Protestant crowd, among them B Specials, was gathering.

This spill-over from the Divis Street rioting – plus, it must be said, blatant provocation on the Catholic side – led, on the evening of the 14th, to the worst rioting the city had known in fifty years. For the Protestants of the 'mixed' streets to a certain extent shared the police interpretation of events, and believed that the Divis Street rioting was part of a coordinated insurrection. When Catholic crowds then began to appear on Percy Street and Dover Street for the *second* night, the Protestants, fortified by the presence in their midst of the B Specials, assumed the worst: their area around the Shankill was going to be invaded. In self-defence, the Protestants prepared to strike back.

As Protestant mobs eddied with mounting anger down from their end of Dover Street and Percy Street, the situation to the south in Divis Street was worsening. The Catholic residents of the tall Divis Flats could see from the roof and from their balconies that the Catholic crowds below were about to be taken in the rear by a police sortie from Hastings Street station. Perhaps the Divis flats complex itself would now be 'invaded'. Barricades went up around the courtyards of Divis Flats. And as the police from the station advanced up Divis Street they were showered with petrol bombs from the roof of one block, and forced to withdraw. The police afterwards said there may have been shooting from the flats, but there is little evidence of this. At this point the situation went mad.

For, unknown to almost all the Catholics around Divis Flats – and so far as can be seen, to the horror of most of those who did know – a crowd of about 100 Catholic youths had marched north from Divis Street up the 'mixed' Dover Street carrying a tricolour and singing the Irish Republic's national anthem, 'A Soldier's Song'. They then cut through into the next 'mixed' street, which was Percy Street. They emerged into full view of the Protestant crowd milling around at the Shankill Road end. It was an act of criminal folly. The hooligans who did it had been involved in the initial attack on Hastings Street police station the night before. They claimed later that they were 'provoked' by the sight of the B Specials mingling with the Protestant crowds in Dover Street and Percy Street. This is unlikely: they began the march at a point from which these B Specials were invisible.

The Protestants were electrified. The Republican invasion was coming. Within seconds, the raging Protestant mob began to counter-attack southward down Dover Street and Percy Street, some armed with sticks and a few with hatchets. The time was about 10.30 p.m. Hundreds of stones and petrol bombs were thrown as the Catholics tried to halt the Protestant advance by tearing down iron hoardings for barricades. But the Protestants came on. And as they came they tossed petrol bombs into Catholic houses on the way. By midnight both streets were ablaze.

According to independent evidence to the Scarman tribunal, the first shots that night came from that Protestant mob. As the Catholics retreated back into Divis Street, a number were wounded. Around midnight the Protestants broke out of the southern end of Percy Street and Dover

134

Street, and into Divis Street – where a Union Jack was then triumphantly planted in the centre of the 'rebel' stronghold.

There were then other, less symbolic, victories to be won. On Divis Street, opposite the southern mouth of Percy Street, stands the Catholic St Comgall's School. The Protestant crowd now began to attack this with petrol bombs. Suddenly, a burst of automatic fire swathed across Divis Street. A Protestant, Herbert Roy, was cut down. Other Protestants were injured. At that moment, three police armoured cars arrived on the scene.

Immediately they heard the burst of fire that cut down Herbert Roy, the police on the ground around the southern entrance to Dover Street opened fire. But the men in the three armoured cars from Hastings Street, hearing *that*, thought they themselves were under fire from Divis Flats. They prepared to shoot back.

In the opinion of District Inspector Cushley, in charge there, it would have been correct for the Shorlands to fire at the flats, if they could see an 'identifiable target'. That made it inevitable that innocent people in the flats would be endangered. One such person was Trooper McCabe, a British soldier at home on leave, lying on his balcony. Another was a nine-year-old boy named Patrick Rooney, who was sheltering in his back bedroom.

Head-Constable Gray first told the armoured car crews they could open fire. Gray was under considerable pressure. 'People were shouting, "A man is dying, a man is dying. What are you going to do?" ' he said later. (The man was Herbert Roy, bleeding to death on the pavement.) Gray's suggestion was that the armoured cars might fire over people's heads; Inspector Cushley amplified this by saying they could engage 'identifiable targets'.

Exactly how the cars came to open fire, and what they

135

thought they were firing at, is not clear from the evidence of
the crews – who appeared at the Scarman tribunal under
code-names. One man thought there was a machine-gunner
by the Divis Flats. Another saw a grenade thrower. It was
quite clear, however, from subsequent investigation that at
least eight bursts of Browning fire hit the Divis flats. The
guns cannot in practice fire fewer than five rounds in a
burst.

Forensic evidence later established that a large area of the
buildings had been sprayed with bullets: at least thirteen
flats were damaged. On his balcony, Trooper McCabe was
killed instantly. And four high-velocity bullets pierced two
walls before entering Patrick Rooney's bedroom and blow-
ing half his head away. Some bursts whizzed past Divis Flats,
travelled two miles westwards across the city, and in landing
struck the front of another police station. The men inside
immediately assumed that they too were under IRA
attack.

The armoured cars went into action again later, around
Divis Street – and in a separate riot to the north, in the
Ardoyne area off the 'mixed' Crumlin Road. There, similar
muddle and over-reaction killed three, and led to the burning, by a crowd including B Specials, of three Catholic
streets. Yet any Catholic armed resistance was slight, and late
in coming. There was machine-gun fire at one point from
Divis Street and a street off it. And three or four men armed
with Thompson sub-machine guns and a revolver opened up
from inside St Comgall's School. Eight Protestants were injured in Percy Street. Most of the 'Catholic' shooting in the
Ardoyne was in fact by the police themselves.

When daylight broke on 15 August, a scene of utter deso-
lation lay around Divis Street and the Ardoyne. Six people
were dead – most of them killed in Catholic areas. Around

150 houses, all Catholic, had been destroyed by fire. From houses still unburnt, lorries and vans were stacked with furniture. Nearly all the Catholic houses still intact in the 'mixed' streets were evacuated that day. (Some evacuees burnt their own homes on leaving.) Nobody was waiting for a second night.

The flow of events now began to submerge both Army and politicians. The tragic result, twelve hours later, was that the British Army went into Belfast too late to protect the Catholics from attack, too early to be prepared, and too sparsely to be effective.

When his troops went into Derry on Thursday the 14th, the Ulster commander, General Freeland, realized that they would have to cover Belfast, too. But although Whitehall had known from midday on Wednesday the 13th that troops would be going into Ulster, *no reinforcements were sent to Freeland until more than forty-eight hours afterwards.* According to an excellent source, this stemmed from a decision on the 14th by Wilson and Callaghan that the troops should only go into Derry. They were still trying to minimize the British military involvement.

That seemed reasonable at the time. But its effect was that when the morning of Friday 15 August dawned in Belfast, General Freeland was in a precarious position. Nominally, he had three battalions at his disposal. One, the First Battalion, the Prince of Wales' Own, had gone across to Derry. But the disturbances there were so bad that, to ring the Bogside, Freeland had also had to strip a further company from his second battalion and send that across to Derry too. So the forces he had for Belfast were tiny. He had the First Battalion, the Royal Regiment of Wales, which had only arrived that week and was so under-manned that it was down to three companies, instead of the usual four – and from this he had stripped the company for Derry. And he had his garrison battalion, the Second Queen's – which was also down to three companies. Instead of a nominal eight companies, therefore, Freeland was left with five to cover Belfast. It could not be done.

On Friday morning, Freeland told Whitehall that because he was so short of troops their deployment in Belfast would need exceptional care. Several of his officers had been 'casing' the city's likely trouble spots from cars for weeks; early on Friday – organized by Freeland's Brigade commander, Brigadier Hudson – they drove through the areas of the previous night's rioting. Hudson's estimate was that the Army would need thirty-six hours. Freeland was unhappy with this: at a meeting in police headquarters, he urged Hudson and the police commisioner, Wolseley, to speed their preparations.

In the meantime, however, in Whitehall, the Vice-Chief of the General Staff, Lieutenant-General Sir Victor Fitzgeorge-Balfour, agreed to the thirty-six hours' grace. (The Chief of the General Staff was on holiday.) When the Home Secretary, Callaghan, got back to his desk on the morning of Friday the 15th, he was told, therefore, that the troops were going into Belfast the next day, Saturday 16 August.

There is conflicting evidence on what followed. Shortly after 9 a.m. on that Friday morning the Home Affairs minister, Porter, saw Wolseley, the Belfast Police Commissioner. Both were gloomy about the RUC's ability to take another night's rioting, though Wolseley knew the Army's view that it would need more time. But around 11.30 the RUC Inspector General, Peacocke, gave Porter his verdict: it looked as if the Army would be needed at once.

The Stormont Cabinet met at noon. Twenty-five minutes later, they agreed to ask London for troops in Belfast. Callaghan had pre-empted them. At noon he had a press briefing scheduled at the Home Office. With the morning papers full of news and photographs of the burning of Belfast, he could hardly have cancelled it. But facing hostile questions, Callaghan reassured his audience. 'Gentlemen,' he announced, 'the troops are going into Belfast.'

Freeland got the news of this abrupt acceleration of the move into Belfast when he happened to tune in to BBC radio's World at One news programme. And the Army minister, Hattersley, was called out of a restaurant to be told by his private office what the Home Secretary had just done. There followed an altercation of no mean proportions, which culminated in this exchange:

Fitzgeorge-Balfour (opposing the move as premature): 'As an old soldier, let me tell you that time spent on reconnaissance is never wasted.'

Hattersley: 'As a young politician, let me tell you that when the Home Secretary says troops are going into Belfast, troops are going into Belfast.'

Three hours later – Stormont's request was 'granted' at 3.10 p.m. – the soldiers were desperately trying to get between the two communities, without any certainty where one ended and the other began. 'We couldn't have been worse off,' said Freeland. Out of the confusion, another Catholic myth was born. That Friday night, a reinforcement battalion, the Third Light Infantry, landed at Aldergrove airport outside the city and drove straight to positions along the Crumlin Road. They were too late. That evening, the Protestants burned an entire Catholic street to the ground.

What happened was, once again, unpremeditated, the product more of fear than of malice, and avoidable with adequate policing. The disturbances began in the Clonard area about 3 p.m. on Friday afternoon. They ended twelve hours later. Once again, the lethal factor was geography.

The Clonard is a small Catholic enclave which juts from the top of the lower Falls area into the Protestant Shankill district.

To the north and east, the Clonard is bordered by the semi-circle of Cupar Street, to the south by the Falls Road, and to the west by Springfield Road. The area is in fact little more than a cluster of tiny streets dominated by the Redemptorist Clonard monastery. The area had a Protestant-Catholic Peace Committee and largely through its influence, peace was maintained – until Friday afternoon.

The spark that was, unwittingly, to ignite the Clonard was once again over-reaction – this time by a Catholic priest. On the afternoon of Thursday the 14th an anonymous telephone call warned a priest that Clonard monastery was to be burnt down. The threat was reported to the police, but the priests felt that the RUC did not then give enough protection. So the rector, Father McLaughlin, began to raise a local vigilante force to protect the monastery. (The police, of course, had other worries.)

In the early hours of Friday the 15th, the Catholics became even more jittery when a sniper was reported to be shooting at their homes from the grounds of the monastery. (The firing was actually that of the police armoured cars blazing away in Divis Street. Some of the bullets from their Browning machine-guns whizzed into Clonard, two-thirds of a mile away.)

News of the riots brought to the monastery two men – one armed with a shotgun, the other with a .22 rifle. There already were Catholics patrolling the grounds outside. But Father McLaughlin, his fears apparently confirmed by the 'sniper', let the two new recruits take up position actually *inside* the monastery, on the top floor. McLaughlin only let them in because he expected an armed attack, and he insisted that they confine their role to a 'completely de-

140

fensive' one. But it was, with hindsight, a calamitous decision.

For when the Protestants learned in the course of Friday of the two 'IRA gunmen' – as they immediately called them – in the monastery, there was hysteria. The Peace Committee met at 2.30 p.m. Friday afternoon, and its members desperately set about calming tempers and giving mutual guarantees of non-aggression. But the Protestant crowds of Cupar Street and Conway Street were now in no mood to consider peace after the 'armed uprising' around Divis Street the night before, and more particularly, the take-over of Clonard by 'IRA gunmen'.

The police at Springfield Road, exhausted, could not meet the Catholic appeals for protection for Clonard. The trouble broke around 3.00 p.m. on Friday afternoon. Within half an hour a Catholic boy – Gerald Macauley, aged fifteen – had been shot dead. As the Protestants invaded the monastery grounds they were fired on. The Protestants fired back. And an entire Catholic street, Bombay Street, was razed. (Meanwhile, in the Ardoyne on the evening of the 15th, another twenty-three Catholic homes were burned out.)

From that spasm of destruction was born the first of many Catholic myths about the British troops in Ulster. The Army, it was said, had stood by and let Bombay Street burn. The truth was that Freeland had just enough men to cover Divis Street. The few he could spare, he did indeed send the half-mile up the Falls Road to the Clonard area. But, relying on advice from the RUC, they were stationed in Cupar Street to protect the Protestants. Meanwhile, some of the residents of Cupar Street were out attacking the monastery. The only troops anywhere near Bombay Street were a handful of Welsh soldiers. And they did not have the faintest idea which side was which.

The myth of Bombay Street, apart, however, there could

be no doubt whose side the Army was thought to have come in on. 'If only the bloody British Army hadn't come in,' a Unionist senator complained at large in the members' dining-room at Stormont, 'we'd have shot ten thousand of them by dawn.'

The bitterness was common to the Protestant community. (It was not the Catholics but Ian Paisley who first compared the British Army to the SS.) And this, together with some fine reforming rhetoric from James Callaghan, obscured for a time the underlying reality: when the Labour Government sent troops to aid 'the civil power' in Ulster, the effect was to support the Orange supremacy. In at least one quarter, however, the truth was realized. Aboard the Thames houseboat which is his London residence, Captain Lawrence Orr, leader of the Unionist MPs at Westminster and Grand Master of the Grand Orange Council of the World, exulted. 'We're getting the troops,' he said, 'and we're getting them without strings.'

Chapter 9
Labour Takes the Soft Option

A few days after Britain thus entered its most significant military commitment for a generation, there was a meeting at which the Labour Cabinet solemnly asked themselves if there might not be some Oxford academics who could perhaps advise them on Northern Ireland matters. After the advice which the Cabinet had got from Whitehall's 'experts' on Ulster that there was a good chance of the August parades passing off peacefully, ministers were not disposed to listen to them again. On the other hand, Westminster's self-imposed ignorance of Ulster's affairs was such that nobody else knew anything about the place.

Yet the Labour Government, chiefly through the presence of James Callaghan, managed to give the impression of being more or less in control of Ulster. This is something that the Tories failed to do, but in retrospect this had more to do with the fact that Labour were lucky to lose the General Election before the new season of Orange marches began, and before the emergence, late in the drama, of the IRA gunmen. The truth is that Labour's policy on Ulster was short-term and limited in its objectives. The Cabinet's Northern Ireland Committee – Wilson, Callaghan, Jenkins, Stewart, Healey, Gardiner, Crossman – decided this quite deliberately. Their discussions now throw an interesting light on what, in August 1969, reasonable men thought the trouble was about in Ulster.

In the Committee's mind, the first need was urgency: the first criterion by which to judge any reform proposal the likely speed of its effect. From this standpoint, what one of its members later called 'identifiable social grievances' loomed much larger for the Committee than the political problems. The police had to be reformed and the B Specials wound up. That – in the wake of the riots – was the Committee's first and unsurprising decision. The ending of discrimination in housing, and of the gerrymandering of local authorities were, they decided, the next priorities.

Simple caution played a part in this. The Ulster Prime Minister's brother, the Westminster MP Robin Chichester-Clark, had lobbied fellow MPs vigorously that week with the proposition that, for the moment, the rights and wrongs of the Unionist position scarcely mattered, since they were after all the legally-constituted government of the majority. Besides, as he informed one MP in a nice blend of constitutionalism and *force majeure*: 'They have had power for fifty years; they are not going to give it up now.' The Cabinet's Northern Ireland Committee were all aware that without the commitment of a daunting number of troops the Army would be hard pressed to cope with more trouble just yet, and that – as Robin Chichester-Clark had hinted – nothing would inflame the Protestant majority faster than tinkering with Stormont.

The Committee did discuss whether to introduce proportional representation in Ulster. (At its simplest, this means that voters signify not merely their first choice but also their second: the victor is the candidate with most overall community support. The outcome, in a context such as Ulster, would in theory be that this support would go mainly

to moderates.) But the committee postponed action on proportional representation. They could not agree what form it
ought to take. They feared the communities were so polar-
ized that for a long time no moderates would emerge. They
also considered that, until the Catholics could first obtain
basic civil rights, their community's political demands were
unlikely to be articulated with any precision: was proportional representation what the Catholics wanted?

Above all, the Committee shelved proportional representation for the characteristic Wilsonian reason that it was a
long-term measure; and in August 1969 Wilson and his colleagues were interested only in immediate steps in Ulster.
The decision, and the policy it symbolized, are well described in the words of a civil servant: 'We chose the least
disturbing option every time.'

After those decisions, the Committee relapsed in the
months that followed, until it was, as one of its members put
it, 'mainly concerned with sorting out the endless disputes
between Freeland and the police or between the Ministry of
Defence and the Home Office'. Yet it was the working out of
the Committee's own policies on the streets that produced
these disputes. Indeed, the first tangible result of Labour
policy was a misunderstanding which almost destroyed the
authority of the British Government's chosen agent of
reform, James Chichester-Clark.

On 19 August 1969 – four days after the troops had gone
into Belfast – the Ulster Prime Minister escorted by Faulkner and Porter came to London for his first five-hour bar-
gaining session with Wilson, Callaghan and Healey.
Discussing strategy before the Downing Street meeting,
Chichester-Clark and Porter had realized that Labour
would want the B Specials disbanded. They also perceived
that it would be political suicide to agree. They devised a
scheme, and when the B men came up, Chichester-Clark

145

sprang it. Why not, he proposed, put not only police but also the B Specials under Army command? (He knew that was what Labour wanted to do with the police.) 'I think you could fairly say,' he reported later, 'that a pin might have been heard to drop.' While Wilson struggled to make conversation, Callaghan and Healey retired to consider this suspicious surrender. When they returned, accepting it, Chichester-Clark thought that he was home. He agreed to their suggestion that the B Specials should also be 'phased out' of riot control.

The meeting broke up just as ITN's News at Ten was beginning. Television cameras had been set up inside Number Ten, at one end of the long Pillared Room on the first floor. Seated in front of a lacquer screen, Wilson proceeded to spell out on News at Ten his agreement with Chichester-Clark. And he said, 'the B Specials are being phased out'. Horrified viewers in Ulster took this to mean disbandment. That was exactly what it did mean in the mind of Denis Healey at least. But it had not been agreed at the meeting. And, of course, it was not what Chichester-Clark had in mind at all. But he was at the other end of the Pillared Room, being made up, and he did not hear what Wilson was saying.

So when he followed Wilson on to the programme and muttered a few standard sentiments, he appeared to acquiesce in the destruction of the B men. He had no idea what he had done – or what had been done to him – until he landed at Belfast Airport in the early hours and was met by his incredulous wife, who had watched the programme. At once, a feeling of doom overcame Chichester-Clark.

In retrospect, he felt that he never really recovered from the damage the episode did him. Later that day, 20 August, a meeting of his troubled parliamentary party was called at Stormont Castle: he and his ministers managed to quieten the backbenchers with brave talk of mass ministerial resignations if the Specials were indeed disbanded. Frantic telephone calls came to Whitehall from Chichester-Clark and Porter, trying to 'clarify' the position. But Whitehall realized that, by one means or another, they had got what they wanted.

The Unionist confusion deepened the following day with the announcement that Lord Hunt, the man who had organized the first successful ascent of Everest, was to look into the whole structure of the Ulster police forces. Uneasy Unionists were not assuaged by reports that Lord Hunt was descended through his mother from one of the original thirteen apprentice boys who had shut the gates of Derry against its Catholic besiegers.

Nor were they reassured when, a few days later, Sir Leslie Scarman, a High Court Judge, was appointed to head a full judicial tribunal of inquiry into the disorders between April and August 1969. Lord Cameron had not yet reported on the disturbances in the five months before that. Northern Ireland was under extensive scrutiny. What, the Unionists wondered, would the findings be?

Into this atmosphere of uncertainty and fear James Callaghan now thrust his imposing presence. On 27 August the Home Secretary came to Belfast. It was a last-minute decision. The day before, he had sat patiently in Cabinet while his colleagues wrangled about whether the reforms contained in the Wilson–Chichester-Clark 'Downing Street Declaration' of 19 August would do the trick. The gloomy consensus was that they would not be enough, and that the Government had in the end only a slim chance of avoiding direct rule in Ulster. But, bored by all this talk, Callaghan finally announced: 'People are getting hurt over there. I'm not waiting, I'm going over.'

The Downing Street Declaration

... reaffirmed that in all legislation and executive decisions of Government every citizen of Northern Ireland is entitled to the same equality of treatment and freedom from discrimination as obtains in the rest of the United Kingdom, irrespective of political views or religion.

But it manifestly hedged on the crucial question of who called the shots on security: the Northern Ireland Government only promised 'to take into the fullest account' the views of the UK Government. The demonstration of whether or not there was any real firmness of purpose in the UK Government now rested with its Home Secretary in Belfast.

Callaghan had not at that point been any more notable a success as Home Secretary than he had as Chancellor of the Exchequer. Indeed, in twenty-one months in the job, he had already presided over the two most disreputable things the Wilson Government did in nearly six years: the passing of the Commonwealth Immigrants Act 1968, which deprived certain British citizens and passport-holders – East African Asians – of the right of entry into Britain; and the refusal to implement due and impartially recommended changes in parliamentary constituency boundaries which would have lost seats for Labour.

Ulster re-established him as a considerable figure. Callaghan defied history; he was the only British politician ever to improve his reputation by dealings with Ireland. There was something about the Ulster theatre of action which appealed to him: long afterwards he used still to speak with a lively relish of the sight of 'naked force' at work. And there was something about Callaghan which appealed to Ulster: he combined gravity with professionalism. Stormont civil servants, comparing him with their own stammering and tactless rulers, reflected how nice it would be to work for someone who did at least know the business.

For professionalism was what Callaghan exuded on that

first visit to Ulster. The O'Neill reform plans of the previous autumn were beginning to make a little progress. A suggested scheme for allocating council houses on a system of points according to need – the English way – had been sent out by Faulkner at the Ministry of Development; most councils had said they would adopt it or something like it. An ombudsman had been appointed to look into grievances against the central government: the new man held the same office at Westminster – Sir Edmund Compton. The Derry Commission was already building houses not with the aid of a ward map but according to an area plan drawn up by outside consultants. Undertakings to reform local government franchise, boundaries and functions had been renewed during the summer. Only the Special Powers Act was untouched.

But Callaghan could see that, except for what was being done in Derry, all this changed nothing. Local councils could still cheat on housing so long as the points scheme was neither rigorous nor mandatory. Nothing had been done about job discrimination even in the public sector, let alone the private. And relations between the two communities were hardly likely to settle down while a paper like Paisley's *Protestant Telegraph* (motto: 'The Truth shall Set you Free') could claim with impunity that any shortage of houses and jobs was all the fault of the Papists, since 'these people breed like rabbits and multiply like vermin'.

Still, the beginnings of movement were here: what was important was to sustain the momentum. Callaghan met Chichester-Clark and his cabinet, addressed them briskly – 'As I see it, these are the problems . . .' – and proceeded to enumerate the various sorts of discrimination still untouched. There was, according to one witness, practically a sigh of relief from the Cabinet. (Some, at least, had been expecting the dreaded words 'constitutional position' would come up.) 'I couldn't agree with you more,' Chichester-Clark said, 'indeed, I think everyone in this room agrees. What we cannot agree is what to do about it.' Callaghan: 'Well, I'll tell you what to do . . .' And did.

He decreed the setting-up of three working parties – on house allocation, job discrimination and community relations – their membership to comprise officials of both governments. And they had a deadline. Callaghan would be back in mid-October. In the meantime, they were left under the eye of the first 'UK representative', sent over by the British Government and installed in an office at Stormont Castle, Oliver Wright.

In the wake of the Downing Street Declaration, Wilson had considered sending a minister to Northern Ireland to keep an eye on Stormont. His Lord Privy Seal, Lord Shackleton, was the politician selected. The idea was dropped, partly because it would obviously have weakened Chichester-Clark's position, but mainly because nobody could work out whether Shackleton would be answerable to the Westminster Parliament and if so, for what. The Government sent a civil servant instead, borrowing for the purpose a Foreign Office diplomat. (Which immediately caused an argument in Whitehall, since the Foreign Office were incredulous that one of its senior fellows should be expected to report to Home Office men. A compromise was struck: he reported to both.)

Oliver Wright had been British ambassador in Denmark before coming to Belfast. His business at Stormont was to keep open the lines to Whitehall. He had good ones himself: before his Copenhagen posting he had been in Wilson's private office at Downing Street (from where he had gone, for instance, as an emissary to Rhodesia). He turned out to be very good at talking to Unionists. 'If I let the lines of communication go unused for a single day, they begin to silt up,' he once told Callaghan. This very facility had its drawbacks, though. 'I'm not saying Oliver went native, but he did begin to exaggerate the difficulties on the ground,' one minister recalled. Another remembers arriving at Stormont Castle, to find Wright – a burly figure 'in what I take it was a Prince of Wales check' – warming himself before the baronial fireplace. 'Ah,' the minister greeted him, 'the Squire of Stormont Hall.'

Wright could never quite conceal his feeling that he had not joined the foreign service to come to Belfast – his witty dispatches from this Ultima Thule were passed around the Foreign Office with great amusement. More importantly, Wright was of the school of thought which held that the Irish were the Irish, and that – 'a settler problem plus a tribal problem' – explained much of the trouble. While the Unionists on principle did not trust him, therefore – 'the Ambassador from England', they called him – the Catholics rapidly came to feel that he was in Stormont's pocket.

Already, the equation of British power with Orange supremacy was being drawn by the more perceptive Catholics. The only question was how long this conclusion would take to filter into the ghettoes of Belfast. Just how raw-edged the relationship was between the Catholic community and the British Army was demonstrated by, paradoxically, the first Army 'victory' in Ulster. In September, the Army got the Catholic barricades down – peacefully. It did so by talking with the local vigilantes – which meant the IRA.

It began like this. In the week after the riots, as the soldiers became a fixture along the Falls Road, they manned an official 'peace line', in parts a solidly constructed wall of corrugated iron and barbed wire, at other less sensitive points merely a notional line dividing rival ghettoes. The barricades which the Catholics had thrown up along spinal traffic roads, such as Divis Street and the Falls Road itself,

151

were dismantled within a few hours. But the barricades across the roads branching off this spine and into the Catholic ghetto remained in place. The Army's job was to get them down.

The Army, it must be remembered, had no idea of the tensions and factions within the Catholic community. Indeed, they seem at this early stage to have taken most of their information about the Catholics from the Unionists. The 'Sinn Fein Oath' provides a fascinating example of this.

The Army rapidly produced a booklet, called 'Notes on Northern Ireland', with the praiseworthy aim of giving its men some idea what the trouble was all about. (Considerably more use to the average squaddy was a map of Belfast equally speedily run off by the Army cartographers, showing by means of a colour code the religious complexion of the ghettoes throughout the city – 'our tribal map', the Army proudly called it.) But the booklet printed in full what purported to be the oath of the IRA's political wing, Sinn Fein. As a case-study in psychosis, it deserves reprinting:

'I swear by Almighty God . . . by the Blessed Virgin Mary . . . by her tears and wailings . . . by the Blessed Rosary and Holy Beads . . . to fight until we die, wading in the fields of Red Gore of the Saxon Tyrants and Murderers of the Glorious Cause of Nationality, and if spared, to fight until there is not a single vestige and a space for a footpath left to tell that the Holy Soil of Ireland was trodden on by the Saxon Tyrants and the murderers, and moreover, when the English Protestant Robbers and Beasts in Ireland shall be driven into the sea like the swine that Jesus Christ caused to be drowned, we shall embark for, and take, England, root out every vestige of the accursed Blood of the Heretics, Adulterers and Murderers of Henry VIII and possess ourselves of the treasures of the Beasts that have so long kept our Be-

loved Isle of Saints . . . in bondage . . . and we shall not give up the conquest until we have our Holy Father complete ruler of the British Isles . . . so help me God.'

The interesting point is that this oath was never taken by members of Sinn Fein. Sinn Fein, indeed, had no oath of any kind. The version the Army got dated from 1918, when it was forged by a group of over-heated Unionists. It has since appeared regularly in Loyalist Ulster news-sheets, most recently in Paisley's *Protestant Telegraph*. It bears exactly the same relation to reality as the Protocols of the Elders of Zion – indeed, in its constant dwelling on blood, it has much in common with the Protocols. As a document, therefore, it tells one nothing about Sinn Fein, though quite a lot about the impulses to violence in Unionism.

In this attitude of optimistic ignorance, the Army began to try to talk down the barricades. The first contact came when one or two officers in the regiment along the Falls expressed an interest in precisely what weaponry had been available during the riots. They asked the local priest, the able, beefy and extremely tough Father Padraig Murphy – who, in turn, 'did some asking around', as he delicately put it.

About 20 August there was a meeting in an upstairs room at Murphy's home, St Peter's Presbytery: the colonel of the regiment, the major and another officer – and the handful of men who had defended St Comgall's School when the Protestants swept into Divis Street. It was, according to one present, 'a technical discussion, between military men'. The IRA men – which is what they were – said they had had two pistols, but had sent a car chasing down to Dundalk, just over the border, to pick up three Thompson sub-machine guns. 'That explains it,' said the colonel. 'We thought we recognized forty-five calibre bullet holes.'

It was all very amicable. But Callaghan's visit on 27 August increased the pressure on the Army: the Unionists complained to the Home Secretary about the continued existence of the Catholic barricades; Paisley was beginning to make capital out of them. On 30 August Chichester-Clark went on television: his appeal for understanding was anodyne, but he specifically mentioned the barricades. Two days later, on 2 September, General Freeland – who up till then had had too much to do simply organizing his forces, now swollen to 6,000 men – made his first approach to the Central Citizens' Defence Committee, the CCDC.

The CCDC, based above the seedy Long Bar in Leeson Street, was the headquarters of the Belfast Catholics' various ad-hoc community defence groups. It would, emphatically, be false to equate the CCDC with the IRA. One of its most prominent figures, for instance, was the Social Democratic and Labour MP for the Falls, Paddy Devlin, and its chairman was later a Belfast produce broker, Tom Conaty. In the nature of things, though, this 'defence committee' did contain quite a few self-styled community defenders, which in Belfast meant the convinced Republicans, like Jim Sullivan, the Republican leader in the Lower Falls. It was to this uneasy coalition that Freeland now appealed – without success. After the armoured cars, the CCDC wanted guarantees that no RUC men would be allowed back into the Falls. Freeland could not possibly agree.

On 4 September the Army moved in at dawn and removed the barricades from Turf Lodge estate, a Catholic estate on the outskirts of Belfast west of the Falls. The residents were shaken – women formed a chain across the road – and though it passed off peacefully, the Army had taken a risk. And the Falls barricades were clearly next on the list.

The men who began talking were Sullivan, Murphy, the

remarkable Lower Falls priest, and Freeland's Chief of Staff, Tony Dyball, by then a Major-General. They had met on the so-called 'Peace Conference', a piece of window-dressing stitched together by Chichester-Clark before he set off for the 19 August meeting with Wilson. It was supposed to represent all sections of the community, but it fizzled out in October. Its only useful contribution, in fact, seems to have been as the means of introducing to each other the Army representative Dyball, Murphy, and the produce broker Tom Conaty – who had come, as he said later, as the Chamber of Commerce's 'tame Catholic'. (Over the next year, it should be said, Conaty speedily became less tame. Indeed, the radicalization of a peaceful, able, middle-class, non-sectarian Catholic like Tom Conaty should have warned the Army how disastrously things were going wrong.)

When Murphy, Sullivan and Dyball met on 5 September, things still looked hopeful. They agreed that some barricades – three big ones in Albert Street – would come down next day. The Army would come to St Peter's Presbytery at 9 a.m. – by which time everyone would be awake, breakfasted and unafraid. But at 6.30 a.m. next day, Murphy was woken to be told that the Army had already rolled up to the bar-ricades with cranes and armaments and was 'scaring hell out of everybody'. Murphy went to the barricades to meet Dyball. 'I get my orders,' Dyball said. There was a hasty compromise. Murphy, complete with megaphone, Paddy Devlin MP, and the local Republican leader Jim Sullivan, toured the area reassuring everyone. The residents took down the barricades themselves.

Perhaps things would have continued so pacifically. But later that same day, Saturday 6 September, Freeland him-self went to St Peter's Presbytery – for a follow-up to the 20 August meeting between the colonel and the IRA de-

155

fenders of St Comgall's School. There he met Murphy, Tom Conaty, and Jim Sullivan and what Murphy called 'six or eight good men and true' accompanying him.

Disastrously, in the Army view, news of the meeting reached Tony Geraghty of the *Sunday Times*, and next day we carried a report that the Army was negotiating with the IRA. It was one of those hard cases where a true report has unhappy consequences. That night, there was a Protestant riot in Belfast, and on Monday 8 September, Chichester-Clark had to go on television and announce in the most peremptory terms that the barricades were an act of defiance, and must come down in twenty-four hours. Both Army and Catholic leaders were horrified, and everyone began to play for time. The idea came up of a delegation to Callaghan – who promptly agreed to see whoever the Catholics might send at 2 p.m. on Thursday the 11th, four days later. In the meantime the threat of barricade removal was held over.

In this crisis, the UK representative Oliver Wright was helpless: he had made the mistake of endorsing Chichester-Clark's broadcast. At a meeting on Wednesday 10 September, Murphy and Conaty angrily asked him why he was putting them, the moderates, in this impossible position. Wright reportedly replied that it was all a mess, and what was he supposed to do? Murphy could not contain himself: 'Why won't you realize,' he shouted, 'that you are dining with a bunch of well-dressed rogues?'

After hasty factional debate, a formidable team was assembled to see Callaghan: Conaty and Murphy of the Peace Committee; Paddy Devlin and Paddy Kennedy, both MPs in the Catholic minority at Stormont for the central areas of Belfast; Gerry Fitt, a colleague at Stormont and also the Westminster MP for Belfast West; Jim Sullivan, the Falls Republican leader and chairman of the CCDC, and a lawyer named Jim McSparran – everyone thought they would need a sharp lawyer to cope with Whitehall.

The meeting lasted seven hours. Callaghan said that he couldn't see Sullivan, because of the rumpus over the *Sunday Times* story, so Sullivan and Paddy Kennedy repaired to the Irish Club. (According to Conaty, they later came back secretly to meet Callaghan in his ante-room.) The meeting was a formal negotiating session, and it ended in agreement – with Callaghan's personal assurance that if the barricades came down there would be soldiers at the ends of every street to prevent Protestant incursions.

The weekend was spent trying to sell this deal to the rest of the CCDC. At the CCDC headquarters, a two-day meeting began of 120 or so men from all over Belfast – a tough crew who inspired the two strangers, Murphy and Conaty, with something like awe. There was a good deal of dissent from the Callaghan package. And the dissent was led by Francis Card, Billy McKee and Leo Martin – the three men who were later to emerge as leaders of the Provisional IRA. This was the first meeting at which this identifiable hard-line group emerged inside the Catholic community. On Monday, when the Army was getting desperate, Father Murphy had to involve the power of the Church to get the deal through: he called in his bishop, Dr Philbin, Bishop of Down and Connor, to work over the CCDC leadership.

Just before midnight on Monday 15 September, Major-General Dyball rang Murphy, and the priest said it looked all right for Tuesday morning, but not too early, for God's sake. Murphy still needed time to explain things, to get some sleep, and get back on the street for the demolition. They agreed on 11 a.m. Then Dyball called back to suggest 9 a.m. Murphy said it was too early – even when the Bishop then called, at Freeland's instigation, also to ask for 9 a.m.

Murphy fell into bed at 5.30, to be awakened at 8.30 with the news that the Army had arrived.

When Murphy refused to come out, the Army waited patiently till 11 a.m., when Murphy and his bishop, Dr Philbin, turned up and the demolition began. In front of the TV cameras, the Bishop received a long denunciation from one of the future Provisionals. But all the barricades were down by Wednesday morning. When three Catholic houses were then promptly burnt out by Protestants, the barricades went up again. This time Murphy negotiated direct with Freeland. Once more they were removed.

Looking back on this knife-edged relationship, what neither side seems to have appreciated were the pressures operating on the other. Freeland knew little if anything about the bitterness welling up between the factions within the CCDC. And Murphy and Conaty did not know, because Freeland would not have stooped to tell them, the pressures he was under. When the Army waited those few hours before clearing the first barricades from Albert Street on 6 September, for instance, Freeland had abuse flung at him by prominent Unionists. One called him 'an enemy of the state'. And the leader of the Westminster Unionists, Captain Willy Orr, sent him a letter which Freeland later described merely as 'abusive'.

What, in particular, the Catholics did not know was that at a critical stage of the CCDC's debate on the Callaghan package, throughout Monday 15 September, Freeland's intervention had been decisive. In London that Monday, Wilson and Healey were listening to Callaghan describe his weekend negotiations with the Catholic delegation. Freeland and the Chief of the General Staff, Sir Geoffrey Baker, were there. Suddenly, while one of Wilson's secretaries came in with the news that Chichester-Clark proposed to go on television that evening to demand the removal of the barricades, Freeland asked Wilson to stop this irreparable folly. Wilson immediately ordered the Ulster Prime Minister to postpone the broadcast while they listened to Freeland – who proceeded to enthrall the more martial among them by spreading his maps of Belfast all over the Cabinet table. His case was persuasive: either the Army talked down the barricades, or it would have to fight its way through the Falls (which, of course, was just what many Unionists wanted to see). Wilson ordered Chichester-Clark to cancel his broadcast altogether.

That, under such pressures, a workable relationship between the Army and the Catholics should have survived through the autumn and into 1970 was an amazing feat of human relations. But the underlying danger remained – the fact that no Army, however well it conducts itself, is really adapted for police work. It was, however, the Protestants who first proved the point.

Chapter 10
Law versus Order

The Hunt Report on the Ulster police, issued on 10 October 1969, came as an appalling shock to Protestant opinion. Its release on a Friday night was admirably timed to fit in with the weekly rhythms of Belfast violence: Friday night is boozing night. (The mistake has not been repeated.) And it provoked riots on the Protestant Shankill Road as bad as anything since 1922.

Two events had already eroded the Unionists' crumbling self-assurance. One was the publication in September of the Cameron report on the violence that had attended the Civil Rights movement after the Derry march of October 1968. Chichester-Clark's Government made what it could of Lord Cameron's concession that among the Civil Rights movement and other advocates of reform were 'revolutionary and subversive elements'. But Cameron's evidence of the need for reform, whoever advocated it, was damning.

The other disquieting event for Unionists was the Conservative party conference which began at Brighton on 8 October. Quintin Hogg, in a speech larded with New Testament tags, got his biggest round of applause for the statement that 'There can be no justification at all for any discrimination whatever on the grounds of religion in our

160

United Kingdom.' And Hogg had been in Ulster the week-end before, too. Was there, the Unionists wondered, no justification for discrimination in the Catholic wish to sur-render part of the United Kingdom to a foreign power? The Unionist part of the Conservative Party's name had come to mean very little.

When Callaghan came back to Ulster, as he had warned, on 9 October, Chichester-Clark saw no alternative but to do his bidding. He had already appointed a Minister for Com-munity Relations and brought in a Bill appointing a Com-missioner for Complaints, to hear allegations of discrimination by local councils over jobs or houses. He now promised to review the law on incitement to religious hatred. There was to be an anti-discrimination clause in government contracts: public bodies were to make a de-claration of equality of employment opportunity and to adopt a code of employment procedure. A Local Govern-ment Staff Commission was to advise councils on filling senior posts.

On housing, the working party created under Callaghan's aegis had concluded that – with so many slums to rebuild – the only answer was to take the problem out of local author-ity hands altogether: there was to be a new central housing authority. (The Labour Cabinet Committee had in fact already decided upon that, as the only means of ending dis-crimination in housing allocation.) With local Govern-ment's main function thus removed, the plans for reorganizing it would have to be drawn up again. This actu-ally saved Chichester-Clark from an embarrassing rejection of the plans by his own supporters.

Finally the draught was sweetened with a little money. The rate of investment grant payable in Northern Ireland went up by five per cent to as much as fifty per cent, which made the province the cheapest place in the kingdom for

161

an industrialist to build a new plant. And two million pounds were to be spent on the relief of unemployment that winter.

Callaghan, as he arrived in Belfast on 9 October, believed that Ulster had passed through the valley of the shadow and was now on the upward climb. There were a number of reasons why he proved to be mistaken. One was that reforms like these could only bear fruit over a matter of years, while Catholics now pardonably expected them within months.

The deeper reason was that the structure of power was left intact. Catholics might get fairer representation than before; but they would still be a permanent minority, with no prospect of taking part in government at the centre, and no entitlement to seats on public bodies except by Protestant grace. Indeed, with the patronage these reforms placed in the gift of central government, the power of the unreformed Stormont was actually increased.

This impasse Callaghan himself endorsed. 'That speech of Jim's,' one of his colleagues later groaned. 'He just about said that the only thing wrong with Stormont was that the wrong party got elected.' As a summary of Callaghan's review of the reforms in the House of Commons on 3 October, that is slightly unfair. But, certainly, reform of Stormont was not on his list. In the months that followed, this speech was the framework within which the Labour Cabinet operated.

The Cabinet's deliberations on Northern Ireland were, as we have said, governed initially by a desire for quick results. By October 1969, it is reasonable to expect, their view might have broadened. It had not, for several reasons. One was that, temperamentally, several of the Northern Ireland Committee members – certainly Jenkins, Crossman, Stewart, and Healey – favoured as the only long-term solution

162

a united Ireland. But the thought of what would happen if this should leak appalled them. So they did not discuss it.

This attitude – 'the low-profile approach', one minister later called it – was bolstered by Whitehall. For the civil service regarded Ulster as an administrative problem much like any other: susceptible to the gradualist approach of 'good government'. Only when it became apparent that simple administrative reforms were insufficient did the question of political reform arise. The civil service in Britain prides itself, after all, on its ability to *respond* to articulated political demands; it does not create them. And in Ulster in 1969, the Catholic demands – whatever their root cause – were couched in the old bread-and-butter, Civil Rights terms. The vogue word was one of Callaghan's: 'amelioration'. One of his colleagues said later: 'Jim was terribly good on steadfastness, toughness, and fairness. He was not so hot on political reform.' But nobody, in politics or the press, made the point at the time.

Nor did the Cabinet Committee, preoccupied with the minutiae of Callaghan's reform programme, give any impetus. Not until Easter 1970 did the pressure of passing affairs slacken upon them. 'I think we could fairly be accused of wasting the last three months in office,' said one Committee member. 'But in the dying months of a government, you can never do much.'

During Callaghan's October 1969 visit, however, the lesson he might have learned from the events of the weekend which followed, was that the Army could not for long remain a neutral presence. It was too obtrusive; its methods potentially too rough. In particular there was a danger that in keeping order, it would increasingly seem to be protecting the established order, which was Orange. And this danger would be heightened if reform were slow or if the Chichester-Clark Government were ever to reassert its claim, inconclusively dismissed by the Downing Street Declaration, to be the Army's master.

Ironically, though, the common assumption in October 1969 was still that the British Government was on the Catholics' side – and the Protestants had this confirmed on 10 October, when Lord Hunt reported on the police, and Callaghan compelled the adoption of most of his report. The RUC was to be disarmed and made more like a British force. It was to be run by a new police authority with Catholics on it; and it was to have a British chief officer. Peacocke was retired early; and in came Sir Arthur Young, a humane and intelligent policeman of considerable colonial experience who had been running the City of London force. Far worse for the Protestants than all that was that the B Specials were indeed to be disbanded.

After the television muddle at Downing Street, of course, it looked as if Chichester-Clark had connived in the plot. He fought for time, to be told by Callaghan: 'If Stormont won't disband the B Specials, Westminster will.' He was allowed two ersatz replacements: a corps of part-time traffic policemen, and a new citizens' militia to be controlled by Westminster. But even the plans for this militia were drawn up in the Ministry of Defence. Chichester-Clark was allowed only to choose their name: the Ulster Defence Regiment. It sealed the Unionist grassroots distrust of him. But at the time, this was overlooked in the bloodshed along the Shankill Road on the night of 11–12 October.

It was the first day in Ulster of the new police chief, Sir Arthur Young, and he later described that Protestant rising in words approaching biblical force:

They rose in their wrath to demonstrate against the vile things Hunt had said about their wonderful police. They came in their thousands down the Shankill Road, appearing like animals, as if by magic. Then they marched to burn the Catholics out of the nearby flats. And as they came down the street, they were halted by a cordon of exactly the police they were marching to defend.

A reporter who was there adds: 'From fifty yards away you could smell the beer fumes coming off the crowd so strongly that you had the impression you could see them.'

An RUC constable, Victor Arbuckle, was then shot; no policeman, surely, could die a more ironic death than to be killed by a mob protesting against the disarmament of his own force. It was this rising which was to make the Protestant backlash a living threat in Chichester-Clark's mind. But, in retrospect, even more significant was the manner in which the Army put it down.

Freeland woke Callaghan to tell him: 'British troops are under fire,' and that he was going to fire back. 'Excitable chap,' Callaghan murmured afterwards.

The Army claimed later that the rioters fired more than 1,000 rounds from weapons which included a machine-gun and several sub-machine guns. Even if that figure is a little high, there can be no doubt that the Shankill riots were a considerable affray. The Army held its fire for an hour-and-a-half, during which time twenty-two soldiers were injured. The troops then opened fire: sixty-six shots, which killed two Protestants and wounded many more. The Army riot squads then moved in; their reaction was vigorous. 'We gave them a bloody nose,' said Freeland.

The heartiness of that euphemism begins to convey the difference between civilian and military scales of violence. Two years later, a police surgeon still recalled those riot casualties as the worst he had seen. He had found one man in a police cell twenty-four hours later with blood still coming from his nose and ears – one symptom of a possible fractured skull.

Edward Bawman, a thirty-two-year-old plumber's mate,

was one of the injured. Bawman and two friends were among those later accused of disorderly behaviour. An Army sergeant said that he had seen three men throwing stones: when they fled down a side street, he was ordered to pursue and arrest them. Bawman's story was that he and the other two had been talking outside his house when soldiers charged down the street. They fled indoors to avoid trouble. Seconds later the soldiers burst in. The evidence of violence was not arguable: Bawman had a broken arm, and at the hearing another was still in hospital with a fractured skull. 'They beat us and beat us and beat us,' he said. The case against Bawman and his friends was dismissed. The magistrate could find no clear pattern in the evidence, he said, except that violence had clearly been used and the accused men had been the recipients.

Given the savagery of the Shankill mêlée, the ruggedness of the military approach to law and order was understandable. But the evidence later given in court by Sergeant William Power, of the Third Battalion, the Light Infantry, raised deeper questions – foreshadowing very precisely the consequences of pretending that an army can be a substitute for a police force.

Sergeant Power was an outstanding soldier; he led one of the Army riot squads in the Shankill that night, and he won the B.E.M. for his courage. He gave evidence in at least a dozen cases – mostly charges of disorderly behaviour – arising from them. (Court records are not precise on the total.) In four, convictions were overturned on appeal when striking inconsistencies emerged from Army evidence.

One of the four concerned a twenty-six-year-old welder, John Malcolmson. In the magistrate's court on 13 October, Power said that he had seen Malcolmson throwing stones. A private in the 'snatch squads' corroborated this. At the higher court two months later, on 11 December, Power said

166

that he had seen Malcolmson throw a petrol bomb on the Shankill. Malcolmson said that he had thrown nothing, and even disputed that he had been arrested on the Shankill.

I was going home from the city centre using side streets. When I arrived at Diamond Street [a turning off the Shankill] the Army had started moving up it. I was clubbed on the head by the troops ...

He said there had been 'no mobs or hundreds of people charging up and down' – and Diamond Street, besides being on his way home, was indeed some way along the Shankill from the centre of the riot. The jury acquitted Malcolmson of throwing a petrol bomb.

A second of Power's cases was overturned on appeal for similar reasons. The man had been charged with stone-throwing in one street; Power's evidence put him in another. The magistrate had convicted.

The case of Cyril Brinkley, a thirty-one-year-old labourer, raised the most eyebrows. Power said that about midnight he saw Brinkley come forward from the crowd of about 800 and throw a petrol bomb. The Army fired tear gas, and Power dashed forward to arrest him. Brinkley told, in detail, a different story.

After watching Match of the Day on television, I was out for a walk about midnight when I heard someone say that a man had been shot. I went to Mansfield Street, where I saw a man who I knew lying on the ground. I took a white cloth and eventually reached the Shankill Road, where I went up to a military barricade and asked if I could phone for an ambulance. I was told to shut up. The next thing I knew I was lying on the ground. My face was busted, also my right eye ... The nearest I ever got to a petrol bomb was seeing them on TV.

Brinkley was convicted in the magistrate's court, but acquitted on appeal. When we subsequently checked the Army log for that night, 11–12 October, we found it recorded that shortly after midnight a petrol bomber was shot in Hopeton Street (just by Mansfield Street). A few minutes later, the log records, men with white cloths did come forward to the Army positions in the Shankill.

Such incidents do not remotely justify Ian Paisley's claim at the time that the British Army was emulating the SS. Nor do they show that Sergeant Power was deliberately lying. What they do support is the reasoned complaint of a senior police officer that 'the Army quite often had no idea who they had arrested, when or where'. This is scarcely surprising: soldiers are not trained to make arrests and note evidence. But the result is that the Army can be used for community pacification only with certain clear risks to relations between the community and the Executive.

The random nature of Power's cases made a supplementary point of equal subsequent importance. If the quartet demonstrated anything beyond a commendable military determination to secure conviction, it was that *anyone* in the vicinity of trouble stood a fair chance of being collared; and that the evidence of the arresting soldier would overwhelmingly secure conviction at magistrate's court level. It was a dangerous power to put in the hands of an armed force untrained for a police role.

Ironically, it was precisely the severity of the Army's reaction on the Shankill that blinded its commanders to the dangers thereby revealed. The extraordinary fact is that the gun virtually vanished from the Belfast streets after that riot: Freeland and his officers reasoned, probably rightly, that the troops had given the Protestants a nasty shock. The Army's wholly military interpretation of its police and peace-keeping role was unwavering after that – as a long dispute between Freeland, the new police chief Young, and the Minister of Home Affairs, Porter, was to demonstrate.

On his arrival in Ulster to reform the police in October 1969, Sir Arthur Young – fresh from the City of London force – was appalled to find that the RUC's standard response to disorder was a baton charge. Young once defined this as 'each man taking out his baton and using it to thump the nearest member of the public'. (The Cameron Commission had much the same opinion.) The irony also struck him that, just at the moment when he was coming to Ulster to introduce less indiscriminate methods to the police, the Army should have taken over not only the policemen's old role, but their old methods as well.

Freeland's original orders, defined by the Downing Street Declaration of August, had been 'to command and task' the RUC as well as the Army when it came to 'security operations'. Young, when he arrived, got that changed, though he had to threaten resignation to overcome Whitehall's intransigence. Freeland's responsibility now became to 'coordinate' Army and police. But what 'security operations' meant, as distinct from normal policing, was never adequately defined, and in Young's eyes Freeland's definition brought the Army far too often on to the streets.

This dispute over the Army's role was fundamental. Yet there was no mechanism for resolving it. The British Government was split in precisely the same manner. Healey ran the Army directly; Callaghan, through Porter, ran the police. Neither would cede power, and plans for a joint Ulster Department in Whitehall were scrapped in August 1969. Callaghan went on his first trip to Ulster – 'and came back a saint', as one civil servant put it. After that, it was impossible to envisage any other minister taking over. The separate Ulster Department was stillborn.

In theory, difficulties should have been solved at Stormont's Joint Security Committee, chaired by Robert Porter, with Freeland and Young as its most powerful members.

But Freeland, retaining sole charge of 'security operations', had finally the power to mount Army road-blocks, searches, vehicle curfews and the like without necessarily consulting the Committee, though he was punctilious about doing so. But as Young continued to argue, the presence of the Army on the streets kept the tension screwed up and made it virtually impossible to get any civilian policing under way.

Whitehall compounded the problem. When, on 13 October, the young Labour MP Ivor Richard arrived at the Ministry of Defence as another junior minister he – being a lawyer – inquired what the legal basis was for all this Army activity. The 'common-law solution' propounded before the troops went in by the Attorney-General, Sir Elwyn Jones, covered situations where violence *had been* committed; but in law it did not allow the Army to mount road blocks and other purely preventive measures. 'There was,' recalls one of those at the meeting, 'a shifty sort of silence.' After much searching by Treasury counsel, the only legal basis that could be found lay in the ample provisions of the Ulster Special Powers Act. Thus, to bolster the Army's role, the British Government was forced to rely upon the very piece of repressive legislation which it was supposedly committed to abolishing as soon as it could.

In this Alice-in-Wonderland context, the most apt if most exasperated comment came from the new police chief, Young: 'How can the Army be going to the aid of the civil power? There isn't one.'

'My task,' Young used to say, 'is to talk the police back into the Falls.' It was a piece of shorthand for a job which fell into two complex parts: expunging the RUC's anti-Catholic reputation, and straightforward modernization. Modernization, along the lines published in Lord Hunt's report on the day of Young's arrival, was the easier task. 'The RUC was run like an antique English county force,' one expert said. In one week, Young and a colleague from the East Anglian force made 400 promotions in the RUC, with another 200 later. The political task was harder.

The Unionist and the general Protestant position was that when the Army had arrived in August and separated the two communities, it had 'expelled' the police from the Catholic areas. These were the famous 'no-go' areas behind the barricades, with which Ian Paisley made such play. Since the Army had expelled the police from the Falls, said the Unionists, the Army must somehow put them back. The truth was that the RUC had not patrolled the Falls area for five years, except in pairs of armed Land-Rovers. Indeed, in the days when Craig was Home Affairs minister they had even closed a station in the Falls, just as they had in the Bogside of Derry. But although Freeland, Young and Porter all knew this, none of them could say it publicly.

The first task was to somehow win the Catholics' confidence, and Young's policy was simply to talk to anyone. Seated beneath tricolour flags, listening to beery Republican songs, Young got an ovation from the Central Citizens' Defence Committee above a bar in the Lower Falls, and if he heard the sound of previous RUC officers revolving in their graves he gave no sign. The method scarcely commended itself to Protestant opinion, and three days after the Shankill riots, with Young in London for the day, Porter announced that the police were going back into the Falls – if necessary, with military backing. (It is fair to say that Porter was under immense back-bench pressure at the time.) Trying to repair the damage Young spent the next day, 16 October, touring the Falls. Unfortunately, television cameras caught him talking to Jim Sullivan, the CCDC and Republican leader. Protestant outrage was little soothed by the fact that the IRA had still not yet made a single aggres-

171

sive move. 'The man's a political liability,' Chichester-Clark muttered.

What drove Young to such risks was shortage of time. He knew that the 'honeymoon' with the Catholics could not last while executive power lay with Protestant Stormont. He was also convinced that the peace would end all the quicker with the Army crashing around. In November 1969 he proposed a bold solution to Freeland. The basic riot squad, he suggested, should be 100–200 soldiers armed only with batons, plus 100 policemen similarly equipped. Porter seized on the idea as a way of appeasing his back-benchers. He wanted unarmed troops – 'batons and gym shoes' – to accompany RUC men on patrols into Catholic areas. Gradually, he believed, it would be possible to withdraw the soldiers.

In retrospect it looks a risk worth the taking: it might just have appeased Porter's back-benchers without alarming the Catholics. But after a joint Army–police study of the proposals Freeland rejected both original idea and elaboration. 'Soldiers in riot situations,' Freeland told the Joint Security Committee, 'must carry guns, and show they mean business.' A man with a gun, of course, means only one kind of business – but in the end, that is the business the Army is in.

Freeland certainly had good grounds apart from military convention for his decision. There was a question whether the RUC was yet fit for such a task. Young had arrived to find a force which was not only partisan and disposed to violence, but also under strength, out of date, and demoralized by what it saw as a straightforward defeat in the August siege of the Bogside. Young's promotions helped somewhat, and with little difficulty the RUC was also relieved of the distinction of being the only armed police force in the UK. But to get the force back in charge of the streets was another matter. Here Freeland and his officers neither shared Young's confidence in swift reform nor considered the Catholics did.

Young's position vis-à-vis the Catholics was fatally weakened by the evidence of police brutality revealed at the inquest in Derry on Samuel Devenney. The Devenney affair began before the troops went in; it remains unsolved still. The inquest of December 1969 was probably its point of maximum impact upon the Catholic community. The recital there of what had happened in the Devenneys' front room in the Bogside in April 1969 was damaging enough to Young's hopes of a rapprochement with them. Even worse was his inability to identify and punish the six or eight policemen responsible. Even the Scotland Yard detectives Young called in were defeated by what he publicly called 'a conspiracy of silence' in the Derry force.

The Catholics were deeply suspicious: Young, it was rumoured, had decided that a prosecution would lower already sagging police morale. The truth was that the Derry police were so disorganized that the Yard investigation foundered for lack of the paperwork – the station log books, for example, kept by any disciplined force – from which the men responsible could be traced. By hard questioning, the Yard men did identify four likely culprits, but there was no proof. Even so, Young considered charging them in the knowledge that they would be acquitted, simply *pour encourager les autres*. He rejected the idea. There were legal complications (certain offences had been amnestied); and besides, political trials for whatever motive were, he reckoned, a bad start to a reform programme. The Catholics, of course, did not forgive the failure.

The Army already thought RUC staff work semi-literate ('You couldn't get them to number paragraphs,' said one of Freeland's officers, 'because they used to write like Mark Twain – start a new paragraph when you feel like a drink.')

And they thought its intelligence was years out of date. Basically they considered the RUC as not really a police force at all, but an undisciplined para-military body.

That impression was largely derived from the Army officers' discovery of how the RUC had used their armoured cars on the Falls Road. But it was strengthened when, at Young's request, they cleared the RUC armoury at Sprucefield. 'We took enough out of there to equip a division,' said an officer.

If the RUC cut loose again, Freeland feared, the Army's own knife-edge relationship with the Catholic minority would he imperilled. Talking down the barricades, the Army had listened for hours to diatribes against the RUC. There had even been unofficial 'back-of-envelope treaties', as one officer called them, guaranteeing that the police would *not* come back in. Young, the distinguished stranger from the City of London, might be accepted; Freeland did not think Young's men would be – and he did not think Young believed that either.

Freeland based this belief upon the fact that at Joint Security Committee meetings he was always pressing Young to involve the police in Army activities like road-blocks and searches. Young declined, for reasons which Freeland quite misunderstood. He put it down to police laziness, but in fact Young held firmly that the proper police function is essentially a passive one. 'You can't just leave an Army standing around,' he once said. 'They always have to be *doing* something.' And he was scornful of the staff at Lisburn Army headquarters 'always dreaming up things to do'. A policeman, on the other hand, is doing his job, Young believed, just walking around – a visible symbol of the law and order which the presence of a soldier visibly destroys. Freeland himself knew these dangers: he had constantly to resist demands for 'action' from Chichester-Clark's ministers. 'All

174

these old Unionists,' he commented after one bout, 'think you are achieving something if you are interfering with normal life.' But he did not connect this with Young's resistance to activity: 'The Army was left holding the baby through no wish of its own,' he said later.

Freeland and Young never understood one another on this central issue. In the meantime, the Army continued to act as policemen. Yet, as the ambiguities of the Shankill cases had demonstrated, they were not merely inefficient policemen. The law they were trying to enforce was, in practice, a blunt instrument which, unless used with precise care, would come to seem more a weapon of repression than of justice.

Chapter 11
Birth of the Provisionals

If this book can be said to advance a thesis, it is broadly that the question to be answered by any analysis of the present Ulster crisis is not, why does the Provisional IRA exist? The significant question is, why do the Provisionals command the support among the Catholic population that they evidently do?

One common answer to this runs along the theological lines of 'the Irish are the Irish'. Other people are satisfied with the answer, touted by the Army and by Stormont, that the Catholics are all cowed by IRA intimidation – though the manpower required to intimidate half-a-million people is surely such that the answer begs the question: why are there so many 'intimidators' in the first place? The most plausible answer, as we have begun to outline in the last chapter, is to be found in the nature of the decisions made and the policies followed since 1969 by Westminster and Stormont, and the consequences of these upon the Catholic population.

If that is so, however, there are other questions: why and how did the nucleus of the Provisionals come into existence – ready ruthlessly to exploit inside their community the real and imagined grievances that these policies induced? The common answer to that is equally simple: the Provisionals arose from the failure of the established IRA to protect the Catholics in the riots of Belfast in August 1969. That is only the surface of the story.

As we showed in chapter 5, the IRA in Belfast was split from 1964: on one side were those willing to follow Goulding and the Dublin hierarchy away from a simple and violent dedication to a thirty-two-county Republic and into new-fangled Socialism; against them were the old sweats who prophesied no good would come of it. In 1969, as the Orange parades approached and with them the probability of imminent violence, these old sweats – men like Jimmy Steele, who gave the Barnes and McCormack funeral oration – began to drift back into the movement. Here, once more, was a situation they understood: all they needed was weapons.

But from February 1969 – when that emissary from political figures in the south first came to the South Derry IRA commander with his offer of guns on certain conditions – the Dublin IRA command had in Belfast's eyes deliberately stalled. When the riots broke in August and the Dublin command had still not produced weapons, those in the north who supported Goulding were instantly discredited. 'IRA – I Ran Away' was scrawled derisively over the walls of the Catholic ghettoes. The only group to salvage their reputations were the leaders in the Lower Falls. On the night of 14–15 August they managed to bring three Thompson sub-machine guns from Dundalk, over the border – in a baker's van, it is said – in time to defend St Comgall's school in Divis Street from Protestant attack.

It is now part of the Provisionals' mythology that the official Dublin leadership of the IRA actually planned that the Belfast Catholics should be left defenceless before Protestant attack in 1969. The theory, supposedly, was that

177

there would be a terrible massacre which would bring down Stormont and, as a bonus, eliminate the troublesome Belfast dissidents at the same time. 'It was the Russians and the Warsaw Ghetto all over again,' said Leo Martin, one of the Provisionals, with heroic over-statement.

Whatever happened, a break-away group of Belfast IRA men something like the present Provisionals would have emerged after that experience. But the precise nature and timing of their appearance did not in fact depend upon events in Belfast at all, but upon manoeuvrings inside Jack Lynch's Government south of the border in the Irish Republic.

Lynch had succeeded Sean Lemass as Prime Minister in 1966, as a compromise between two stronger men, George Colley – who became Lynch's Minister of Industry and Commerce – and Charles Haughey, his Minister of Finance. So it was unfortunate that his first major crisis in office should have concerned an issue so set about with emotion as Ulster. An unequivocal Irish policy was never so necessary: under pressure it became exactly the opposite. When Lynch went on record throughout 1969, it was frequently to say what his Government would not do about the position in the north: it could not long stand idly by, and so on. What Lynch's Government *would* do was never made clear either to his country or to his Cabinet.

As British troops gathered ready to move into Derry on 13 August 1969, Lynch's shaky position as the moderate leader of a disparate coalition became even less secure. Correspondingly, the influence of Neil Blaney, his Minister of Agriculture, grew. Blaney was the head of the tough caucus of 'northerners' – men who had family ties in Ulster – inside Lynch's cabinet. Through the summer of 1969, as we showed earlier, various Dublin political figures, plus men in the ruling Fianna Fail party's fund-raising club, Taca, had already been negotiating to supply arms to the north. Now, as the RUC besieged the Bogside, the northerners in Lynch's Cabinet put a firm hand on policy. They were fed up with Lynch's unwillingness to go to the aid of their fellow Catholics. They decided to do something about it.

Blaney was a heavyweight inside Fianna Fail. Lynch had found it necessary to keep him as Minister of Agriculture after the 1969 Irish General Election, in spite of Blaney's unwillingness to give an undertaking to support him as leader. And Blaney had the determined support of two fellow northerners in the Cabinet: Lynch's rival Charles Haughey, and Kevin Boland.

Haughey, the Minister of Finance, was a native of Swatragh in County Derry and retained bitter childhood memories of his family being forced out of the area under Protestant pressure. Kevin Boland, on the other hand, had been born with impeccable Republican credentials. His father had founded Fianna Fail with De Valera. His uncle had worked with Michael Collins, the most charismatic Irish guerrilla leader, and his brother helped create Taca. It therefore caused no surprise when Kevin Boland became a minister on the day of his election to the Irish Parliament in 1957. By 1969 in Lynch's Cabinet, he was joint secretary of Fianna Fail and Minister of Local Government.

This triumvirate – Haughey, Blaney and Boland – could bring Lynch down. And Lynch knew it when, on Tuesday morning, 13 August 1969, his first emergency Cabinet met to consider the situation in the besieged Bogside.

The half-dozen Cabinet meetings that took place that week were eventually to lead to the departure of those three ministers as a result of a gun-running scandal, and to the formation of the Provisional IRA. At the time, though, Lynch had only one preoccupation: to reach an accommodation with his hard men. The accommodation he reached was, in

179

effect, to let them all but dictate the pace of his Government's policy. He had little choice. In all the manoeuvrings which followed, therefore, there is no reason to suppose that the northerners in Lynch's Cabinet did anything but act in a way which they thought Lynch and the Cabinet had at least tacitly approved.

When the Cabinet battle began on 13 August, the northerners' demands were at once uncompromising and unrealistic. The Irish Army must invade the north. They might, however, have perceived drawbacks to this policy – not the least being the state of the Irish 'shock troops', the so-called Sixth Brigade. This had been stamping around the Donegal border area ever since the RUC's excursion into the Bogside in April. (Their detailed planning left something to be desired: a camping site outlined on maps provided by GHQ Dublin turned out now to be a council estate.) But the Irish Army did actually have an invasion plan.

The excuse for the invasion was to be a specially created border incident at the Craigavon Bridge into Derry. A doctor in Derry would telephone for an ambulance from a hospital over the border in Donegal. Arrangements had been made for this to be fired on when it crossed the border. Outraged, the Irish Army would then take Craigavon Bridge and enter Derry. Meanwhile, in the south-east corner of Ulster, the Sixth Brigade were to advance north across the border and take Lurgan and Toome Bridge, giving themselves control of the top and bottom of Lough Neagh which separates Belfast from the rest of the province. Derry and Newry – the two Catholic border cities – would be occupied. When reinforcements arrived, the 'spearhead' Sixth Brigade would move on from Lough Neagh into Belfast.

The tricky question of resistance by British troops, or indeed by the outraged Protestant inhabitants of the province, was glossed over. In Armagh, for instance, British soldiers were simply to be asked to confine themselves to barracks, or at least to the city's Protestant area.

Whether Whitehall knew of this plan is uncertain. But the Ministry of Defence's view of the capabilities of the Irish Army can be indicated. One source in Ireland talked to us of the plan being the creation of 'the Irish Rommel'. Whitehall was more sceptical: when the Ministry was working out Ulster contingency plans it allocated, to deal with what it saw as the remote chance of Irish Army intervention, precisely half an armoured car squadron.

Still, the plan was the best the Irish Army could think up. And on 13 August Boland threatened in Cabinet that unless Lynch agreed to mobilize the Army, he, Haughey and Blaney would resign. Lynch's Defence Minister, Jim Gibbons, the Minister of Justice, Martin O'Morain and Sean Flanagan, Minister of Lands, looked ready to follow.

Lynch reached a compromise. A Northern Sub-Committee of the Cabinet was created, consisting of Haughey, Blaney, and two other ministers. This group took over the day-to-day running of Government policy on Ulster. Lynch, meanwhile, went on television to call for a United Nations force in Ulster and to announce that units of the Irish Army were erecting four field-hospitals along the border. (A British Army officer who covertly inspected them reported: 'They're just a lot of dirty tents.')

If Lynch thought he had headed off trouble, he was speedily disabused. Within forty-eight hours, groups from the north were arriving in Dublin to demand guns. Their champion in Lynch's Cabinet was Neil Blaney. One of the first to arrive from the north, about 15 August, was John Kelly. A Belfast IRA man – he had served eight years in Crumlin jail for possessing arms and ammunition during the abortive 1956–62 campaign – Kelly now came as leader of one of the

181

Belfast Citizens' Defence Committees. Inevitably, he met Captain James Kelly of Army Intelligence – who earlier in the month, as we have already narrated, had been up to Belfast, and had then reported to his boss that the Catholics there needed help.

Captain Kelly's boss, Colonel Michael Hefferon, the director of Irish Military Intelligence, had taken this report seriously. Hefferon had distrusted the Stormont Government's intentions – and the Westminster Government's ability to control these – since 1957, when he had learned of Bill Craig's construction of the Shorland armoured cars. Hefferon had regarded this as being in breach of a secret clause in Ireland's 1938 Treaty with Britain laying down that the north would not construct weapons which could be used against the south. So, when Kelly reported to him, Hefferon was ready to believe the worst of Stormont. Now he in turn reported Kelly's visit to his boss, the Defence minister Jim Gibbons – who was already sympathetic, as his support of the northerners in the Cabinet a few days before had shown. The date was now mid-August. But the agreed policy which Lynch had pushed through his divided Cabinet was that the Irish Government would not officially supply the northern Catholics with arms.

Other moves were already afoot, however, to help them. On Sunday 17 August Cathal Goulding, the IRA Chief of Staff, received a telephone call in Dublin from a Catholic priest in north London. The priest said that he was acting as a go-between for somebody offering unlimited cash to buy arms for the north – so long as the arms were sent there directly, and not via the Republic. If Goulding were interested, said the priest, he should fly to London. Goulding did so. When he arrived at the presbytery on 18 August he found an emissary from a political figure in Dublin. Their discussion was business-like. The emissary asked whether

Goulding knew a willing small-arms supplier. Goulding said he did, but that the supplier wanted at least £50,000 before he would agree to anything. As a token of goodwill, the emissary handed over £1,500 on the spot.

But a problem then arose. There were, the emissary said, certain conditions. As the man who had received the report from the South Derry commander of the IRA back in February about a similar offer from another Dublin politician, Goulding thought the terms had a familiar ring. The main ones were, once again, that the IRA should cease political involvement south of the border and that a separate Belfast command should be set up. Goulding, Mac Stiofain and the rest of the IRA Dublin command were still arguing bitterly over the similar offer put to them in the Shelbourne Hotel back in June. While they argued, that deal had remained in abeyance. Now, in north London, virtually the same offer was being repeated. Goulding was wary.

His wariness was heightened by the record of this particular north London emissary in the matter of raising arms for the northern cause. The emissary had in fact been to London on several occasions in 1969: all he had achieved was a modest but profitable coup for the British intelligence services. Accompanied by a representative of Saor Eire, the extremist and violent Republican group, the emissary had early in 1969 contacted a London arms dealer by the name of Captain Peter Markham Randall. Randall operated under cover of a small insurance company based in Oxford Street. He was sympathetic, and apparently able to offer almost any kind of arms. He even took the two men to a warehouse at Eltham, just outside London, where they inspected a consignment of Sterling sub-machine guns. The emissary paid a deposit of £6,000. The agreeable Captain Randall then offered to return to Dublin with the two men until his arms arrived, as evidence of his bona fides.

Randall's presence in Dublin for several weeks awaiting the arms aroused no suspicion, until he tactlessly asked to visit an IRA training camp. Only Captain Kelly prevented his being shot for this and he was sent packing back to London. When the IRA then tried to check him out, they discovered that his insurance company no longer existed; nor could they trace any Captain Randall. They were forced to the conclusion, correctly, that Randall was a British intelligence officer – who had been privy to their organization in Dublin for nearly two months.

Still, at the August meeting in London, this same emissary's role was less ambitious. He merely provided Goulding with money and food for thought. For obvious reasons a separate Belfast command did not appeal to Goulding; nor did political concessions. Yet unless Goulding and his Dublin HQ could supply the northern Catholics with guns and cash, Goulding knew that a break-away command in the north would probably be established anyway. That was exactly the possibility which Captain Kelly was at that moment reporting back to the Northern Sub-Committee of the Lynch Cabinet.

Captain Kelly had been north again to see what the situation was in the aftermath of the British troops' appearance on the scene. Now, he told Blaney and his colleagues, the IRA men in Belfast and Derry were disgusted at the lack of support from the south during the riots in their cities. They were not in the least concerned with political or other deals between the Dublin IRA and the Fianna Fail. All they wanted was guns.

A week later, Kelly's assessment was borne out by a meeting of Belfast IRA men held in a social club in west Belfast on Sunday 24 August. The meeting was called to decide the future of the IRA north of the border. Most of the senior IRA men in the north were there. So was Captain James

Kelly – accompanied by a Dublin politician. The notable absentees, however, were the men who had led the IRA in the north along its Civil Rights, non-violent line for the previous five years. They boycotted the Belfast meeting because they still agreed with Goulding's approach.

Those who did attend the meeting were given an optimistic account of events. They were told that boatloads of arms were about to arrive in the Republic – which was untrue. They were also told, correctly, that the intelligence director of the Dublin IRA command, Sean Mac Stiofain, favoured a break with the official leadership. (Back at the Shelbourne Hotel meeting in June, Mac Stiofain had been the main advocate in favour of the deal: the north-south split should be accepted if it brought arms, he said.) With that sort of news, the outcome of the Belfast meeting was inevitable. Those present agreed that the official IRA command in Belfast should somehow be overthrown and a separate northern command established.

This meeting and, in particular, the presence at it of Captain James Kelly, intelligence officer and liaison man, convinced Goulding and his allies in the Dublin command that Fianna Fail and the various politicians, far from trying to reach an agreement with the IRA in return for supporting the northern Catholics, were in fact engaged in an ingenious Lynch plot to split and weaken the IRA throughout Ireland.

Goulding's conviction was reinforced by what happened next. In the first ten days of September, less than three weeks after the Belfast meeting, another gathering of northern IRA men was called in the village of Moville, twenty miles from Derry over the border in Donegal. The Moville meeting led directly to the emergence of the Provisional IRA as an autonomous group. Moville is so modest a place that there was some difficulty finding a room big enough for

185

everyone, because, along with the northern IRA stalwarts, came men from Taca, the Fianna Fail fund-raising club, several minor Fianna Fail politicians, a prominent Dublin businessman and the same Dublin politician who had been with the Taca men at the divisive Shelbourne Hotel meeting.

This time the message to the northern IRA men from Dublin was unequivocal. They were to set up a separate Belfast command and abandon political operations in the Republic. In return they would receive at least £200,000 for guns and ammunition. Ten businessmen were named as having pledged £20,000 apiece – if the conditions were met.

If the deal were agreed in principle, the Dublin politician said, details could be worked out quickly enough. He himself, he said, had no doubt about the right decision. In anticipation, indeed, a planning meeting was already called, he said, for Sunday 14 September, in Belfast. That was enough for the IRA men. They went away to plan the immediate removal of the existing northern command.

There was now, however, a mysterious intervention. When the IRA men attended that pre-arranged meeting in Belfast on 14 September, they found that a stranger had been invited to talk to them. He was introduced as a well-known political columnist and TV commentator from Dublin; he delivered a rousing indictment of the Dublin IRA's lethargy, warmly commending the establishment of a separate northern command. On the following Thursday, 18 September, he said, yet another Dublin politician whose views coincided with theirs would meet them in Dundalk, just over the border, to see what help he too could provide. His name was given.

When the IRA men, by now thoroughly aroused, obediently trooped once more across the border four days later, a politician was indeed waiting for them. But he was not the man named. This odd discrepancy caused inquiries to be made about the eloquent speaker at the previous week's meeting. He turned out to bear no resemblance to the political commentator he had claimed to be. (As television transmissions from Radio Telefis Eireann in Dublin cannot be regularly picked up in Belfast, that had not been immediately apparent.) Who was this 'journalist'? Weeks later, the IRA in Dublin discovered that he had been an intelligence man *for the Dublin government.*

To the northern IRA men at the Dundalk meeting however, the main interest was not some mysterious stranger of a week past, but the politician's offer. He took it for granted that the deal was on. It was. Next day, 19 September, a bank account for the purchase of arms was opened with a token deposit of £5. The northern IRA men assumed that the promised £200,000 would rapidly follow. They went away happy – in spirit already separated from their colleagues in the south.

The central thread through the events we have just described is that nobody has ever discovered whether the politicians involved were following 'official' Dublin policy or not. There were, to start with, so many possible definitions of 'official': approved by Lynch; approved by the Northern Sub-Committee; approved by a majority of the Cabinet; approved by the apparatchiks of Fianna Fail; approved in nod-and-wink fashion by the senior civil servants who knew what was going on.

All that is certain is that nobody who did know what was going on said no; but that, afterwards, everyone denied having said yes. John Kelly, liaison man for the desperate Catholics of the north, said later: 'We did not ask for blankets or feeding bottles. We asked for guns – and no one from Lynch down refused that request or told us that this was contrary to Government policy.'

Kelly made the comment on 14 October 1970, the seventh day of what became known as the Dublin Arms Trial – the arraignment of Lynch's Finance minister Haughey, Captain James Kelly, John Kelly himself, and an Irish-naturalized Belgian import/export dealer, on a charge of conspiring to import arms illegally. In court, Haughey denied all knowledge of the contents of the consignment concerned, for which his department had granted import customs exemption. The others claimed that what they had done in attempting to import the consignment of 500 pistols and ammunition had Cabinet approval. The jury acquitted all four defendants. Lynch subsequently sacked Haughey and Blaney. Boland resigned in protest at this. (The British Cabinet thought the trial purely political – a cynical judgement, for the reason why Lynch had to mount it at all was that the British Government, told by its intelligence services what was afoot, secretly leaked the whole plot to the Opposition leaders in Dublin, who promptly confronted Lynch.)

But back in September 1969 – with the northern IRA men now set upon splitting from the south – there were two areas in which the Dublin Government finally considered it could officially help: finance and training. The essential, though, was secrecy. Because the Ministries of Finance and Defence would be involved, their Ministers, Charles Haughey and Jim Gibbons, were deputed by the Irish Cabinet to devise ways of implementing the following plans.

A total of £175,000 was to be made available to help the northern community – £75,000 of it for propaganda purposes, the rest for 'general relief of suffering'. A Dublin public relations man named Seamus Brady was sent up north (he was a native of Derry) to organize propaganda: one of his creations there was a news-sheet called *Voice of the North*. Brady was assisted in running this by three people: the liaison man John Kelly, his brother Billy Kelly

188

(later commander of the Provisionals' Third Belfast Battalion) and Sean Keenan, the Republican leader in Derry who had run the Derry Citizens' Defence Association which organized the defence of the Bogside.

Running this propaganda exercise from Dublin was easy enough. But the transfer of the £100,000 balance to the north presented the Irish Government with problems. Haughey had not specified what constituted 'relief' when allocating the money: the object was merely to get it to the defence committees in Belfast and elsewhere as rapidly as possible – naturally, without arousing public interest. If the committees then decided that 'relief' included the purchase of guns and ammunition that was, ultimately, not under Dublin's control. But the Irish Cabinet recognized, of course, that there would be an unholy international row if Westminster or Stormont heard of this.

To disguise the operation, therefore, Haughey gave the £100,000 to the Irish Red Cross. (This expenditure was not actually approved in the Irish Parliament until May 1970, seven months later, by which time the bulk of it had been spent.) But Haughey's recipients, the Irish Red Cross, do not operate in Ulster. So they in turn handed over the money to a committee of half a dozen respectable Ulster Catholics – who banked it with the Bank of Ireland in Clones, south of the border in County Monaghan. The account was in the name of the 'Belfast Fund for the Relief of Distress'. On 12 November this account was transferred to the Leinster and Munster Bank in Lower Baggot Street, Dublin, where two subsidiary accounts were also opened in the fictitious names of Anne O'Brien and George Dixon. The money from the Finance Ministry was handed to the Red Cross who then paid it into the Distress Committee account from which it was transferred into these subsidiaries. The 'George Dixon' account was used for arms purchases; 'Anne O'Brien' financed the propaganda activities of Seamus Brady.

In all, the Belfast Fund for the Relief of Distress received, in six months, a total of £78,993-10s. The details of how this money was actually spent have been the subject of some dispute ever since. What is certain is that more than £30,000 vanished in the attempt to import 500 pistols and ammunition which led directly to the Dublin arms trial of September–October 1970. The accounts kept by one of those involved suggest, however, that another £7,000–£8,000 passed through the 'George Dixon' arms account. Whether this did provide arms for the north we do not know.

While Finance minister Haughey grappled on his Government's behalf with these problems of finance, the training of men from the various citizens' defence committees in the north produced similar problems for the Defence minister, Jim Gibbons. On no account could the Dublin Government be seen to be supporting an illegally armed force. A simple solution was devised. No 'civilians' would be offered arms training by the Irish Government. Instead, the northern Catholics would be required to enlist for seven days in the FCA (Forsai Cosanta Aitula), the Irish Army Territorials.

In the last week in September, with Gibbons's authority the first intake of men from the Bogside arrived at Fort Dunree, an Irish Army camp in County Donegal. There were nine of them. They received a week's elementary arms training. It was a useless exercise, and to the Dublin Government immensely damaging, because Lynch knew nothing about it – he was on holiday in West Cork – but the local press in Donegal found out almost immediately. At the end of the week, around 30 September, Colonel Hefferon contacted Gibbons and, in a state approaching panic, urged him to abandon the project. By this time, too, Lynch had returned from holiday: he was told of the training by Gibbons. He immediately ordered it to stop.

So, over the weekend of 4–5 October Captain James Kelly had to tell a meeting of fifteen delegates from the northern defence committees (held at his home town of Bailieboro, County Cavan) that the training was now halted. The delegates were upset but they understood the halt to be temporary. It was in fact permanent. From the Irish Government's point of view, though, this came too late: Stormont knew all about the affair.

By now, however, the southern politicians' main aim was achieved: the IRA in Belfast was visibly divided into two camps. The bitterness at the leadership's failure to provide the arms was compounded in September when the same leadership seemed willing to negotiate away the Catholics' only protection in Belfast, their barricades, in talks with the Army. When, on 13 September, the Central Citizens' Defence Committee went over to Whitehall to negotiate with Callaghan, it was the last straw. The row that followed as men from the various defence committees throughout Belfast debated that weekend whether to accept the proposals the group brought back, signalled the first emergence of an identifiable dissident group; the trio most vocal against accepting Callaghan's offer were Billy McKee, Francis Card, and Leo Martin.

On the afternoon of 22 September sixteen of the old-time Belfast IRA men now coming back into the movement met at a hall in North Queen Street in the centre of the city with the two sympathizers who had stayed in the Belfast hierarchy throughout the sixties, Leo Martin and Sean Mac-Nally. They decided to confront the official Belfast Battalion staff. A meeting of the Battalion staff and all the company commanders was in fact scheduled for a couple of hours' time, at a room in Cyprus Street off the Falls Road. The

191

sixteen old-timers burst in – and made it clear that, by the gun if necessary, they were forcing a split with Dublin, thereby complying with the deal offered by the southern politicians.

For a few minutes, it looked as though there would be a bloodbath. (One of the sixteen mutineers had suggested beforehand that the only solution was to machine-gun the entire leadership.) The official battalion commander, Billy McMillen, said he had to leave the meeting to summon his adjutant-general. As he was heading down the stairs, a guard posted by the mutineers pulled a gun and there was a scuffle, but nobody was hurt. When McMillen returned with his allies, his first move was to reassert democracy: he demanded a vote of confidence and got it.

A compromise was then tacked together. The Belfast command would be increased from six to eleven for a period of three months, allowing all shades of opinion to be represented in tactical discussions. If the trial period was unsatisfactory, four moves would be carried out. Firstly, four members of the IRA's most senior body, the Army Council, would be removed – among them Cathal Goulding. Secondly, the northern command would become autonomous. Thirdly, all socialist political programmes would be abandoned, and finally the breakaway group would not attend the 'Army convention' – roughly, the IRA annual conference – to be held in Dublin in November.

In the meantime, three hard-liners were co-opted on to the Belfast Battalion staff: Billy McKee, Sean MacNally and Seamus Twomey. McKee was the most charismatic of the three: he had been head of the Belfast IRA until 1964, when he was overthrown by McMillen and gradually 'eased out' of the movement. McKee's prestige, based largely upon a reputation for bravery, was such that many Provos afterwards considered that the split would never have succeeded but for his personal standing. Seamus Twomey was much less well known: he too had dropped out of the movement in the mid-sixties. Sean MacNally was about the youngest of all the dissidents: he had stayed in the Gouldingite IRA, on the Battalion staff in fact, until 1967 when he resigned in disgust. Since he had been the Battalion's 'intelligence officer' and thus knew more about the personnel in the movement than anyone else, his conversion to the dissident faction gave the Provos a head-start in the lobbying which now began throughout the province.

During the next three months, September-November 1969, the existing Belfast command and the would-be usurpers each made strenuous attempts to enlist the support of the rank-and-file to their cause. The unofficial representative of the Irish Government, Captain James Kelly, tried to keep in touch with both wings and with his Dublin masters. On one occasion in October the lobbying of the Citizen's Defence groups grew so hectic that the official Belfast leadership called a meeting in a Monaghan hotel on the same day as the unofficial group called a similar meeting of its own in Belfast. The harassed Captain Kelly found himself forced to keep in touch with Monaghan by telephone from Belfast as the meetings continued.

The dissidents soon claimed that McMillen had welched on the agreement reached in Cyprus Street. They had intercepted letters between him and Cathal Goulding in Dublin showing, they said, that the Belfast leadership still considered itself under southern command.

From that moment, it was probably too late for compromise. But in a final attempt at reconciliation, Sean Mac Stiofain made a special trip to Belfast in November to see Billy McMillen and impress upon him the necessity for all the Belfast men to attend the IRA Army convention in Dublin the next week. He made no impression. Nobody

193

from Belfast attended: a compromise was impossible. At the conference, Goulding's men won: the conference voted thirty-nine to twelve to recognize *de facto* the two Irish Governments and Westminster. Mac Stiofain himself and the others walked out, announcing the establishment of the 'Provisional Army Council' with the ringing declaration:

We declare our allegiance to the thirty-two-county Irish Republic proclaimed at Easter 1916, established by the first Dail Eireann in 1919, overthrown by force of arms in 1922 and suppressed to this day ...

The political wing, Sinn Fein, split soon after. The Provisionals had emerged.

The first Chief of Staff of the Provisionals in Belfast was Billy McKee. Francis Card was in charge of propaganda. Leo Martin had some responsibility for operations. Others on that first Brigade staff included Seamus Twomey, Billy Kelly and Sean MacNally. The common factor uniting these men was traditionalism. As one observer put it: 'The Officials go to Mass once a year; the Provos once a week.' The other factor they had in common was violence. Cahill barely escaped hanging for his part in the murder of a policeman in 1942. As a priest who knew them said: 'Mostly, they are damaged people – damaged by unemployment, by the long years they have spent in confinement, by the sheer hopelessness of their vision of life in Belfast.'

In the weeks before Christmas 1969, these sad men began to turn themselves once again into an armed force. How badly the split affected the IRA can be judged from the fact that before it happened, the eleven members of the Battalion staff had comprised four hard-liners, four Goulding-ites and three fence-sitters who when the split came stayed with McMillen and what were now the Gouldingite 'Officials'. At the time of the split, the total IRA strength in Belfast was

194

about 150 – of whom perhaps eighty were activists. Of these no more than thirty joined the Provisionals. While seven of the eleven old Battalion staff stayed with the 'Officials', the split at the grassroots looked, on paper, more promising for the Provisionals. Of the eleven companies in the IRA Belfast Battalion at that time, the officers of nine declared for them. But the people who mattered there were the company quartermasters, because each held his company's stock of arms. Almost without exception, they stayed 'Official'.

This lack of numbers did not worry the embryo Provisionals. They reckoned that, if it ever came to it, they could mount effective urban guerrilla warfare with fifty people. But the shortage of arms, and a dire shortage of cash, did worry them. Their first weapons came via more or less orthodox theft. On the night of 8–9 December 1969, ordinary unpolitical thieves stole fifteen rifles and a Luger pistol with quantities of ammunition from a Belfast gunsmith's. They tried to sell this loot to the Provisionals for around £500, only to have it seized 'in the name of the Republic'. A few days later, units of the Officials in three counties over the border switched allegiance to the Provisionals and sent their weapons up to Belfast: thirty Thompson sub-machine-guns, twenty-seven rifles and assorted pistols.

The cash to buy more came from what little of the Haughey 'distress' fund reached them. The £8,000 or so unaccounted for in the 'George Dixon' bank account may have come to Belfast. Certainly, some cash did, and was split between the rival factions. One prominent Belfast Catholic was appointed to act as neutral 'bagman' for both – and proceeded to embezzle impartially. The £200,000 from southern business did not arrive. This shortage of cash caused real hardship in some cases. In theory, full-time Provisionals got paid: on paper, the pay rates allowed an experienced 'soldier' about ten pounds a week. But there was embezzlement here too: some men were recorded as being paid more than they actually received. Some Provisionals at the outset collected a mere twenty-five bob a week – and most of them were either too wary or too proud to queue up for unemployment benefit.

Still, the Provisionals came to dominate the Belfast IRA within a couple of months. A few pockets of Republicanism preferred to go their own way. The Catholics clustered round the Short Strand in east Belfast trusted only in themselves and set up their own 'community defence association' – to this day, the area remains something of a no-man's-land for either IRA faction. The Ardoyne Catholics went even further. According to envious Officials, the local activists sent their own representatives to America at the beginning of 1970 to negotiate, successfully, for arms and cash – before, in mid-1970, joining the Provisionals.

Only the Lower Falls remained a stronghold of the Officials – plus the Turf Lodge district of west Belfast, where several hundred old Falls' residents had been re-housed.

Much of the quiescence of the first six months of 1970 can be accounted for by these rivalries and re-groupings in Belfast. The Provisionals and some of the neighbourhood defence militia went training that spring over the border in Donegal, Cork and Wicklow. There was much reading of guerrilla manuals, notably the writings of General Grivas. The Provisionals were simply not strong enough to take anyone on – even if they had wanted to.

But did they want to? Remarkably, until the summer of 1970, the only traceable incidents for which the Provisionals were definitely responsible were one shooting and one bombing. The shooting was on 28 September 1969, when a Protestant crowd made to storm the isolated Unity Walk Catholic flats near the city centre and a Provisional inside –

this was, of course, before the group was known by that name; but he was of their persuasion – opened up on the crowd with a Sterling sub-machine-gun stolen from the British Army. (Sixteen bullet cases were found on the pavement below the flats.) And on 27 January 1970 in an obscure act of retaliation for an alleged act of Army misbehaviour, the Provisionals blew a hole in the wall of an old police barracks by Unity Walk – the soldiers billeted inside narrowly escaping injury.

The Army's relations with the Catholics were, of course, good as 1969 turned into 1970 – though to a large degree this merely reflected the fact that relations with the Protestants were bad. There is some evidence that the Provisionals were unhappy about this fraternization and missed few chances to spread a little disaffection.

Yet the Provisionals themselves do not seem to have known what they wanted. Only Leo Martin among their leadership was really talking about a united Ireland: the others were still concerned with ensuring that they were in a position to 'defend' their communities should the need arise. They remained a small group: they could do nothing, even if they wanted to, without community support. In reality, therefore, a Provisional 'campaign' was never possible until certain pre-conditions had been met. The most important of these was that the British Army had to become cemented in Catholic eyes into the structure of Unionist supremacy. In the event, this was achieved in 1970 by simple passage of time working upon the vacuous British policy of legislative reform without political change.

Chapter 12
'The greatest single miscalculation...'

As 1969 drew to a close, the Labour Government still managed to maintain a confident demeanour. This was largely because of Callaghan's deftness, as his fellow ministers recognized. 'Just as well Roy isn't still Home Secretary,' one of Jenkins's Cabinet colleagues remarked at the time. 'If he had announced he was going to Ireland, the way Jim did, I would have said: "Prime Minister, we must back him with artillery." '

Ministers in Belfast and London could turn their minds to an Ulster problem more abiding even than violence: unemployment. In the province as a whole, seven per cent of the working population were out of a job that winter – in Derry, twelve per cent. The trade union movement had played a creditable part in the containment of violence, particularly in the Belfast shipyards; but the violence that had not been contained was quite enough to frighten off industrialists. Investment to create new jobs was dropping. Chichester-Clark had to defend himself against backbenchers unhappy about Faulkner's zeal as Minister of Development in moving towards a Central Housing Authority, and Young's in civilianizing the RUC. But when he came to London in January 1970 to see Callaghan, the talk was mainly economic. Ulster

was off the front page, at any rate. Yet the quiet was danger-
ously deceptive – and perilous in itself, for it induced a false
sense of security in the British Government and in British
public opinion. Whitehall was congratulating itself on the
excellence of the troops' relations with the Catholic population – which was, of course, a simple inverse product of
the fact that relations were at that stage bad between the
Army and the Protestants.

Freeland's officers, encountering day-to-day the tension
on the streets, appreciated that relations with the Catholics
could not much longer be maintained, however friendly the
soldiers, while the mechanism of Unionist supremacy remained. But Freeland himself, after an outspoken comment
on television about the need for political reform, was
muzzled by the Ministry of Defence. Even the Cabinet's
thoughts on the introduction of proportional representation
in Ulster faded, for a singularly petty reason. One man who,
at this time, passed on to Labour the tip that even the re-
surgent IRA might consider this a major concession, was
given a cool reception by Callaghan's deputy at the Home
Office, Shirley Williams. 'Think what Jeremy Thorpe and
the Liberals would make of it,' he was told.

Labour began to lose its sense of urgency, and with it a
grasp of the scale of change needed. Callaghan himself was
affected by the mood. By the end of 1969 a small group
under the Ulster Attorney-General, Basil Kelly, had spent
four months examining the Special Powers Act, the key-
stone of the system of supremacy. Perhaps surprisingly,
Kelly's group – which at times included Whitehall Home
Office men – reported in the early days of January 1970 that
it was time to make an end of the Special Powers, at least in
the form in which they stood.

The Act, they said, was demonstrably despotic, and much
of it meaningless or unenforceable or both. Two of the least

199

useful additions had been made during the Craig régime: membership of 'Republican Clubs' had been made illegal; and sale of the Sinn Fein paper, the *United Irishman,* had been proscribed.

The first was unenforceable, there being no sensible way of defining a Republican club. The second was bigotry, since on the whole the *United Irishman* (the voice of the Official, or 'political' IRA) was – certainly in Young's view, for instance – scarcely more inflammatory than such Protestant journals as the *News Letter,* Belfast's ardently Unionist morning paper.

Attorney-General Kelly's working party advised that out of the Special Powers Act and its sub-structure of regulations only the power of internment really mattered. But instead of that being dependent upon the signature only of the Minister of Home Affairs, it should, under a new Act, become possible to introduce it only with the prior consent of Parliament. Virtually everything else, such as the right to suspend inquests, and the police right to hold a man indefinitely on suspicion, should be scrapped.

This did not altogether represent a change of Unionist heart. Apparently, Kelly and his colleagues feared that Labour would want to repeal the Special Powers Act entire: therefore, this series of concessions was offered to preserve the internment power in a workable form. If so, they over-estimated Labour's reforming zeal – and underestimated the legal tangle Labour had woven for itself in relying on parts of the Special Powers Act as the legal basis for much of the Army's activity.

So extensive a remodelling of the Act required Westminster approval: and this Callaghan refused to give. He was confronted with a golden opportunity to make a gesture to the Catholics which the Protestants would accept. He turned it down. Rather than incur the odium of drafting a new Act deliberately to re-introduce the power of internment, would it not be better, he said, to 'let the old Act fall into disuse'?

The calculation almost certainly underestimated what a hindrance the Act was to Catholic acceptance of a reformed RUC. The peripheral clauses of the old Act, after all, loaded down the police with fearsome powers. Why should the Catholics believe the police no longer wanted them? And it must have been a rosy future James Callaghan saw, in which Special Powers could 'fall into disuse'.

But any instant of calm in Ulster is enough to generate hundredweights of official optimism. People discover that the worst is over or – more recently – that the gunman is being mastered. One of the clearer voices raised in this cause during the peaceful early days of 1970 was that of Oliver Wright, the first 'UK representative' in Ulster. As Wright's tour of duty ended in March, he gave an ebullient press conference. 'Cheer up!' was his message. 'Things are better than you think.' Within a month, Ian Paisley had been elected a Stormont MP for Terence O'Neill's old seat: O'Neill had gone to the Lords. But British politicians were now preoccupied with the run-up to the 1970 General Election.

The diplomat who succeeded Wright was Ronald Burroughs, a bespectacled expert on Portuguese affairs. He had come to Wilson's notice as one of the Foreign Office's most effective guardians of Rhodesian sanctions at the Lisbon embassy from 1965 to 1967. (Beira, in Portuguese Mozambique, was Rhodesia's main sanctions-busting port: Lisbon the European centre for illicit deals.) Burrough's flippant manner, and a certain talent for mimicry, masked a concerned mind. He saw at once that danger sprang from the new series of Protestant marches. On cue, an Orange parade sparked on 1 April 1970 the first conflict between

British troops and Irish Catholic civilians for two generations.

The rather special social structure of the Ballymurphy housing estate on the western edge of Belfast had already engaged the interest of Queen's University Social Studies department. A ramshackle product of the late 1940s, Ballymurphy was, one academic said, 'the worst housing estate in the British Isles'. A creation of the then acknowledged Belfast housing policy of religious apartheid, its population was entirely Catholic. Its attributes included high rates of birth, unemployment (twenty per cent), juvenile delinquency, crime and VD; low incomes (£20 a week for the average family of eight) – and a burning sense of Irish nationalism: 'Coming home on the bus at week-ends you sat listening to "Kevin Barry" and "the Soldier's Song" ' a local Protestant complained.

1 April 1970 was Easter Tuesday. On the hill overlooking Ballymurphy come two new Protestant estates – Highfield and New Barnsley. Up this hill, a decent distance away, the Junior Orangemen were preparing for an out-of-town rally. In spite of warnings that parades into Belfast could start trouble, the Junior Orange band marched straight up the Springfield Road where it overhangs Ballymurphy and paraded through the Protestant estate of New Barnsley. A Catholic married to a Protestant in Ballymurphy recalled: 'They marched up and down that road playing for a full two hours before they left for Bangor.'

Freeland impartially disliked all parades, Catholic or Protestant. 'Grown men! Pathetic! Ridiculous!' he once exploded. But the Orange bands – and, more particularly, the followers they attracted – were his pet hate. 'Run the lot of them in,' he once advised Chichester-Clark, who not unnaturally quailed. An ineffective system of licensing bandsmen had been introduced instead.

When the Orangemen returned to Belfast that night, still playing 'The Sash', an angry Catholic crowd lined the route, throwing bottles and hurley sticks at the marchers – some of whom were only fourteen or fifteen years old. Fist fights started in the Lower Falls Road. But most of these were between Catholics disputing whether or not to let the march proceed, and Jim Sullivan, the Republican leader of the Lower Falls – an area by now identified with the 'Official' faction – was visibly trying to cool the situation.

The marchers got through the Falls safely but, meanwhile, another section of the parade was on its way back to the Orange Hall near Ballymurphy. There was going to be trouble anyway. But according to Paddy Devlin, the Social Democratic MP who was on the spot trying to avert a replay of the August 1969 rioting, the Army did not help matters by sending a lorry 'screaming up Springfield Road putting barricades on every corner to prevent the Catholics coming out'. But this was largely Devlin's own doing. At Army headquarters at Lisburn, Freeland and the Army minister Roy Hattersley – over for the day – were having a quiet drink when Devlin telephoned. 'The boyos are out to make trouble tonight,' he said, and he appealed for troops to come quickly.

When they did, however, a Catholic mob of about 400 schoolboys and teenagers built up, throwing stones and bottles. Facing them were a mere seventy Royal Scots – and behind them an increasingly excited crowd of Protestants. Before the night was out, twenty-five soldiers had been injured. Next day, Belfast was loud with Unionist complaints that the security forces had fallen down on the job. 'The question everyone was asking this morning,' said a local newspaper, 'was why only seventy men of the Royal Scots Regiment were deployed to quell the disturbances.'

It had its effect. When a second night's rioting began in Ballymurphy on the evening of 2 April, 600 troops sup-

Ulster

ported by five Saracen armoured cars moved into the estate. As a show of force it was counter-productive. The Catholic mob showered the troops with stones and bottles. 'I'm not having my men stoned like that,' a senior officer said. The order to use CS was given.

The smoke rolled in clouds down the streets and gulleys of the estate, choking rioters and peaceful citizens in their homes alike. The Army never grasped how 'radicalizing' in its effect CS was; but that first Ballymurphy riot – when they fired 104 canisters – was a classic demonstration of the fact. A weapon so general produces, inevitably, a common reaction among its victims: it creates solidarity where there was none before. One knowledgeable local thought afterwards that those Ballymurphy riots gave the first great boost to the Provisional IRA recruiting campaign.

Which was deeply ironic. Freeland let it be known that 'sinister people' were behind the teenagers who had attacked his soldiers; and in one sense he was right. The Provisional IRA was present in Ballymurphy – but trying to *stop* the rioting. 'Even when the crunch came,' the *Belfast Telegraph* reported, 'Catholic vigilantes continued to appeal for a return to sanity and were caught in the no man's land between the mob and soldiers ... Many vigilantes were injured.' They were, largely, IRA men of both persuasions. One of the leading Provisionals – as we write, still at large – bears the scar caused by a bottle thrown at Ballymurphy by a youth he was trying to restrain. His story is plausible, besides being supported by other sources: 'The Provos had been in existence only four months at that time,' he said. 'Our full-time active strength was no more than thirty. The last thing we wanted was a confrontation with the British Army or the Protestants.'

If they did not draw any lessons from the CS, the observ-

204

ers on the ground, Freeland and Burroughs, did get the point that the 1970 Orange marches were going, once again, to cause real trouble. Nobody in Whitehall would listen. Britain was preoccupied with the 18 June General Election campaign, and its sequel in a new Tory Government, as the balance of tension began to change dramatically in Ulster. The failure to ban the 1970 Orange parades, and the massive arms search and curfew of the Lower Falls Catholic ghetto which followed, were, one senior civil servant thinks now, 'the turning point in our policy in Ulster'. In his judgement: 'It was then that the Army began to be viewed in a different light. Before they had been regarded by the bulk of the Catholic population as protectors. That operation turned things absolutely upside down.'

The trouble began with great promptitude on 3 June 1970. One of the first Orange marches – a 'transfer-of-banner parade' the Orangemen solemnly said – was making its way back from the city centre along the Crumlin Road. The march's route would take it right along the southern boundary of the Ardoyne, an isolated and therefore militant Catholic sector. Indeed, the march was heading for two sensitive spots: the mouth of Hooker Street, full of burnt-out houses, and the Ardoyne Catholic Church, which is cut off from its parish by the width of the Crumlin Road.

The colonel locally in charge got his first intimation when, to his horror, he saw the march coming up the Crumlin Road. Somehow, the police had neglected to tell him of the route. Improvising, he tried to divert the marchers at Tennent Street, a couple of hundred yards before the Ardoyne – and found himself with two nights of Protestant rioting, accompanied by gunfire.

When the Joint Security Committee met at Stormont Castle on Wednesday 24 June to consider the next weekend's Protestant marches, everyone was scared. The pro-

205

posed Orange routes went past just too many predictable
trouble spots. For example, one was along Cupar Street,
which forms the northern boundary of the Catholic Clonard. This would take it right past Bombay Street, burnt out
in 1969. Fighting was inevitable. The moderate Catholics
foresaw that the inevitable riots could only strengthen the
Provisional IRA. The police knew that fresh rioting would
re-open the barely healing wounds of August 1969.

Ronald Burroughs and Arthur Young of the RUC
thought that the only course was to ban the marches. Both
had excellent Catholic contacts, and had been warned that if
the Protestants were allowed to march over the ground of
their previous 'victories', there would be attempts to repel
them. But the Prime Minister, Chichester-Clark, maintained, exactly as he had the previous year, that his followers
would destroy him if the marches were banned.

At this point, Freeland's contribution was vital. He
agreed with Burroughs and Young that the marches should
not go ahead. Since his men would have to bear the brunt of
the consequences, he felt if anything more strongly than they
did. But he also agreed with Chichester-Clark that they
could not be banned – though for tactical rather than political reasons. The 3 June riots after the Orangemen had been
forcibly redirected persuaded him that the Protestants
would march, whether legally or not. Legal marches would
simply be easier to control. According to two accounts, he
told the Committee: 'It is easier to push them through the
Ardoyne than to control the Shankill.'

That was the policy of last resort, though. What Freeland
recommended, and the Joint Security Committee accepted,
was that the police – the ultimate arbiters of such matters –
should negotiate with the Orangemen to re-route the
parades.

But the routes of Ulster marches are difficult to change,

because each one is based on a set of closely-argued territorial precedents. The Orangemen's game is to take in 'new ground' – march through a new street even closer to the Catholic heartland – each year, and the next year claim the right to do so again on the grounds that a 'tradition' has now been set. In 1970 the Orangemen were not allowed to take in 'new ground'. But the police, in the person of one of Young's senior officers, failed to get any significant re-routing. By the time the Joint Security Committee learned of the police failure, on Friday 26 June, they decided that it was too late to do anything but let the marchers go ahead.

Ronald Burroughs disagreed. As a diplomat, he was naturally averse to deliberately allowing a confrontation. He also knew that technically the Catholics had no legal right to try to repel Protestant marchers, but that fear and anger are stronger than respect for legal technicalities.

That evening, after a dinner at the Wellington Park Hotel, Burroughs took the Catholic leader, the produce broker Tom Conaty, aside in the car park and told him of the Security Committee's decision. Conaty, who was by now chairman of the CCDC (an organization he had originally been shy of because of its 'Republican' connections) knew that this meant illegal 'defenders' (i.e., IRA men) would offer their services to the Catholic ghetto-dwellers. It was a point which Burroughs also understood.

Burroughs, as appalled as Conaty by this prospect, said that he would do all he could to get the decision changed, to the extent of exercising his right of personal access to the British Prime Minister. At midnight, Burroughs got a call through to Edward Heath. The new Prime Minister had then been in Downing Street just eight days.

Burroughs, in some agitation, told Heath that bloodshed over the weekend was now inevitable – unless Heath stepped in and banned the Protestant marches. Heath listened

207

coolly, and said that he would consult the new Home Secretary, Reginald Maudling. We do not know what happened after that. What is certain is that all Maudling's intervention achieved was a minor, and irrelevant, piece of re-routing. The marches were not banned.

Early on the morning of Saturday 27 June thousands of Orangemen made their way in groups across the city towards the Shankill Road, where the major Orange parade was to begin. Most groups had their bands, and were singing Orange songs. (Orange songs vary from the traditional 'Boyne' and 'The Sash', to more hair-raising freelance efforts, such as: 'If guns are made for shooting, then skulls are made to crack/You've never seen a better Taig, than with a bullet in his back.')

The first trouble was stoning between Protestant and Catholic crowds on the Catholic Springfield Road. This led into a battle on the nearby Ballymurphy estate between Catholic youths and the Army, who fired numerous CS canisters into the estate, but with relatively little effect. There was rioting, more or less severe, all over Belfast throughout the day: the Army was stretched perilously thin, and in all 276 people were injured. (Things were not made easier by the fact that Bernadette Devlin, newly re-elected as Westminster MP for Mid-Ulster, was taken that evening to Armagh Jail. She had finally lost her appeal against a six-month sentence for incitement to riot and riotous behaviour in Derry the previous August. 'A ridiculous piece of timing,' Freeland said of her arrest.)

But it was the two shooting affrays which were really serious. The first was in the Ardoyne. It began when an Orange lodge marched up the Crumlin Road past the burnt Catholic homes of Hooker Street. They then retreated a little way into Palmer Street, on the Protestant side of the road, and stoning began between the crowds on either side.

Suddenly, gunfire broke out, and there were exchanges for roughly thirty minutes. At the end, three Protestants lay dead. When five Ardoyne men were tried (and acquitted) on murder charges, the police gave evidence that a group of gunmen emerged suddenly from the mouth of Hooker Street and fired without warning into the Protestant crowd. The local IRA Provisional commander is equally adamant that the first shots came from the Protestant side.

The second engagement began in the east Belfast ghetto called the Short Strand, around Seaforde Street, which is even smaller and more exposed than the Ardoyne – a pocket of about 6,000 Catholics huddled among 60,000 Protestants along the east shore of the Lagan river which divides Belfast. The key to this small Catholic enclave is St Matthew's Church and churchyard, which stands on Newtownards Road facing a group of tough Protestant streets to the north. One of these is Gertrude Street, whose Orange band is famous for its zest and repertoire. As the band passed St Matthew's on its way home that Saturday evening, someone flaunted a tricolour from Seaforde Street, and the stones began to fly. A few shots were fired, without anybody being hurt, and things died down quite suddenly. But the scene was set for a bloody night – and also for a decisive one. For the first time, the Provisional IRA went into battle.

There was more shooting in the Short Strand, again without casualties, around 10 p.m. Shortly afterwards a Protestant group tried to set fire to the church with petrol bombs: the sexton's house, near by, was set alight. By this time the Stormont MP, Paddy Kennedy, was there, and he went to the Mountpottinger RUC station near by to ask for protection for the church. He was told that the Army was already over-stretched on the west of the river, and nothing could be done.

209

Ulster

Also on the scene were the Belfast brigade commander of the Provisional IRA, Billy McKee; its 'Third Battalion' commander, Billy Kelly, plus some local 'freelances' with guns. (Kelly had been mending his car when these freelances in east Belfast had telephoned to ask for help.) At around the time that Kennedy went to the police station, Kelly says that he approached a group of policemen in the Newtownards Road but they refused to help.

Kelly goes on that he then approached the officer in charge of a small Army patrol, but was told: 'You can stew in your own fat.' Whether all the details of these exchanges are accurate is hard to say, but whatever was the case in the Ardoyne earlier, the IRA men in the Short Strand enclave seem to have had only defensive intentions. What frightened them was that the Army had blocked the bridges leading from west Belfast. The Catholics of the Short Strand were thus trapped, without hope of reinforcement. (In fact, Freeland had blocked the bridges mainly to prevent Protestants flowing over from the rioting in the Shankill.)

Around 11 p.m. Protestant groups, under covering fire from the streets to the north, began to attack St Matthew's Church with petrol bombs. Kelly and his men, established in the churchyard, began to shoot back, and Billy McKee joined in the battle, over Kelly's strongly-voiced objections. (This was a breach of the rules by McKee: in any local situation, even the Chief of Staff is supposed to defer to the local commander.)

The shooting went on until 5 a.m., when the Army at last arrived. By then two Protestants had been killed, another two died later from their injuries, and several more were wounded. (As the attackers, the Protestants were the more exposed.)

McKee himself had also been seriously wounded. He and another Provisional called McIlhone suddenly came face-
210

to-face with a Protestant gunman who had actually got inside the churchyard. The man opened fire with a carbine, hitting McKee. McIlhone hesitated for a fatal moment. The Protestant gunman had faster reflexes or fewer inhibitions. He shot McIlhone through the chest.

The fact that so long a gun-battle could go on was, of course, a simple failure by the Army in its basic task of getting between the two sides. Catholic imagination soon added new dimensions: it was said in the Short Strand that the Army had sealed the bridges over the river so that the attackers could finish the task at leisure. The truth was that just as Kennedy had been told the Army was just so busy in west Belfast that for three hours they could not look the other way. The one platoon Freeland could spare had tried to get up the Newtownards Road at the height of the battle, but was beaten back by the Protestants.

It was, just as it had been in August 1969, a case of too little, too late. That weekend, Freeland had barely two battalions in Belfast. The reinforcements which the Ministry of Defence were sending him to cope with the trouble expected from the Orange marches of 12 July – an extra three and a half battalions and two armoured squadrons – did not arrive for another week.

But even if Freeland's judgement that he simply did not have enough men to relieve the Catholics was correct, the conclusions which the Provisionals drew from the St Matthew's shoot-out remained intact. If the 60,000 Protestants of east Belfast *had* risen against the 6,000 Catholics in their midst, who – in the absence of troops – would have defended the Catholics, except that small group of Provisionals and the Short Strand's own neighbourhood militia? Either way, the St Matthew's battle pointed towards a doctrine of militant self-help. (The Provisionals naturally ignored the inconvenient fact that the Protestants had not risen: all the

211

Provos had been doing was fighting a Protestant gang much like themselves.)

Surveying the wreckage of the weekend, which claimed six lives in all, and £500,000 worth of damage, Ronald Burroughs said to a friend: 'That was the greatest single miscalculation I have ever seen made in the course of my whole life.' There was worse to come.

*

The new Home Secretary was Reginald Maudling. He had been the Conservatives' deputy leader ever since he had narrowly lost the leadership to Edward Heath in 1965 – the first time it had been balloted for. 'The best brain in the Tory party,' a senior colleague said of him shortly before the 1970 election. 'He'd be a different man if he was leader. Not getting the leadership affected him more than people thought.'

The visible effect was to make Maudling sit a little loose in his parliamentary responsibilities and devote himself to his business interests, not all of them well chosen. This impression of indolence was strengthened by his considerable girth and shuffling gait. To some extent it was a matter of style. Even at the Treasury in 1962–4, when the Tories were last in office, he had preferred not to intervene until he had identified something which could usefully be done.

But non-interventionism, for a British Home Secretary dealing with Ulster, was a dangerous relapse into the past. Maudling had little previous knowledge of Ulster, and had not shadowed Home Office affairs in opposition: the man who had, Quintin Hogg, was now Lord Chancellor.

In the wake of the June riots Maudling paid a prompt visit to Belfast – the following Tuesday, 30 June. He was so ill-provided with ideas and even information that the trip was a damaging anticlimax. It was quickly apparent that here was no Callaghan. 'Tell me,' said one of those who met Maudling, 'is he really as innocent as he seems? He didn't appear to grasp the first thing of what was going on.' The military verdict was much the same: 'He seemed amazed at the ghastly situation.'

Maudling's own feelings were made clear as his plane gathered height on the way back to London on 1 July. 'For God's sake bring me a large Scotch,' he said. 'What a bloody awful country.'

At approximately the time when Maudling boarded his plane to leave Ulster, a small group of men approached the occupant of 24 Balkan Street, a terrace house in one of the maze of streets threading the Lower Falls Catholic enclave in the centre of Belfast. They were from the leadership of the Official wing of the IRA. (The Falls, the main Catholic ghetto, is the homeland of the Officials – the more aggressive Provisionals being dominant in the outlying areas.) The occupant of No. 24 was an 'auxiliary', which is to say he was not a member of the Officials but that, in the aftermath of the burnings of August 1969, he had volunteered to do some arms drill in case a Falls militia were needed.

The Officials now asked this man to store a load of arms. The auxiliary was horrified. He had a wife and children; and this was more than he had bargained for. Reluctantly, he agreed – on condition that the arms stayed only twenty-four hours. The consignment was twelve pistols, a Schmeisser sub-machine-gun (a Second World War relic in perfect condition, though minus its magazine) and assorted explosives and ammunition.

When the twenty-four hours were up, the Officials said there had been a mix-up. On the morning of 3 July, therefore, when the auxiliary left for work, his wife went once more to the Officials. They reassured her: the arms would be removed after dusk. But the next visitors to No. 24 were not

Ulster

the IRA. Shortly after 4.30 p.m. a police car and two Army
Land-Rovers roared into Balkan Street. While four or five
lorryloads of Royal Scots sealed both ends of the street, the
police and a major in the Royal Scots searched the house.

That account of the background to the Balkan Street
arms haul – the biggest by the Army up to that time – was
pieced together later by a local priest. It fits in with the
Army's own subsequent analysis. It was said later that the
Army's information about the Balkan Street arms had come
as a tip-off from the Falls. According to a senior Army
officer, that was just a cover story. The information actually
came as a result of three police raids at Hammersmith in
west London on 2 July, which had themselves produced
four Bren light machine-guns, twelve rifles and 17,000
rounds of assorted ammunition. On 3 July the CID officer
who had led the Hammersmith raids arrived in Ulster, and
the troops moved into Balkan Street only hours later.

No doubt they were glad to get a good tip about illegal
arms. But it seems doubtful that anyone at Army HQ in
Lisburn had considered the cumulative effect of an arms
raid on this most sensitive of Catholic areas, only six days
after the mayhem following the Orange parades, which the
Army had inevitably been seen to be protecting. Against a
background of open jubilation by the Stormont Unionists at
the Tory election triumph in England, it did not need an
overly paranoid Catholic to discern a political-military
plot.

In a sense, that view was correct. The arms search was a
straightforward military operation – albeit, one stamped
with political naïvety. But the Army's behaviour in the
aftermath was indeed the consequence of a deliberate decision in which the Unionist Government had a large hand,
and which the new Conservative Government's junior Minister of Defence, Lord Balneil, personally endorsed.

214

On Wednesday 1 July, there was a meeting of the Joint Security Committee. The members were much as usual: among them Porter, Freeland, and Young, though on this occasion Chichester-Clark himself seems to have turned up. The main topic was, inevitably, the bloodshed which had engulfed Belfast after the marches of the previous weekend. And the committee came to a remarkable conclusion. The trouble had spread, they decided, because the Army had not been tough enough when it first broke out. On this basis, they decided future policy: what was required to restore the peace was a demonstration of force. The *very next* incident which sparked trouble in Belfast should be put down by the Army with maximum force.

Maudling was, of course, in Belfast at the time; but while it is likely that he knew of this decision, we have no evidence to that effect. But on 2 July Maudling's colleague, Balneil, arrived in Ulster. In a briefing at Lisburn Army headquarters, he was warned that the Unionists would tell him that the Army had failed the previous weekend, and he was told of the policy that had now been agreed to restore the military image. He assented to it. Twenty-four hours later, the Falls Road curfew was the result.

The Balkan Street arms search was completed by 5.30 p.m. The three vehicles bearing the arms drove out of the Falls on to the main road, Grosvenor Road. But crowds had inevitably gathered at either end of Balkan Street. When the soldiers cordoning the street tried to get back to their vehicles, the crowd blocked their path. The troops pushed their way aboard, but now the crowd jostled their armoured personnel carriers. Endeavouring to manoeuvre past them, one of the drivers reversed – and crushed a man against some railings. The crowd, now with something to be angry about, began to throw stones.

Where trouble is brewing, the Army stays around, on the

215

theory that a military presence damps it down. The practice, at least as often as not, is that the military presence both increases the tension and provides a handy target. Anyway, when the stones hit the last vehicle, its troops dismounted – and once more faced the crowd.

It was an imprudent thing to do: by 5.30 p.m. one platoon of troops was effectively besieged in the middle of the Falls half-way along one of the exit routes from Balkan Street to the main road. Farther along the same route, the other troops, this time a company, were also stranded. Somehow, the Army had to get them out. It was precisely the sort of opportunity for a show of force that the Joint Security Committee had envisaged.

The only distinct thread in the subsequent confusion is that the Army duly over-reacted. They also compounded their own muddle. A company of the Gloucesters and one from the Second Queen's went into the Falls to rescue one lot of troops: a company of reserves went in to rescue the other. But to extract one of the stranded squads, their rescuers had to fire CS – which, of course, promptly drifted into nearby streets and incensed their residents. The confusion grew still further when the reserves sent in to rescue one of the original squads achieved this only at the price of becoming trapped themselves. They began to fire CS too. The time was now 5.40 p.m. and the Falls was going mad. (The residents' temper was not calmed by the gothic and baseless rumour that in searching the house in Balkan Street, the troops had lifted a dead child from her coffin.) Then, of course, more troops had to go in to rescue the rescuers. So the military presence grew. The Army's radio log reveals considerable confusion, with heavy radio traffic as the troops on the ground appealed to regimental and command headquarters for guidance and reinforcements.

The inhabitants, alarmed at such disorganized behaviour,

took it for an invasion. By 5.50 p.m. nail bombs and petrol bombs were being thrown, and later two, perhaps three, grenades injured five soldiers – luckily with splinter rather than blast wounds.

Until about 7 p.m. things remained more or less under control, because the Chief of the Brigade Staff, Brigadier Hudson, was directing events from a helicopter. Suddenly, Hudson and his pilot heard a loud clang in the airframe. The pilot, thinking it might be the impact of a bullet, put the machine down in the grounds of the Royal Victoria Hospital. By the time Hudson was on the move again, things were seriously out of control.

The only way to regain order was to pull the troops out of the Falls altogether and, once everyone had been 'rescued', this is what Hudson did. The Army began to regroup its forces on the main roads bordering the area. Meanwhile, of course, the Falls' residents threw up barricades against them. What had begun as a simple arms raid had now escalated to a major confrontation. Freeland was convinced that there had been some sort of concerted ambush of his men in the Falls, and he thought that IRA men from all over the city would now join in. Once the troops had pulled out, his first move was to order Hudson to cordon the area. He was partially correct. Around 6.30 p.m. the Provisional IRA leader, Billy McKee, telephoned one of the leaders of the Official IRA in the Falls, to ask if he needed help. 'We're going to take on the British Army,' the Falls IRA man said. McKee thought he was mad, and told him so. The Provisionals did not budge.

A show of Army force was now required – and even if it were not, the Falls had somehow to be brought under control. At 8.20 p.m. the Army invaded the area. The local IRA opened fire on them. Among their targets were troops of the Black Watch and Life Guards, so new to Belfast that they had driven straight from the ferry when it berthed at Belfast docks. 'They were absolutely terrified,' Hudson admitted later. There was, in consequence, a good deal of gunfire from the Army. One official report puts the Army's expenditure of ammunition at fourteen rounds of the 7.62 mm bullets from the troops' self loading rifles, and one .303 round. This frugality simply does not accord with eyewitness accounts. Nor does it tally with the private log of one officer involved, which records *1500* rounds of 7.62 mm ammunition fired, seventeen rounds of .303, and ten rounds of 9 mm pistol ammunition. If his figures are correct, one would have to have a low opinion of Army marksmanship to believe that all this was fired, in accordance with policy, only at 'identifiable targets'.

The troops also deluged the area with CS. The matchbox houses provided no refuge from the choking clouds. Some of the canisters broke enough roof tiles in falling to smash into attics and fill the houses with smoke. There was no escape for the occupants: the streets outside were also saturated. 'The women were white-faced with panic,' Father Murphy recalls. By 10 p.m. Freeland believed that the only way to stop widespread bloodshed was to get everyone off the streets. He declared a curfew over the whole Falls area, and he did not lift it until Sunday morning, thirty-five hours later.

The decision was entirely Freeland's own. He did not have time to consult the rest of Stormont's Joint Security Committee. There was much argument later about the legality of this curfew, or 'restriction on public movement', as the Army afterwards preferred to call it. (For this reason, none of the Falls people arrested for curfew-breaking were prosecuted.) Apart from its dubious legality, though, Freeland himself had given the best argument against a curfew at a press conference almost eleven months before, on 18

218

August 1969. 'What do you do if people disobey it?' he said.
'Shoot them?' In the Lower Falls three people were shot
dead.

While the curfew lasted, the Army took the opportunity
to conduct a house-to-house search of the whole area – and
this obvious military course was also the consequence of a
political decision. At the 1 July Joint Security Committee
meeting, it had been agreed that when arms were found in a
house, the entire street should be searched. Whether this was
a genuine military judgement, or merely to introduce a punitive element, we cannot say. But the policy of more general-
ized arms searches was dear to Chichester-Clark's heart, and
on his brief visit Maudling had suggested that the Army
might do a little more to make Chichester-Clark's life
easier. Normally, the military refused to consider 'area'
searches on the grounds that the opprobrium incurred out-
weighed any advantage. But since they had incurred the opprobrium anyway, Chichester-Clark might as well be given a
leg-up.

Just as the soldiers had always prophesied, the returns
were not large by Ulster standards – especially if it was considered as the arsenal of 20,000 people. The Army H.Q.
log lists: twenty-eight rifles, two carbines, fifty-two pistols
or revolvers, twenty-four shotguns, 100 'incendiary devices',
twenty pounds of gelignite, and 20,000 rounds of ammunition. The weapons would just about have equipped a rather
down-at-heel infantry company. The ammunition, on the
other hand, would have supplied a couple of battalions.

For this haul, the Army paid a very high price. Four civilians were dead: one run over by the Army, and three shot.
None of the dead was alleged to be connected with the IRA;
but it is perhaps fortunate, in view of the volume of fire, that
more people did not die.

Illegal confinement, summary search and exposure to unprecedented amounts of CS gas outraged large sections of the Falls Road population. Their conviction that the 'invasion' had been politically motivated was confirmed, as they saw it, when the Army drove two beaming Unionist ministers, Captains William Long and John Brooke, on a tour round the subjugated Falls.

On top of this, men from two of the regiments involved, the Black Watch and the Devon and Dorsets, were accused of smashing and sometimes looting the houses they searched. Characteristically, the Catholics later undermined their genuine grievances on this score by absurd inflation: 'At least one would like an explanation from General Freeland of why the Ulster Society for the Prevention of Cruelty to Animals was not alerted ...' ran one of the more imaginative efforts. But when he arrived in Ulster a couple of months later as GOC Land Forces, under Freeland, Major-General Anthony Farrar-Hockley, after inquiries, came to the conclusion that this had indeed happened in about sixty cases, though he could not get evidence to justify legal charges. He found that although the Falls Road citizens wanted to vent their wrath against the Army, they would not 'inform' upon individual soldiers. (Farrar-Hockley was a stocky veteran of the Gloucesters' stand at Imjin in Korea, and hero of several subsequent attempts to escape from Chinese camps. He was also a military historian of some distinction.)

The writer Conor Cruise O'Brien says he was in the Falls Road when the confined people came boiling out of their homes on Sunday morning. An Army helicopter was cruising by, with a British officer calling through a loudspeaker: 'We are your friends, we are here to help you.' Men and women alike shook their fists and impotently hurled stones.

Father Murphy saw an abrupt change in many of his parishioners. 'Women who had been giving soldiers cups of tea, those very same women, were now out on the streets shouting: 'Go home, you bums; go home, you bums . . .' – to the tune of 'Auld Lang Syne', in fact. There is an element of Celtic exaggeration in this. The Army officer responsible for the Falls for four months before the curfew said later that only two householders used to give his men tea. The pre-curfew months should certainly not be elevated to a lost Golden Age. But 3–5 July 1970 did convert what was perhaps, only an increasingly sullen Catholic acceptance of the Army into outright communal hostility.

It was not quite the end of relations between the Army and the Catholics, but it was the decisive change. From then on, it was all, or nearly all, downhill. Brigadier Hudson, who saw all too clearly what had happened, called a meeting of community leaders on the day the curfew was lifted. 'Let's keep talking,' he said. 'What's the use?' he was asked. Not everybody in Ulster was upset and angry, though. As the Falls Road arms haul was displayed in the yard of Springfield Road police station, Captain John Brooke squeezed the arm of a young constable. 'It's a grand day for us,' he said.

In the months that followed, recruitment to the Provisionals was dizzily fast: the movement grew from fewer than a hundred activists in May–June to nearly 800 by December. Time was running out.

Chapter 13
Firm Measures

James Callaghan, Labour's Home Secretary, was already planning direct rule in Ulster – control of the province from London – when Labour lost the election in June 1970. He had a three-clause bill ready. Few of his colleagues knew. The Prime Minister, Harold Wilson, did know and was 'dithering', so Callaghan remarked at the time. The Cabinet had not been approached.

Callaghan's mind appears to have been made up. He now tends to say merely that he was 'reviewing' the situation; but we have no reason to doubt a detailed account of his intentions which he gave privately at the time. In view of what has happened since, it is worth examining both the reasons for Callaghan's direct rule plan and the difficulties his civil servants then foresaw.

Callaghan was fed up. He thought that the Catholics were stringing the British Government along, making fresh demands as soon as old ones were met. On the other side, he had also come to doubt whether the pace of reform at Stormont could last much longer – or, indeed, whether it was Chichester-Clark's wish that it should. Callaghan saw Ulster bedevilling British politics for years, unless some decisive move were made.

'It's absurd,' Callaghan said of Stormont, a few days before the 1970 election. 'Here they are, with all the panoply of government – even a prime minister – and a population no bigger than four London boroughs. They don't need a prime minister, they need a good Mayor of Lewisham.' (As a model of government, Lewisham may not habitually spring to mind, but Callaghan's wife used to be a GLC councillor there.) With some misgivings, his civil servants agreed.

Much Whitehall staff work had gone into the mechanism for direct rule. At the Home Office, Callaghan – who had been mightily impressed at the Treasury by their contingency planning for devaluation – had a similar 'black book' drawn up examining five possible ways of taking over Ulster. (Since then the document has grown: under the Conservatives, various combinations of these plans have also been compiled.)

It was later said that direct rule would entail a full-scale military invasion of Ulster, followed by an army of Whitehall officials to replace what was seen as a potentially mutinous bureaucracy. That indeed may have to be the scale of any future operation: the 1970 plan was less dramatic.

About 15,000 troops would have gone over – 1,000 more than we have there now. Many of the troops, it was thought, could be withdrawn again in a few days. The Ulster Civil Service would carry on, it was now known: only a handful of Whitehall men, already selected and briefed, were to go over to improve the quality of administration at key points.

The timing of the direct rule intervention depended on the British General Election (18 June 1970) and events in Ulster. The 'season' of Orange marches (June to August) was just about to begin. For a variety of reasons – including the practical difficulty of enforcing a ban – Callaghan was proposing to let the marches go ahead, though several of his colleagues feared bloodshed. If there had been trouble, it would, he recognized, have at least the virtue of justifying direct rule.

This, of course, was the crucial moment when government and the Ulster problem unexpectedly fell into the lap of the Tories and of Reginald Maudling, the new Home Secretary. It is possible that Maudling did not even know what Callaghan had in mind, because of the Whitehall custom of not telling ministers of new governments what their predecessors had been up to. A whole new group of politicians had to learn their way round Ulster from scratch.

New or not, Conservative ministers had very little excuse for not realizing that Britain's Ulster policy was now going badly wrong. Dr Patrick Hillery, External Affairs minister of the Republic of Ireland, went to London on 8 July to see the British Foreign Secretary, Sir Alec Douglas-Home. He told Home that Britain's political aims – to make Catholics into full and willing citizens of the north – were being frustrated by its new military aggressiveness. He spoke with authority; two days before he had been on the Falls Road himself, and he had seen the signs of growing Catholic estrangement after the curfew.

Hillery had driven north alone with an official of his ministry. The secret visit, publicized afterwards, was intended as a gesture of solidarity: the Irish Government liked to think that northern Catholics would look to Dublin as the guarantor of their civil rights. But Hillery, like his Prime Minister, Jack Lynch, is a soft-voiced, unforceful man. Home and Maudling thought his Falls trip impertinent and his evidence unpersuasive. They saw no reason to depart from their new policy of 'firm measures'.

Anyone who supposes that 'firm measures' alone are the cure for the ills of Ulster should examine the next episode with care, for it is hard to imagine that there was ever a

measure which was firmer, in its way, than the Criminal
Justice (Temporary Provisions) Act, 1970.

On Monday 29 June 1970, after the rioting and shooting
which followed from the Orange marches, the Ulster Cabinet met in a state of something like panic. In anticipation,
the Minister of Home Affairs, Robert Porter, and the Attorney General, a bluff Belfast lawyer called Basil Kelly, had
spent the weekend putting such finishing touches as they
could to a new piece of legislation. It provided *mandatory*
prison sentences for rioters.

The Cabinet had been toying with this for five or six
months. One of its advocates had been Phelim O'Neill, the
jovial Agriculture Minister, which gave the measure a certain gloss of respectability: as one of the very few Unionist
politicians not a member of the Orange Order, he was a
card-carrying liberal. Outside the Cabinet, its chief backer
was Freeland. He had always pressed for two changes in the
law: stiffer sentences, and a new blanket charge to cover
people who might be merely present at a riot. The difficulties
the Army had encountered in its efforts to arrest rioters
among the lanes of Ballymurphy in April had persuaded
Freeland of the need for these.

The Cabinet knew the risks. The major legal one was privately pointed out at the time by Porter himself: 'There is
always a tendency to convict when you have mandatory sentences, because the court feels the accused would not have
been brought there unless he had done something fairly
serious.'

Yet without dissent, the Cabinet approved a Bill which
laid down minimum six-month jail terms for anyone convicted of 'riotous behaviour', 'disorderly behaviour' or 'behaviour likely to cause a breach of the peace'. Inevitably, the
Army was going to be the chief instrument for applying this
crude legal device – because the Army would be doing the

arresting in riots. The theory was that the Army would hand over anyone arrested to the RUC for charging. But the Cabinet never consulted the police. The first that Sir Arthur Young, the Callaghan-appointed head of the RUC, heard about it was when one of his officers, Bill Meharg, burst into his office as the Cabinet broke up and said: 'You'll never guess what they've done now.' Young was appalled.

Freeland saw no problems. He complained at the next meeting of the Security Committee that it was 'too little, too late'. But the more thoughtful members of the RUC saw the peril. It was, as Porter more or less admitted in Stormont, unnecessary on a strictly legal basis. Already, there was an ample battery of charges to deal with trouble on the streets, ranging from breach of the peace through disorderly and riotous behaviour, unlawful wounding, grievous bodily harm, and even arson, with further penalties for weapons. But all these charges, of course, needed the specialist disciplines and skills of a police force to make them work. These were the skills the Army lacked. Now, as the police saw it, the law was being bent for the Army's benefit.

The legislation was unstoppable: Stormont rushed it through in a record eighteen-hour debate. Only two MPs challenged it line by line: Ian Paisley, who had just been elected in rapid succession to Stormont and Westminster, and his ally William Beattie. (Paisley is one of the few men at Stormont with any sort of consistent record in opposing military excess and despotic law. Most people affect to see this as nothing more than concern for the necks of his own more extreme supporters, but there is a certain gristly integrity to Paisley's mind which separates him from the Eatanswill traditions of Stormont at large.)

One of Paisley's complaints was that the Bill was so ill-drafted as not to make sense in parts; and Basil Kelly's own words must surely be unique for an attorney-general commending a piece of legislation to a Parliament. 'Inevitably,' he said, 'harsh cases will arise as a result of this Bill, perhaps even wrong convictions on the basis of mistaken identity.' The spirit in which this warning was received was encapsulated in the words of Captain Robert Mitchell, MP for North Armagh. 'It brings in,' he said with satisfaction, 'an element of ruthlessness.'

The new Act's most immediate effect, however, was to bring chaos to the magistrates' courts. For in their enthusiasm to decree minimum sentences not just for 'riotous behaviour' but also for 'disorderly behaviour' and 'behaviour likely to cause a breach of the peace', the Unionists forgot that the two minor charges were the RUC's standard device for handling Saturday night pub-brawls and other non-sectarian rituals of city life. Normal police work thus became even harder throughout the province.

And even in the area for which it was designed, the disastrous results of this hasty legislation were soon made apparent. On 1 August 1970, in a disturbance in Belfast, the former chairman of the Civil Rights Association, a dentist called Frank Gogarty, was recording the sounds with a microphone and tape. He was stopped by an Army patrol, bundled against a wall and searched, being thrown against the wall twice in the process. When he protested, he was cursed, kicked and thrown into a jeep – at which he said: 'Stop kicking me, you British bastard.'

Gogarty was charged with disorderly behaviour and, because of his 'insulting and abusive' language, with behaviour likely to cause a breach of the peace. In court, the soldiers agreed with Gogarty's account of his arrest – as a private put it, he had not been 'handled with kid gloves'. The magistrate dismissed the disorderly behaviour charge, and the language he found nothing worse than 'a case of bad manners'. It did, however, constitute behaviour likely to cause a breach of the peace. Gogarty had to get the mandatory six months – the magistrate saying that he would support a petition for his reprieve. On appeal, however, Gogarty's sentence was actually *increased*: he was now bound over for two years as well as being gaoled. Gogarty's father had to come out of retirement to patch up the practice. There may be faster methods of alienating moderates, but it is hard to think what they might be.

A Belfast docker, twenty-year-old John Benson, was the next celebrated victim. He painted 'No Tea Here' on the wall of his street – a reference to the now defunct practice of giving tea to the troops. Beside such ubiquitous Belfast graffiti as 'Up the UVF' or 'Taig Bastards Out', this contribution was scarcely inflammatory. But the Army complained to the police, and a constable traced Benson by following the trail of red paint drips back to Benson's kitchen. Deciding that the slogan was 'an obvious attempt to intimidate people', the magistrate gave Benson the requisite six months for breach of the peace.

This sort of case was so clearly disastrous that Attorney-General Kelly approached the police. Could they, he suggested, 'bend the law' a little, to find new charges that did not carry mandatory sentences? There was, according to police sources, an argument of some heat when Young said flatly that the only solution was a repeal of the Act. The judiciary – particularly the magistrates – took the same view. The Cabinet finally succumbed to pressure in December 1970, and with some sleight of hand repealed mandatory sentences for everything except riotous behaviour.

But by Christmas 1970 the damage was done. The Ministry of Home Affairs' statistics reveal the fearsome range of the Act. Between 1 July and 17 December 1970 – when repeal took effect – 269 people were charged with riotous or disorderly behaviour. The police withdrew 129 of

228

these before they came to court; and reduced the charges in twenty-two cases. (Nine cases dragged on and had still not been heard when the statistics were assembled.) In the end, therefore, 109 defendants went to court on charges carrying mandatory prison sentences. *Every single one was convicted*. Only four of seventeen sentences that went to appeal were reversed.

But the fact that of 269 charged only 109 finally came to court shows that, in effect, the police were sabotaging the Act by introducing an element of discretion into its working. This sounds wise; but the Catholics maintained, with some justice, that this discretion was consistently exercised in Protestant favour. The Act's partial repeal in December only made this worse. By giving the authorities power to choose between riotous behaviour (meaning inevitable imprisonment) and disorderly behaviour (reduced now to a fine), the police were handed precisely the weapon of potential discrimination which ministers like Porter had supposedly hoped the new legislation would remove.

Afterwards, the moderates – among them Porter himself – put about this justification that the unmodified Bill had at least stopped the courts from discriminating between Protestants and Catholics. Even ignoring the oddity of this rationale – and the fact that the police sabotaged it anyway – it is hard to accept this as a motive behind the Bill. Catholic complaints focused at that time on the political bias in higher judicial appointments – which the Cabinet did not tackle – and not upon the lower courts' treatment of rioters. Predictably, too, the new Act in operation, so far from expunging bias, became in Catholic eyes the second most repressive piece of legislation (after the Special Powers Act) at the Unionists' command. *And the Army was the instrument which enforced it.*

In addition, the men who might have checked this tendency in Stormont towards harsher and harsher measures were disappearing. Porter had seen the snags in the Criminal Justice Act; but he was exhausted, he had long wanted to leave office, and in August 1970 he managed it. His effective replacement (though only with the rank of Minister of State, since Chichester-Clark nominally took on the Home Affairs ministry himself), was a young authoritarian named John Taylor. Later in the year, Young went home to London: his successor as chief constable (RUC ranks were anglicized now) was a long-service Protestant Ulsterman, Graham Shillington. Polarization between the two communities was steadily increasing. And as it did so, Chichester-Clark's own position steadily weakened.

*

Chichester-Clark was among the optimists of Ulster. When the troops moved into Derry and Belfast in the 1969 riots, he thought they would be back in barracks within twelve months. When those twelve months, in fact, ended with the Orange parades and the Falls curfew, he thought the first a success and the second justified. When the winter of 1970 seemed quiet, Chichester-Clark and his Cabinet colleagues began to murmur that the trouble was over. The Army was disconcerted. 'We used to tell them "For God's sake, your troubles are ahead of you",' one senior Army officer recalled. 'But they wouldn't listen.'

The root of Chichester-Clark's optimism did him credit, however. In 1969 he, like most Ulstermen, had blamed the trouble on the IRA. But while some of his Cabinet colleagues had remained of that fundamentalist persuasion, Chichester-Clark had by 1970 come to believe that the IRA was at that time secondary. 'The trouble really is communal discontent,' he once said privately. And this he thought his reform programme would assuage.

230

Few people appreciated the pressures Chichester-Clark was under from his own backbenchers through the latter half of 1970, or the ways in which deliberate steps to ease tension had to be postponed for fear of alienating them. In the late summer of 1970, for instance, Young told Chichester-Clark that the border was so irrelevant that some of the RUC's stations along it might as well be closed to save manpower. A Northern Ireland 'presence' there could safely be left to the Customs and an occasional Army patrol. Chichester-Clark agreed, but said that his backbenchers would never accept the idea.

A few weeks later, Young was again summoned to see Chichester-Clark. He arrived to find the Prime Minister flanked by Porter, Faulkner and the Secretary to the Cabinet, Black. Chichester-Clark announced that all police stations must be re-armed. Young resisted strongly, pointing out that they were under no attack; if and when they were, he said, the Army could defend them. After a long argument, Chichester-Clark agreed with the logic of this, but put in a final plea: 'What am I going to tell my backbenchers? Couldn't we agree on, say, one shotgun per station?'

On the other side, the Army was pressing in the Joint Security Committee for the province to be disarmed. Freeland and his fellow officers thought it was absurd that in a country as tense as Ulster, about 100,000 weapons should legally be in private hands. Shotguns did not worry them – as one officer put it: 'Anyone who tries conclusions with a soldier armed only with a shotgun would be mad.' But the Army did want to take in all rifles and revolvers, and the category of weapons which police records rather sinisterly called merely 'other'. Operationally, they saw no difficulty. The Army plan was to sweep the province, picking up arms in three stages: border areas first, then everywhere except Belfast, finally Belfast itself.

All they needed was police cooperation and political backing. They got neither. The police claimed 'pressure of work' as the reason why they could not break down the records of gun licences, district by district. Finally, the Army offered to do the job for them. At this point, Chichester-Clark compromised. He ordered that all privately held weapons in Belfast should be withdrawn, and that, elsewhere in the province, nobody should be allowed to hold more than one weapon. (The Army had encountered one prominent Unionist in Armagh with eight.) Even this turned out to be 'impossible'.

In a sense, Chichester-Clark was the victim of the Conservative Government's policy urged upon it by his own brother at Westminster, Robin. To borrow a phrase from the American Supreme Court, Maudling took a 'strict constructionist' view of Ulster: Stormont had an elected government: they should get on with it. 'Be fair,' one civil servant enjoined us. 'When Maudling wanted to push something he did it discreetly and through Chichester-Clark. When Callaghan had an idea, he used to rush round telling everyone. There wasn't much doing-good-by-stealth with Jim.' But, he cautiously admitted, Maudling's attitude was such that 'you could say the inaction was greater than it had been under Labour'.

This quietist approach extended to the military, too. Under Labour, scarcely a day had passed when, say, Hattersley was not on the phone, querying decisions as apparently trivial as the use of water-cannon. Freeland liked the comparative silence of Balneil: 'Not so many back-seat drivers,' he said approvingly. But it fretted some of his colleagues. 'When you're in unknown territory, it is useful to have native guides,' Farrar-Hockley once remarked.

But, more significantly, the silence left Chichester-Clark isolated – without public pressure from Westminster to pit against the pressure from his backbenchers. As 1970 drew to a close, the only consistent reformist pressure came from the British representative in Ulster, Ronald Burroughs – who, being a Wilson protégé, was known not to be close to Heath or Maudling. But around November 1970, for instance, Chichester-Clark had to postpone a proposal by Burroughs that the chairmanship of certain committees in Stormont should be given to the opposition parties. Faulkner finally accepted the idea the following June. Every proposal in Faulkner's Green Paper on political reform, issued in the late summer of 1971, had in fact been discussed in 1970 by Chichester-Clark. Faulkner himself remarked somewhat bitterly to a friend that his own working copy of the Green Paper was actually the draft prepared for Chichester-Clark, with his own handwritten notes in the margin.

Yet even this inability to deliver political reforms did not dent Chichester-Clark's optimism. When he told Burroughs that they were 'not practical', he meant merely that he could not yet force them through his party. He expected the Catholics to understand and trust his intentions. He felt he had earned that. And, indeed, during the first twenty months of Chichester-Clark's premiership, up till the end of 1970, a good deal of progress had in fact been made with the legislative and administrative preliminaries of reform.

A police Act had established the principle of a civilianized and unarmed police force, and set up a Police Authority to run it. The Parliamentary Commissioner Act (Northern Ireland) had set up an Ombudsman to look into grievances against central government, and the Commissioner for Complaints Act (Northern Ireland) had set up a similar arbiter of grievances against local government.

The first of two Electoral Law Acts had brought the franchise into line with Britain's. To check abuses over council housing, local councils had been sent a scheme of allocation

233

by points, which they were broadly required to follow. On council jobs, an interim Local Government Staff Commission now existed to give advice.

Chichester-Clark had created a Ministry of Community Relations: it had been charged with collecting from local councils their promise to abide by a declaration of equality of opportunity and a code of employment procedure. He had also set up a Community Relations Commission, and his Government had passed an act outlawing incitement to religious hatred.

The moves on electoral law, council housing and council jobs – three of the main areas of Catholic grievance – had come from Brian Faulkner's Ministry of Development. A good many things remained to do, even on the legislative front; and the bulk of them, too, were the Ministry of Development's business. Of specific commitments in the Callaghan communiqué of October 1969, local government boundaries and functions were still unreorganized; and the central body which was to take charge of all public-authority house-building had not yet been set up. (A lot of work had been done on local government reorganization, which is a slow business; a Housing Executive Act became law on 25 February 1971; and on the same day Faulkner also got a second Electoral Law Act through Stormont which extended the new local-government franchise to by-elections, the only form of election likely to take place for some time.)

Three other important commitments not yet fulfilled at the end of 1970 were the appointment of a public prosecutor separate from the police; the introduction of an anti-discrimination clause into government contracts; and the withdrawal of such parts of the Special Powers Act as conflicted with international obligations.

Even so, a respectable body of work had been got through. The mistake which Chichester-Clark appears to

234

have made was to expect quick results, in terms of cheerful and grateful Catholic cooperation, from actions taken in the clear air of Stormont which could not possibly have had time to filter down into the miasmal streets of Belfast below. Change could only be gradual: institutions might be altered in form, but a real difference in their practice was not likely to be produced except by the slow replacement of the generation which had been running them.

Time on that scale was not to be had. At the beginning of 1971 Chichester-Clark knew that many of his Protestant supporters believed reform irrelevant, and he feared a Protestant rising if communal peace were not restored. What happened next inclined him to take their views more and more seriously.

Chapter 14
The Tories say No – once

The riots in the Ballymurphy estate in west Belfast in January 1971 began a double political process: Chichester-Clark's disenchantment with reform, and his increasing attachment to strong measures. But the riots were remarkable for something else: a secret attempt by the Army to enlist the Provisionals of the IRA in keeping the peace.

The Second Royal Anglians had assumed the task of controlling Ballymurphy and a wedge of west Belfast some months before. Although the Anglians are a notably unflappable regiment, the help of the community leaders was clearly needed to keep the peace.

Quietly, the Anglians' colonel, Dick Gerrard Wright, resurrected the practice of his predecessor and began to talk to the local Provisionals. The men he met were a formidable trio: Francis Card, number three on the Provisional Brigade Staff, who lived by Kashmir Road in the Clonard; Liam Hannaway, also on the Brigade Staff, and his brother, Kevin, commander of the Provisionals' Second Battalion – covering both Clonard and Ballymurphy – who lived in Cawnpore Street by the Clonard monastery.

The contacts continued on a regular basis through the months of sporadic rioting in Belfast at the end of 1970.

Both sides seem to have seen them as an inexpensive intelligence operation. Neither side can have guessed what they would become.

Early in December, however, the Anglians found a new use for their Ballymurphy headquarters, the converted Presbyterian chapel now called the Henry Taggart Memorial Hall. They opened a discotheque. It was for the soldiers' recreation: the local girls were invited, the boys were not. Within a couple of weeks lurid rumours were spreading through Ballymurphy about girls being 'drunk, raped, even drugged' as one incredulous officer put it. The girls did have to show their birth certificates, one of the Anglians' officers having discovered that the age of consent in Ulster is seventeen, not sixteen as in the rest of the United Kingdom. Perhaps the locals merely drew their own conclusions. For those who did not, there were quite enough troublemakers on the estate who would. It was fruitful ground for agitation, and by Christmas local women had taken to parading outside the hall: much of their placarded indignation had the unmistakable whiff of propaganda.

The discotheque was promptly closed. But local girls continued to go to film shows. As a group were leaving the hall on the evening of 10 January, they were stoned. On 11 January full scale rioting broke out – and continued, spreading to other parts of the city, for a week.

In the first couple of days at Ballymurphy, the rioting consisted mainly of teenagers throwing petrol bombs at the Henry Taggart Hall. While this was dangerous, it was clearly random hooliganism: 'At no time,' says the Army headquarters log for that period, 'was there aggressive action by organized groups.' There is eye-witness evidence that the rioting might have been bloodier on the night of 12–13 January 1971, but for the fact that the Provisional leadership was working to stop it. According to two sources, one an academic who was doing sociology research on the estate at the time, the Provisionals actually placed some youths under armed arrest.

Perhaps the Army saw the same things. For on 13 January, so far as the participants can now remember, the Army got in touch with the Provisional leadership to appeal for help in cooling Ballymurphy.

The sequence of events – agreed by IRA and Army sources – is that Francis Card was invited to an Army post in North Howard Street, to be warned of a rumoured threat against his life. The subject of Ballymurphy was raised – and at a meeting later in the house in Cawnpore Street, Liam Hannaway told the Army: 'If you get out of Ballymurphy, we can control it without your assistance.'

The Army now asked to speak to more senior Provisionals. At a further meeting lasting a couple of hours, Leo Martin came from the Brigade Staff. He was unhappy at the very idea of talking to the Army, and made the toughest demands. But both sides explored possible solutions. The Provisionals rejected a suggestion that the RUC should go back into Ballymurphy in place of the troops. A group of Ballymurphy residents had, in fact, requested that only a week before: which led some Army officers to think that the Provisionals had promptly started the riots to 're-radicalize' the area. But, at this meeting, the soldiers did not apparently reject the idea that they should allow the IRA to keep order.

The meeting was broken up by renewed rioting in Ballymurphy. And the next morning, 14 January – acting on the orders of 'higher authority' – 700 troops began a house-to-house search of the estate. Before the rioting finished the night after, forty-two petrol bombs and three bottles of sulphuric acid had been thrown. And guns had at last been used, wounding one soldier.

Even for the Provisionals, the thought of taming Bally-murphy was now daunting. One of the leaders told us much later:

We were in control of Ballymurphy in a normal situation. But it is a big area. There are thousands of teenagers there who detest the British uniform. Every time they saw one in these riots they went berserk. And we couldn't start beating people around because they disliked the British, could we? The people we had in Ballymurphy were swamped – say twenty rioters to one non-rioter ...

There is a sliver of evidence that Chichester-Clark learned on 15 January of the Army's discussions. He made the odd public announcement that day to the effect that the Army would not be leaving Ballymurphy 'in response to physical force or to any form of political pressure'.

By the evening of 16 January, however, the Ballymurphy riots had died. Perhaps the Provisionals played a part in this. Perhaps it was because, as the Army concluded, people were just tired of rioting. Whatever the cause, it was, the Army thought, a modest victory. The Ballymurphy rioters had numbered only a few hundred – a handful compared with some previous upsurges. Now, even this had successfully been quelled. In the bar at Lisburn, on the evening of the 16th, Freeland and Farrar-Hockley were just settling down to a celebratory drink when Chichester-Clark telephoned with a shattering message. 'I can't go on,' he said. The response was uniform. 'Why?' they replied, 'we've won.'

Two months and two days later, Chichester-Clark did finally go: 'Jimmy's cliff-hanger,' one civil servant called it. The Conservative Government's immediate reaction was to prop him up. As his price for staying, however, Chichester-Clark made impossible military demands. He wanted more troops. In the weeks that followed, 15,000 was the figure he most often mentioned – 'I think that sounded a nice round sum,' one military source commented. To this the Army was opposed. He also wanted more of every sort of martial activity – in particular, following Ballymurphy, more arrests. 'It went on for night after night,' he complained. 'The Army didn't seem to be trying.' (They had, in fact, arrested around 120 people.)

In the event, all Chichester-Clark got from a visit to Maudling on 18 January was a declaration – which he repeated on returning to Ulster – that the Army 'may now take the offensive' against the IRA. It was never entirely clear what, if anything, this meant; and an Army man later dismissed it wearily as 'all public relations rubbish': 'The poor fellow just wanted any straw he could grasp at,' he said.

The Unionists were not deceived. Within a week, 170 delegates to the party's main body, the 900-strong Unionist Council, were calling on Chichester-Clark to resign. The Army's reaction was straightforward. 'Keep your nerve,' Freeland and Farrar-Hockley insisted. Finally, Chichester-Clark lost his temper with Freeland, saying that he was not there to be lectured while he, the Prime Minister, was carrying the can for things which were Freeland's and Westminster's responsibility.

On 29 January the Defence Secretary, Lord Carrington, went over to Belfast to patch things up. The visit was not a success. Carrington was brusque with the Ulster Cabinet, apparently telling them to 'help themselves to stop moaning'. He referred to 'Her Majesty's Government' so often that in the end he was reminded that they too were Her Majesty's Government. Back in Whitehall, though, the Tories were delighted with Carrington's visit. 'Peter has dragged the Unionists a little way out of the nineteenth century,' one of his Cabinet colleagues said. On the contrary, as Carrington departed, the Unionist Cabinet merely reflected that his tone in office was markedly different from the one he had adopted before the 1970 election, when he came to Ulster to collect the Unionist contribution to the Conservative fighting fund.

But the Army, playing an extraordinary double game, was about to precipitate its most ferocious confrontation with the Catholics so far. Had the Unionists had the wit to see it, the events of the first week in February finally and irrevocably cemented the Army on to the Protestants' side and opened the last door for the Provisionals.

The Army's first reaction to Chichester-Clark's 16 January telephone call was to try to help his survival by keeping the peace on the streets. The Provisionals wanted the political success of an agreement with the Army in Ballymurphy. Both sides were therefore keen to continue talking.

We cannot say how frequently they met during the latter part of January, but contact was apparently 'regular' between Colonel Wright, Francis Card and Liam Hannaway. One officer explained:

We felt that some sort of communication was better than no communication at all. Every meeting was calculated to produce some glimmer of contact, spreading one's net. They thought they were conning us. We thought we were conning them. Neither of us was successful.

The trouble was that the Provisionals could not keep their mouths shut. In late January, one of them, Leo Martin, was foolish enough to talk publicly of the Provisionals enforcing their own law and order in certain areas of Belfast where 'the police are not welcome' – adding the immortal comment: 'We can't allow a state of anarchy to exist. We are Irish . . .' In the wake of that, on 27 January William Craig, the hard-line former Minister for Home Affairs, told a sensational story in Stormont. Two RUC constables, he said, had been patrolling in the Clonard area when a pair of Provisionals had advised them to leave the area if they valued their lives. The police approached an Army patrol, *who confirmed the advice.*

Three points about the anecdote are of interest. The first is that it was roughly correct. The second is that while the Clonard and Ballymurphy areas had for months been virtually 'no go' areas – where the police went only by vehicle and by day – Craig's story of expulsion was, to the Unionists, new and sensational. The third is that when Army officers investigated what had happened, they became suspicious of the whole incident. They found that an Army patrol in the Clonard had indeed come across two policemen stranded in the area, surrounded by an angry crowd among whom there were indeed local Provisionals. The patrol rescued the RUC men and escorted them safely out of the area. But the Army could never answer two questions. Why had the RUC men gone into this 'no go' area in the first place? And how did it come about that, as the Army found, Paisley knew of the incident even before the report of it had reached the desks of senior policemen in Belfast?

But, whatever the genesis of Craig's famous incident, the uncomfortable truth was that the Army was in fact acquiescing in Provisional authority in parts of Belfast. At least, so the Provisionals thought. According to Liam Hannaway, the Provisionals were promised (at a meeting around 1 February, Hannaway thinks) that there would be no military or police activity in the Clonard while talks between the Army and the Provisionals were in progress.

This view is supported independently by another IRA man. The Army's recollection of the date of the meeting is uncertain: either around 20 January or 'early February'. But senior officers passionately deny that any deal resulted from the meeting. It is true that the Army did not want any activity in the Clonard but for the reason, the same officers assert, that the Army had various houses in the area under watch at the time.

What happened next certainly ended any faint chance of agreement. On Wednesday 3 February the Second Royal Anglians, on the orders of Farrar-Hockley, cordoned and searched the Clonard and Ardoyne areas. Army sources say that the RUC Special Branch had learned of Provisional documents – either stolen or compiled by the IRA – giving personal details about Special Branch men. (Whether these were home addresses and details of jobs, or the sort of material that could lead to blackmail, we do not know.) The Army was asked to retrieve the documents, which our sources claim they did – apparently in Hannaway's house.

But in the Clonard, the Army stayed around after the search, and Catholic rioting broke out. Then when Protestant workers from the near by Mackie's engineering works came out to lunch, and began to jeer the Catholic crowds and even pelt them with 'Belfast confetti' – as the local mixture of ballbearings and machine-shop swarf is called – the Army and police ostentatiously turned their backs to the Protestant confetti-throwers and concentrated on the Catholics.

Around four in the afternoon, after a few hours of calm, it was evidently decided to clear the streets before the Mackie's workers were due to come out again. The soldiers did this by roaring up and down in their jeeps. At least two people were knocked down. The operation was a deliberate show of Army toughness. The idea, we have been told, was to 'cut the Provisionals down to size' by demonstrating that the Army could invade their home territory whenever it wished. If the idea was to humiliate the Provisionals, however, its effect was on the contrary to solidify the Clonard behind them.

The rioting over the two nights which followed was the worst the Army had faced in Belfast. In one encounter on the New Lodge Road, five soldiers were wounded in a burst of machine-gun fire. Another had his thigh broken by a gel-ignite bomb. In those two days eight soldiers were wounded, one seriously.

As the riots moved into their second day Farrar-Hockley appeared on Ulster Television. In answer to the point that the searches had caused serious riots, he made a momentous statement: 'We searched this area because we have good evidence that it harbours members of the IRA Provisionals,' he said. Then, fed up with the Unionists' accusations that the Army did not even know who the Provisionals were, he proceeded to name Francis Card, Billy McKee, Leo Martin and Liam and Kevin Hannaway as Provisionals of 'some braggadocio'. Actually, he challenged them to deny that they were Provisionals – apparently on the theory that his remarks would thereby circumvent the laws of defamation. It was a delicate touch, marred only by the fact that Farrar-Hockley neglected to say that these were the same Provisionals with whom the Army had been in talks. Martin, who happened to be watching television when Farrar-Hockley spoke, had an interesting reaction: 'That's a breach of confidence,' he said. It was also exceedingly embarrassing for the Provisionals, *because their own followers did not know about the discussions and might have been outraged to learn of them.*

There were no more talks. The Provisional leadership now felt free to take on the Army. In an amateur way, some of them had been trying to mount an offensive against the Army for some time. (The fact that most of their planning meetings for this had taken place in Liam Hannaway's garage may explain why the Army was keeping a watch in the Clonard.)

On 6 February, the night after the broadcast, Gunner Robert Curtis, aged twenty, of the 94th Locating Regiment in the Royal Artillery, was shot dead in the New Lodge Road. He was the first British soldier killed in the present Ulster emergency. Four of his companions were wounded, one critically.

That same night, three other soldiers were injured. The Army killed one Republican sympathizer, twenty-eight-year-old Bernard Watt, and nineteen-year-old James Saunders, a staff officer in F Company of the Provisionals' Third Battalion.

Curtis's death was the first fruit of the Provisionals' new policy of deliberately killing soldiers. But he was, in a deeper sense, unlucky. A lot of soldiers had previously been wounded, some badly. But most of those had been infantrymen, trained in the cautious art of survival under small-arms fire. It was no coincidence that both Curtis and the second soldier to be killed, on 15 February, were not infantrymen but specialist gunners. The opinion of one senior officer is now that, whatever the Army's manpower shortage, such men should never have been thrown into the lethal street-fighting of Belfast.

The morning after Gunner Curtis had died, Chichester-Clark went on television. 'Northern Ireland is at war with the Irish Republican Army Provisionals,' he announced. Contemplating Chichester-Clark as he said that, the British representative Burroughs sent back a report to the Home Office, advising them not to give in to the Prime Minister's demands for more military force. Whatever they did, he said, 'I think Chichester-Clark has shot his bolt.'

*

But Chichester-Clark survived long enough for his fall to do yet further damage to the fast-disintegrating fabric of Ulster society. The aftermath of the funerals on 9 February of the two men shot the night Gunner Curtis was killed, Bernard Watt and James Saunders, demonstrated to the satisfaction of the Catholics that, with the departure of Sir Arthur Young, the old alliance between the police and Unionist politics was forged once more.

Their funeral processions were followed through Belfast by immense Catholic crowds: they were, patently, IRA parades. The Army stood by quietly; some soldiers on guard even saluted. All that was bad enough to the Protestants watching on television. But when a squad of IRA men fired a volley over Saunders's grave, the Unionists were incensed. One Stormont minister screamed down the telephone to senior Army officers, 'instructing' them to break up the funerals, charge the crowds, and arrest the priest for subversion. Faulkner was with a politician from Westminster at the time. 'If that sort of thing can happen in Belfast, there is no future for a Unionist Government in this province,' Faulkner fumed. The politician thought he had a point, though perhaps not quite in the way he meant.

The Army was relaxed about the affair. 'It is military custom to salute funerals,' an officer explained to Chichester-Clark. 'I would salute Hitler on his way to his last resting place.' Chichester-Clark was not reassured. As for the volley: 'We should have stopped that,' Army headquarters admitted later. 'One of our chaps was a bit wet, that's all.' But the Army did arrest at Saunders's funeral three men who were uniformed in black berets and combat jackets, and bearing that symbol of Gaelic nationalism, the hurley stick. They were charged under the Special Powers Act.

The Unionist reaction to these funerals was so intense

that at the next public demonstration of Catholic militancy, the police were under orders to take a firm line. The clash came on Friday 26 February. When the three arrested at Saunders's funeral appeared at the magistrates' court in the centre of Belfast, two rival demonstrations jostled outside.

A squad of Catholic women paraded in black berets – and some in combat jackets. A counter-demonstration of Protestants jeered, shouted the old Orange slogans, and finally seized and burned one of the women's berets. The police moved in – but solely against the Catholics, arresting twenty women and some six men.

According to a group of lawyers – led by a Protestant who saw what happened and later objected publicly, the police not only made no attempt to arrest agitators in the Protestant crowd, but were actually swapping jokes with them. The lawyers' accusations of police partiality had no discernible effect on the later, mandatory, sentences on the women.

The immediate result was a night of savage Catholic rioting on 27 February in which two policemen were shot dead in the Ardoyne. But the Catholics' view of the courts was to receive its final confirmation during six days in April, with the startling variation in treatment meted out in three separate incidents.

At 5.30 p.m. on 13 April, in one of the first 1971 Easter marches, a Junior Orange Lodge column paraded past the isolated Catholic redoubt of Seaforde Street in east Belfast. As the Army statement put it later:

> A number of people following the march broke through a police cordon and entered a Catholic area. As a result of this, fire was opened at these people and four, including a twelve-year-old boy, were admitted to hospital.

That night, 2,000 Protestants in east Belfast stormed the

247

battered St Matthews Catholic Church on the Newtownards Road – scene of the Provisionals' first gun-battle just a year before. Several soldiers defending the church were set on fire with petrol bombs.

The next day, thirteen Protestants appeared in court. Only three faced the charge of riotous behaviour, carrying the mandatory sentence. A man who struck a sergeant with a rock was given a suspended sentence. A student who stoned the police was fined £15. A man who snatched a soldier's rifle was fined £10.

The same day that these men appeared in court, 14 April, a Catholic labourer named Joseph Patrick Downey was gaoled for a year. His criminal record included two assaults and seven old-style disorderly behaviour convictions; a psychiatrist said he had a mental age of ten-and-a-half. Downey's offence was to have shouted on 13 April 'You shower of bastards, up the IRA' as the Junior Orange Lodge parade passed by.

Five days later, on 19 April, a twenty-two-year-old Protestant arms dealer, Robert Kane, a former B Special and, it was said in court, a friend of many members of the RUC, was found guilty in Belfast on four charges of unlawfully supplying arms. Many of the weapons could not be traced. Kane was given a twelve-month prison sentence – suspended for three years.

It was unlucky that these cases should have fallen in such rapid succession. It has also been argued that the discrepancies in treatment reflected judicial vagaries rather than a common pattern. But among the great mass of Catholics – even Catholic lawyers – the trio of cases signalled the end of any real faith in the reformation of the law in Ulster.

Chichester-Clark was meanwhile putting up a good fight to stay in power – to the surprise of those, like Burroughs, who had predicted his swift collapse. Incidents like the funerals, and – more seriously – the mounting IRA campaign of violence, impelled him to demand still more troops from Britain and tougher action in the Catholic areas. On the advice of the Army, Maudling and Carrington in London turned him down.

Talking at Lisburn shortly before midnight, on Saturday 20 February 1971, Ronald Burroughs and General Farrar-Hockley received a document from the Stormont Cabinet. It subsequently became famous in high Government circles: one of the dozen or so people who saw it called it 'the most astonishing document I have ever seen from a government department in my life'.

It comprised on a single sheet of paper an ill-typed list, with hand-written additions, of the Unionists' military 'demands'. These included – beside such obvious measures as more troops, and more arrests – block searches, total curfews of Catholic areas, sterner action on the border, and a plan to bring the Ulster Defence Regiment, the reformed B Specials, into parallel operations with the Army. But the most startling demand was apparently written in at the foot of the page as an afterthought. So far as we can gather, the Unionists wanted searches of Catholic areas as straight reprisal raids – 'punitive expeditions', we were told.

'It was militarily useless, morally wrong, and in the long term politically self-defeating', was one judgement. Burroughs and Farrar-Hockley submitted a joint memorandum to London saying that the document was unacceptable. (Chichester-Clark's own recollection of the document, it is fair to say, is that it went very little further than a subsequent Stormont speech for which he won praise from Fitt.)

The *coup de grâce* was applied to Chichester-Clark by the Provisionals. On the evening of 10 March three young Scottish soldiers were shot in the back of the head outside a pub

249

on a country road near Belfast. Scotland Yard detectives later concluded that their murderers had been three Provisionals led, ironically, by an ex-British paratrooper. (The Army was satisfied later that the Provo leadership had not sanctioned the killings.) But reaction to them was so intense that, for about forty-eight hours, Chichester-Clark feared that the Protestant 'backlash' had been precipitated at last.

On 16 March he flew to London to see Heath, Carrington and Maudling. He returned to report to Stormont on 18 March that Westminster had agreed to send another 1,300 troops – instead of the 3,000 he had asked for. 'It wasn't anything like enough, and everyone knew it,' he remarked.

The next morning, Friday 19 March, he told Downing Street that he intended to resign. At nine that evening he was in his flat in Stormont Castle eating chicken and chips with three civil servants. The telephone rang. It was Heath.

'I didn't realize it was as critical as that,' Heath said. 'Why on earth didn't you tell me?' (As Chichester-Clark remarked: 'Short of leaping on the Cabinet table at Number Ten, I thought I could hardly have made it clearer.')

But Heath made very little attempt to stop Chichester-Clark going. His main concern was to see that Chichester-Clark, in his resignation statement, did not explain the real reason why he had had enough – that the British Government would not give him everything he asked for in the way of troops and military measures. (The final sticking-place had been a Chichester-Clark demand that troops should be permanently, and suicidally, stationed in Belfast's Catholic-held enclaves. Playing politics with men's lives, Maudling had told him.) Carrington came over next day to reinforce Heath's point. 'I suppose there is nothing we can do for the fellow?' Carrington asked one of his Ulster commanders. 'Not a thing, sir,' was the reply. Chichester-Clark's resignation statement that evening was obediently discreet.

It was a pity. It was almost the only occasion throughout 1971 when the Conservative Government took its courage in its hands and told a Unionist leader that there were military demands which Britain would not meet; and if his followers did not like it, he would have to reconcile them to it or resign.

Chichester-Clark chose resignation. His inevitable successor, elected within the parliamentary Unionist Party by a crushing margin over Bill Craig, was Brian Faulkner. If it had been made clear to everyone that Chichester-Clark had gone because for once Westminster would not help him placate Unionist reactionaries, then they might have understood their own and Faulkner's position a little better; and Heath and Maudling, discovering that a public show of resolution was not so disagreeable after all, might even have chosen to repeat it. But the secret was kept. So the backbenchers very soon renewed their pressure on their leader, and Faulkner passed it on to Westminster, and British ministers – having used up their bisque of bravery for the year – yielded to it, with disastrous results. There is a good deal of irony, in retrospect, in the fact that Britain brought Chichester-Clark down because he was too demanding.

Chapter 15
Faulkner gets his Wish

For a man who was 'as cunning as a wagon-load of monkeys' in a senior Labour minister's estimation, Faulkner had had a slow rise to the top. Now just fifty, he had been a Stormont MP since he was twenty-eight, and had shown evidence of his political flair in the Ministries of Home Affairs, Commerce and Development. Perhaps it was partly that he was not, as his predecessors in the premiership had been, a member of the landed gentry. His father was a wealthy man, but in textiles. 'The little shirt-maker from Comber,' Lord Brookeborough once called him – a phrase which sheds at least as much light on Brookeborough as on Faulkner.

But Faulkner also aroused that slight wariness which is sometimes provoked by men of very quick and flexible minds. Harold Wilson understood him: 'I'm not saying Faulkner could dance on the head of a pin,' he once remarked, 'but he can certainly manoeuvre in a very small area.'

Heath and Maudling could thus be forgiven for not foreseeing Faulkner's form as Prime Minister. He was an enigma. In the past he had upheld the Orange Order as 'the most democratic body in the world'; he had interned IRA suspects when he was at Home Affairs at the end of the fifties; and he had resigned from O'Neill's mildly reformist government at the moment of maximum hurtfulness. Yet now, for the past twenty-three months, he had been himself a mildly reformist Minister of Development. Even here, though, it was hard to say which reflected his real inclinations: the prompt action on certain simple administrative matters, or the much statelier progress on the path of housing and local government reform.

One of the clues to his character is a story which is famous in Unionist circles, and is held to illustrate his most important political gift: agility. It concerns a visit which he paid to the south when Minister of Commerce under O'Neill.

Ulster politicians who happened to hear the Dublin radio that day were startled to hear that Faulkner had visited the Dublin Horse Show – and had been seen in the Presidential box with the arch-Republican, Eamon De Valera himself. They noted that this remarkable event had occurred too late to be reported in the *Belfast Telegraph* (an evening paper). But still they wondered how Faulkner, a man who had risen on the power of the Orange Right, could hope to get away with it.

They understood next day, when the Belfast *News Letter*, a morning paper, carried a report of a vibrant denunciation of the Roman Catholic Church – made by Brian Faulkner in one of the Ulster border counties. Having made his gesture towards the south, Faulkner had jumped into his car and driven rapidly north to redress the balance.

O'Neill, when he was Premier, used to say that the political style of his most brilliant minister was summed up in elaborate trade-offs of this kind. So it was natural that Faulkner, on becoming Prime Minister, should attempt to save the province with a balancing act. He tried to bring the non-Unionist Opposition into the process of government,

253

without alienating his power-base in the Unionist Right.

The collapse of this balancing act led directly to the policy of internment. But Faulkner failed not because he had lost his old instinct for equilibrium: the proximate causes of failure were, firstly, certain rifle-shots fired by the British Army and, secondly, the interplay of personality within the Social Democratic and Labour Party.

The bond between Social Democratic and Labour Party (SDLP) members is less ideological than that all their constituencies have Catholic majorities. The SDLP's leader, Gerry Fitt, has the back-slapping manner of a minor US Senator. The style does not sort particularly well with that of John Hume, the intellectual meritocrat from Derry. And Fitt has had some mighty personal disputes with Paddy Devlin, an enormous man who represents the Falls Road area. (On one memorable occasion, they traded punches in Stormont.)

But these are men of some ability and vitality, frustrated by the prospect of permanent opposition amid the slapstick repartee of Stormont. (Sample: Mr Currie – 'When was the Council of Trent?' Mr Devlin – 'I do not know. It is some bar down around Sandy Row.') On 22 June 1971, during the Stormont debate on the Queen's speech, Faulkner made a considerable gesture towards relieving that frustration.

He proposed to add three new and powerful committees to the existing Public Accounts Committee, which would consider Government policies on social services, industrial development and environmental matters. Much more radically, he proposed that the Opposition should provide salaried chairmen for two of them.

It was an imaginative, even brave, move. Faulkner had taken over against a background of steadily escalating violence. From the end of March the Provisional bombing campaign had really cut loose – thirty-seven major explosions in

April, forty-seven in May, and fifty in June when Faulkner made his offer. (At the start of April Farrar-Hockley wrote a paper predicting bombing as the Provos' main weapon: gun-battles were too risky for them, he said.)

It is possible to show that Ulster's political problems are theoretically insoluble. (Indeed, Professor Richard Rose makes just such a case in *Governing Without Consensus*.) Nevertheless, moments of almost irrational hope illuminate the scene from time to time. Faulkner's offer provided one.

The SDLP members, taken by surprise, reacted guardedly but not disapprovingly. Faulkner's proposals, said Paddy Devlin, 'showed plenty of imagination. It was his best hour since I came into the House ... The Prime Minister has given Hon. Members, and indirectly those outside, an opportunity to share in decision-making.'

John Hume said that 'it should be made clear to all people today who say that no change has taken place, that this is simply not true. There have been changes in this community ...' Another member spoke of 'adulation' coming from both sides of the House; against the background of normal Catholic attitudes 'adulation' was fair.

Six days later, Faulkner 'balanced'. With five members of his Government, including Harry West of the ultra-Right, he made a pilgrimage to Brownlow House, Lurgan, a true shrine of Orange ideals. (Though, to keep the colours straight, Brownlow House is the home, not of the Orange Order itself, but of the Royal Black Institution – the Blackmen being, in the colour-code of loyalty, the *crème de la crème* of Orangemen.)

Faulkner's symbolic gesture to his right wing should, and might, have been tolerable to the Catholics against the substance of his political offer, made in face of mounting Unionist anger about the bombing campaign. But nine days later in the Bogside of Londonderry – John Hume's seat – the

Faulkner initiative was doomed by a series of accidents.

Relations in the Bogside in Derry between the soldiers and the Catholic population deteriorated in the first half of 1971 almost as rapidly as in Catholic Belfast. By the night of 7 July rioting had been going on unbroken for four days, and the Royal Anglians had been fired on sixty times by their count. It says a good deal for the fire discipline of this regiment – the Anglians have a reputation for unusual coolness and restraint – that only three shots were fired in reply.

The night of Wednesday 7 July was noted as 'busy' in the Army log. Rubber bullets were fired on several occasions, and shortly after midnight a patrol began to march down William Street, a main thoroughfare where heavy stoning and petrol bombing had been going on.

A man was seen 'carrying a rifle' in Fahan Street. According to the Anglians, he was ordered to stand still, but moved to a new position and took aim. A marksman fired one round from his self-loading rifle, at short range. The man fell, and was immediately borne away by the crowd. When the patrol reached the spot, there were huge pools of blood. The man and any rifle he carried had vanished.

The shot man was Seamus Cusack, an unemployed welder, aged twenty-eight. He was hit in the femoral artery, causing heavy bleeding. He was put in a car and driven across the border to Letterkenny Hospital, where he died from loss of blood. Immediate treatment, or even the application of a tourniquet in the car, might have saved his life. As the Army see it, Cusack's fatal removal across the border is proof that he was an IRA gunman who could not face the treatment in Ulster. But Bogside people injured in riots regularly cross the border for treatment, because they fear that Ulster hospitals might give their name to the security officers. It was, in other words, a kind of routine to take Cusack to Letterkenny. It appears that sheer inexperience led his rescuers to think that he was not badly hurt.

Cusack was not known to belong to any Republican organization: local opinion is that he was more interested in boxing than politics. Patrick Duffy, a well-known moderate whose peace-keeping efforts have been praised by the Army, says: 'I would swear on oath that Cusack was stooping to pick up a helmet knocked off a soldier.' Other witnesses think that Cusack was trying to remove Duffy's little son from the danger area. What is not in dispute is that, in a tense situation, Cusack – at the very least – was behaving rashly.

Extreme Protestant opinion holds that a few shootings will bring back law and order. But in Derry that afternoon, Cusack's death caused further, bitter rioting. Just after 3 p.m. an Army vehicle was rammed by a hi-jacked lorry. An Anglian patrol in a Saracen armoured car was called to help, and the Army log records that there were three loud explosions from nail bombs. Petrol bombs were also thrown.

At 3.13 an Anglian marksman again fired one round from a self-loading rifle. His target, according to the log, was a man who 'fired at him'. Desmond Beattie, unemployed, aged nineteen, died almost instantly. Father Tony Gillespie who was standing in a group near Beattie, said at the inquest: 'I saw the lad drop to his knees with blood pouring out of him. I could see the hole in his chest.' He said he could see no trace of a bomb or other weapon. Another witness named Henry Curran said that a youth, dressed differently from Beattie, ran past him with 'a cylindrical object wrapped in cloth'. He threw it at the Saracens and it exploded. Beattie was shot immediately afterwards. Forensic scientists found no traces of explosives on Beattie's body, and no sign that he had fired a gun.

The soldier who shot him, described only as Mr A, gave evidence wearing dark glasses, and with his collar turned up to avoid identification. He said that he saw Beattie with a round dark object in one hand, and what appeared to be a flame in the other. This was surprising, as the first reports had spoken of the dead man firing a gun. The inquest also heard that a second bullet had hit Beattie, although it did not hear where the other shot came from. An open verdict was returned on Desmond Beattie. By that time, his death had already become a kind of *cause célèbre*.

John Hume tried to call a meeting of the Social Democratic and Labour Party MPs on the weekend of 10–11 July after the shootings. He collected Ivan Cooper, from neighbouring mid-Derry, plus Austin Currie, Paddy O'Hanlon and Paddy Devlin; but Gerry Fitt was somewhere in Antrim, out of telephone range. When, finally, a message reached the SDLP leader his response was that he was not going to Derry for any meeting called by John Hume.

Hume, then, dominated the meeting. He was emotionally concerned about his two dead constituents, and he was politically concerned about being out-flanked to the Left. During the same weekend O Bradaigh, political chief of the Provisional IRA, came over the border to be rapturously greeted by 2,000 Bogsiders. He gave them, in sharp contrast to Hume's careful reformism, the straight 'sweep them into the sea' line. 'Please God,' he cried, 'we'll fix it this time!' How widely this feeling was shared, John Hume had good reason to know after a bruising encounter with some of his constituents one evening in the week following Faulkner's proposals.

John Hume thus urgently needed to show that he was not the creature of Stormont – a task not eased by the comparative readiness with which he and his colleagues had embraced Faulkner's committees. So he drafted, and the little

258

meeting approved, a long and powerful statement. It gave the British Government until the following Thursday to set up an independent public inquiry into the deaths of Beattie and Cusack. Failing that, the SDLP would leave Stormont and set up an 'alternative Parliament'.

No doubt everyone present knew that Fitt would not approve. He would never have faced Westminster with so crude an ultimatum, nor taken his party out so far on a limb. But Paddy Devlin, presumably one man who might have cooled the tempers, was still fuming over past disputes with Fitt. So Fitt first learned of his party's new policy when he saw the Sunday-night television news. At once, he booked a flight to London for a private chat with Reginald Maudling. Maudling, obviously, could not yield to the ultimatum. But if he could do something – such as bring forward the inquest, and perhaps increase its status by some means – a way might be found for the SDLP to stay inside the system. Maudling, it seems, was willing to help, and for a while the deal seemed likely to work.

But then, back in Ulster, Austin Currie, another SDLP member, was asked by a radio reporter whether any proposal, such as a special inquest, might settle the Beattie–Cusack affair. No, he said, it would not: there must be a new inquiry. On Tuesday Lord Balniel announced in Westminster that there would be no such inquiry: on Thursday 15 July Fitt, fuming, had to lead his men out of Stormont.

It was a symbolic walk-out because Stormont was not sitting at the time. But it was enough – more than enough – to make the Unionists say that the hand of friendship had been bitten. It is, of course, possible to say that Faulkner's gesture would have succeeded but for the deaths of Beattie and Cusack. But by mid-1971, such deaths were becoming so frequent in Ulster as to constitute the ordinary risks of politics.

From Faulkner's election in March to the introduction of internment on 9 August there was an average of two bomb explosions a day. In one hectic twelve hours in July, no fewer than twenty explosions wrecked pubs, shops and banks, injuring a dozen civilians. All told more than 100 civilians were wounded in bombings in this period.

The Army, too, felt the impact of the surge of IRA Provisional activity. Four more soldiers died and twenty-nine were injured between April and August: the Army killed four civilians – one, William Reid, being described as a known Provisional.

The bombings and the collapse of his political initiative gave Brian Faulkner a persuasive case for interning suspected terrorists, and it was his personal achievement that it was finally granted. But internment was not, as it might appear, Faulkner's response to the events of mid-summer. When he took over as Prime Minister on 23 March the issue was not *whether* internment was to come, but *when* and on what scale. By then Faulkner had been an advocate of internment inside Chichester-Clark's Joint Security Committee for six months. 'Month after month, it became quite a ritual,' one minister recalled.

Faulkner had been Minister of Home Affairs from 1959 – the middle of the IRA campaign of 1956–62. Ulster's Catholics had given that campaign no support; but one of Faulkner's more abiding convictions was that internment had been a crucial factor in its defeat. Chichester-Clark, who was on principle against the idea of internment, learned to stave off Faulkner's demands by simply asking the Army and the police for their opinion each time. This never varied: given the likely degree of success, internment would not be worthwhile. The Army and the police did not know whom to arrest.

Even as Chichester-Clark was falling, internment was not

one of his central demands. When Faulkner took over the direction of policy, change was immediate. Some time in April, despite the Army's scepticism about internment as a policy, the Director of Military Intelligence at Lisburn set up with the RUC Special Branch a joint 'internment working party'. Its task was to draw up the list of men who might usefully be interned.

The targets were, from the start, Catholics. The original Ministry of Defence agreement in March 1970 to set up a full scale military intelligence unit in Ulster had been to investigate the Protestant extremists; the IRA bombing campaign had now changed the focus of Army attention.

The working party had no trouble identifying the leading figures in the Officials and the Provisionals. The Officials, pre-1969, had been highly publicized in the Civil Rights campaign. And the Provisional leaders were the old-fashioned Republicans that most Special Branch men knew in their sleep. On specialized areas – the bank accounts through which funds passed for instance – the Army also had good information; and, as we showed, the Secret Intelligence Service in Britain had penetrated parts of the Provisionals' operation very early.

But the younger and newer Provisionals, the actual 'gunmen', were almost wholly unidentified. The Provisionals' command structure was equally unknown. (Though Joe Cahill took over as Provisional Chief of Staff when Billy McKee was arrested in March 1971, for instance, intelligence sources seem not to have learned this for five months.)

Filling in the gaps was difficult. In the new housing estates – such as Ballymurphy and Andersonstown, both Provisional strongholds – the police had almost no informers. And the Army had found it hard to set up an intelligence network. Although it in the end relied (and still relies) upon two MI5 men imported for the task, its intelligence remained an odd mixture of low-grade observations by soldiers in the streets – which houses were frequented in a locality, for instance – plus information from two sources so close to the top Provisional leadership as to be useless except as the broadest strategic outline. On middle-grade, tactical intelligence – operational personnel, bombing targets and the like – the Army was poverty-stricken. And while the RUC Special Branch had been knocked into fairly good shape by Scotland Yard men in 1970, it was still feeling its way.

Much of the working party's time was spent sorting through thousands of photographs taken by Army cameramen at riots, funerals, demonstrations and meetings, and comparing the participants with pictures on RUC police files. (Most of the work was done at the RUC headquarters in east Belfast.) 'The sort of thing that used to happen,' an Army man explained, 'was that we would pick up some new name or address. And the RUC would say: "Oh he drinks with So-and-So; try him. Or, last time round, that house was used by So-and-So." '

But the working party had no direction whether their list was to cover merely the 'gunmen', or all past or present Republicans of any kind. The debate inside the group on this question was interrupted by a kidnapping and a hold-up.

Around 6 a.m. on 16 July four men dressed in medical-looking white coats walked into the Royal Victoria Hospital in central Belfast, strolled up to Ward 10, and – producing Thompson sub-machine-guns from under their coats to quell the guards – they removed an IRA Provisional recently wounded in the leg while placing a gelignite bomb, and drove off with him. The following evening, 17 July, armed men entered the *Daily Mirror* printing plant in Dunmurry, ordered the workers out of the building, and blew up the presses.

The internment decision effectively stems from that moment. On Sunday 19 July Faulkner telephoned Heath in London and said that he thought it was now necessary. Next day, General Harry Tuzo (the diplomatic, Oxford-educated gunner who had taken over as GOC Northern Ireland in February) went to London to collect a knighthood. Carrington gave him less welcome news at the same time. Either the Army came up with an alternative policy to internment – which it still opposed – or Faulkner would have to have his way.

Two separate strands are visible in the events which followed: the last-minute efforts to finalize the 'internment list', and the search by the Army for an alternative.

It took the Army five days to prepare. Then, around dawn on 23 July, 1,800 troops, plus police, raided houses in Belfast and nine other towns in the provinces. The purpose of the raids – muddied at the time with talk of an 'Army offensive' – was straightforward. The internment working party desperately needed material to 'put flesh on the skeleton', as one officer later told us. Apparently, they got it: Provisionals and Officials were wary of keeping documents about their own activities; but each kept excellent files on the other. These, according to military sources, the dawn raids picked up. By the beginning of August, after more raids, the working party reckoned its list was complete.

Then the debate began. The list had rather more than 500 names on it: they fall into three categories. No more than 120–130 were 'gunmen' or officers in either the Officials or the Provos. (The breakdown between the two was roughly seventy to eighty Provos, and the rest Officials.) The other 300–350 were 'sympathizers'. The Provisional 'sympathizers' among them had been weeded from about 1,200 people – the Army estimate of the Provos' total strength at that point. But, in turn, this blanket term 'sympathizer' concealed enormous variation. At one extreme were those who had actively helped the 'gunmen' group: sheltered them, stolen cars for them, and the like. In the middle were a group who were 'too close for comfort': the speechmakers, the propagandists, the radical grassroots activists whose work coincided at points with that of the Officials. And then there was the police contribution: a motley group, 150 or more, whose interest was solely that they had been interned before – and thus were of 'proven' Republican sympathies.

There was, finally, a special group. Eight or ten were on the list not because they were 'gunmen', nor because they had given 'aid and comfort', nor preached violence, nor because they were the old sweats of the movement. They were included simply because they were active politicians who, in the wake of internment, could cause a fuss. Chief among these was the People's Democracy leader, Michael Farrell – veteran of the Civil Rights Campaign.

The problem was how many of these 500 to intern. No answer was ever agreed. The Army and the police mistrusted each other: the Army believed that the police list was politically motivated, and the police believed that the Army's list showed inadequate local knowledge. Further, the Army was divided between those who wanted to do the job quickly before Provisional strength grew any more, and those who urged waiting till more was known about that growth. One school of thought inside the Army had favoured internment back in the spring, when no more than fifty to sixty people would have had to be 'lifted', they reckoned. The perfectionists now wanted another three months to prepare really accurate lists – they were ignored as being quite unrealistic.

Tuzo, unlike some of his officers, did not want internment at all. He remained highly sceptical about what he called 'the Unionists' panacea', and proceeded publicly to say so as often as he dared. But after Faulkner's call to Heath on 19 July, he did accept that the Army had to do something. The bombing campaign was hitting public morale; commercial confidence was sagging. 'The trouble,' Tuzo said wistfully to one of his officers, 'is that this is a very small country.'

In the last days of July, the Army looked anxiously for alternatives to internment. Four were appealing. They could curfew Belfast and perhaps other towns. They could halt and search traffic over wide areas of the province. They could block sections of the border and search vehicles crossing it. They could embark on straightforward repression, such as searching whole blocks at a time in the Catholic areas.

The problem with all these options was that they were unlikely to be more effective than internment. And all except the last carried the unacceptable penalty that they would hit commercial life even harder than it was being hit at present: and thus would lower morale still further. (The fact that, in the aftermath of internment, commercial life might go for a burton anyway seems to have figured less in the calculations.)

One severely practical argument against internment was that only a small proportion of the wanted men might be at home on any given night. (On some nights, when the Army ran an advance check, the proportion was as low as fifteen per cent.) Another was that the sweep was unlikely to be effective with the border open. But the Army knew that there was never a chance that Jack Lynch would collaborate by introducing internment in the south, as had happened in the 1956–62 campaign.

Precisely the same conclusion was reached by the Ulster

Cabinet. Afterwards, it was said that the British Government only sanctioned internment at the request of the Northern Ireland Government. This is not so. Faulkner's Cabinet met on Tuesday 3 August. Internment was the main topic, but although on first impression everyone favoured it, such 'ifs and buts' emerged that in the end the ministers reached no consensus, and made no recommendation either way. Nor did Faulkner ask them to make one. Uncharacteristically, he said little the entire meeting. All that the Ulster Cabinet did agree was that if internment was to be effective, it had to come in the south at the same time. Faulkner said simply, 'London will have to pursue that.'

On Thursday morning, 5 August, the Joint Security Committee met in Stormont Castle: Faulkner in the chair as usual and, round the table, politicians like John Taylor (Minister of State at Home Affairs), a couple of civil servants, the new RUC Chief Constable, Graham Shillington, and the Army contingent led by Tuzo. Even here opinion was against internment. Shillington reported that only a minority of the police favoured it, and those mostly men on the border, not officers in hot spots like Belfast.

That afternoon Faulkner and Tuzo left secretly for London. (The first Faulkner's Cabinet heard of the visit was on television news that evening. They were affronted: 'Who does he think he is?' was their main reaction. The more suspicious of them even flicked their minds back to O'Neill's similarly secret parley with Lemass in 1965.)

At the Ministry of Defence, in the office of the Defence Secretary, Lord Carrington, Tuzo repeated his objections to internment. But in the last analysis he did not object to the policy. He could offer nothing else which held out the hope of checking the violence (ninety-one bomb explosions in July) and he accepted the necessity of doing something to restore the morale and authority of Stormont. Then Carrington strolled across Whitehall and into 10 Downing Street for the Cabinet meeting.

Faulkner was impressive at the Cabinet – 'full of confidence and raring to go', according to one account. Maudling was shrewd enough to see that the analogies Faulkner had been drawing between his success in 1959 and now were shaky. But Maudling was alarmed and anxious at the increasing violence, and he, too, had no other policy: with the Immigration Bill and Ulster it had been a tiring period for Maudling. If Faulkner wanted to try it, why not? He gave his support. So did Carrington and William White-law, the Lord President and Leader of the Commons. There was no real opposition. Tuzo was called in; but not to give his views, merely to answer technical questions about the military requirements of the operation.

Faulkner had got what he wanted. In the small hours of 9 August the machinery was put into motion. The Army had wanted to 'lift' no more than 100–150 people on the joint police-Army list – only those who, they thought, were irre-placeable by the IRA. But the Army technically could only make 'suggestions'. Faulkner, as Minister of Home Affairs, dictated the final size of the list – and he decreed a clean sweep, the 'lifting' of more than 450 people. The Army did its best. By the evening of 9 August 342 people had been arrested all over the province and distributed among three holding centres. They were not charged with any offence: the Special Powers Act did not require it.

The punch had been well telegraphed. Tuzo had himself discussed the pros and cons of internment in an interview with the *Belfast Telegraph*. The Provisionals knew it was coming: they had warned their men, down to NCO level, that the families of any caught at home could expect no subsequent help. And there is some evidence that news of the actual internment sweep leaked about eight hours before the operation took place. As a result, the Provisionals were able to hold a covert press conference four days after the sweep, to claim that their command structure was still largely intact.

The figures for continuing terrorist activity bore out their claim. For internment was not merely followed by a rash of sectarian rioting as bad as anything in August 1969, with two hundred houses burned (many of them Catholic) and refugees pouring south across the Border. Straightforward shootings and bombings increased too, and the increase was sustained. August was the first month in which there were over 100 bomb explosions, mostly in Belfast; and there were thirty-five violent deaths during the month, as against four the month before.

Chapter 16
Internment Fails

The Army had supposed that internment – despite its being a 'distasteful weapon', as Tuzo publicly called it – could at any rate be made to work. Senior soldiers had foreseen that it would provoke a surge of violence and a further estrangement of the Catholic community from the governing authorities; but they had expected that the surge could be contained and would soon fall back.

They were appalled by the intensity of the Catholic reaction. They had foreseen rioting, but not warfare. The bald arithmetic tells the story. In the four months before internment – April to July 1971 – four soldiers were killed, no policemen and four civilians. In the four months after it – August to November – thirty soldiers were killed, eleven members of the RUC and the Ulster Defence Regiment, and seventy-three civilians. Stormont stolidly maintained that without internment things would have been worse. It could only be a matter of assertion.

Still more serious for the survival of Northern Ireland as a governable state was the depth and permanence of the Catholic community's estrangement from the régime. By mid-December, 1,576 people had been arrested by the Army under the Special Powers Act. That meant almost the same number of households – virtually all of them Catholic – which had experienced the actual shock of the arrest, often in the early hours of the morning and often without much personal tenderness displayed: households which were thereafter without the member who was in many cases their main source of livelihood, and which had no idea how long the deprivation would last.

The fact that of those 1,576, no fewer than 934 had (by mid-December 1971) already been released did little to ease this rising mass of resentment. To the families and friends of the released men, it only indicated a chilling carelessness about the way the lists had been drawn up; and the released men themselves seldom came back as tolerant of the régime as they had gone in.

The misuse of internment powers became one of the most potent forces driving moderate Catholics away from the middle ground and, in many cases, into the arms of the IRA. The IRA was well aware of the potential for exploitation. It could not suceed, however, without the Army's apparent readiness to pick people up on the basis of nothing more substantial than an anonymous phone call or vague local gossip. The case of Kevin Duffy illustrates vividly how these tactics can rebound.

Kevin Duffy, an articulate twenty-one-year-old joiner, was lifted at six o'clock on the evening of 2 September. He was watching television in his home at Moy, a village some forty miles from Belfast, when his mother – who was, at the time, under heavy sedation for a nervous complaint – screamed out that there were soldiers all round the house. As the troops, from the 2nd Light Infantry, loudly debated whether to kick the front door in, Mrs Duffy became hysterical. Kevin opened the door, identified himself and was immediately arrested under the Special Powers Act and

270

driven off at speed to Dungannon. Local Protestants laughed and jeered outside the Duffy house.

Kevin Duffy had never been a member of either wing of the IRA, or even of the Republican Party. He had never been connected with any of the Civil Rights groups. His sole 'qualifications' for arrest and possible internment seem to have been membership of the Gaelic Association – where he learned Gaelic, played Gaelic football and studied the history of Eire – and his religion. The Duffys were Catholics.

The most worrying thing about Duffy's arrest, however, was the extent to which Army intelligence seems to have backfired. Kevin's father, John Duffy, a fifty-five-year-old sales manager, was one of the best known and most respected men in the district. For the last five years he had been chairman of the Moy Citizens' Relations Committee, the first purely local group ever established in Ulster to try and bring Catholics – who are in a small minority there – and Protestants closer together. Through a variety of civic projects and social gatherings, the Committee under John Duffy had made considerable progress in improving community relations in Moy. Two years before, for instance, when the local cinema folded, the committee bought it up, refitted it and offered it free to any firm looking for a factory.

Kevin Duffy appeared to have been lifted on the startlingly flimsy basis that, in the words of the RUC Special Branch man who interrogated him, 'There are reports from local people that you are leading young people astray.' What grounds existed for this allegation, Duffy was totally unable to discover. It might have been because there was a steady stream of Catholics into the Duffy house, which was something of a sports and social centre for them. Certainly the Army and the RUC were unable to produce a shred of evidence that Duffy was a potential candidate for internment.

After his arrest, Duffy was taken to Dungannon

271

Territorial Army camp: he was not physically ill-treated, but on arrival he was threatened and sworn at. He was then rushed to the RUC station and left in a damp, freezing cell for two hours: a doctor who passed him 'fit for detention' took no notice of a finger broken in two places and still in plaster. Duffy's interrogation was unsophisticated: 'We know you are an IRA man, so why not tell us? You will eventually.'

The next day he was taken to Holywood Barracks, the only prisoner in a convoy of six armoured vehicles and a police car; an Army officer sat pointing a cocked pistol at his chest throughout the trip. The only rough treatment Duffy received was at Holywood, where he claims that two Military Policemen slammed him against a wall and forced him to do sixty minutes of vigorous exercises which hurt his damaged finger intensely. He was interrogated again, this time by a plain clothes man with a British accent. 'We have proof you are in the IRA,' he was told. 'We can do what we want with you.' He got his first meal thirty hours after being lifted: it was 'slop'.

Duffy was subsequently transferred to the Maidstone prison ship, where he saw his detention order for the first time. On Wednesday 9 September he was called to the office of the Deputy Governor and asked 'If I was your fairy god-mother, what would you ask me for?' He got it – immediate release.

'I really was a moderate before all this,' Duffy said later. 'I had no interest in politics and didn't like the methods the IRA used. Living in my house, you saw that Catholics and Protestants *could* live together peacefully. But everything has changed now.' He was not going to rush out and take up a gun, but his attitudes had changed, at least to the extent that he no longer condemned the IRA for its violent methods.

'How many other people like me have been lifted and are

272

still inside, or got beaten up or lost their jobs while they were being held?' (Duffy lost his.) Duffy's father, the dedicated mediator, was in hospital: his collapse, the family insisted, was mainly due to the arrest of Kevin. 'I don't think he'll change his views when he comes out, but many other Catholics here will be much more wary about trusting the Protestants after this.'

The Army's ham-handedness was the IRA's opportunity. The Provisionals were enabled to extend their influence to communities where they had not exerted it before, and to recover it where they felt in danger of losing it. Indeed, they positively used the Army for that purpose; and the Army allowed themselves to be used. Take the case of the Ardoyne telephone hoax.

The operation began with an anonymous phone call to the Green Howards' headquarters in an ageing mill in Flax Street. The caller gave six names at five addresses in the Ardoyne: these houses, he reported, might be sheltering Provisional gunmen. At dawn the next morning, 19 September, a squad of paratroopers – not noted for their restraint in house searches – drove up in three Saracens, sealed off the streets involved and arrested six men. In full view of a large and angry crowd, the men's hands were tied behind their backs and bags placed over their heads.

The call to the Army was made by a member of the Provisional IRA. (We have talked to the man who made it.) Its purpose was, quite simply, to create trouble between security forces and Ardoyne residents. For the Ardoyne was worrying Provisional leaders: over the previous few weeks they had seen their support in the area – once rock-solid – steadily and severely eroded. This arose partly from a genuine improvement in relations between the Green Howards – responsible for the area – and local residents. Street rioting had virtually stopped.

273

More significantly, at about the same time, the Provisionals were beginning to feel the effects of a wave of revulsion caused by their indiscriminate bombing of crowded buildings in Belfast. The explosion at the Electricity Board premises in August – which had killed one youth and maimed several teenage girls – and four more in the city centre in September, had filled the newspapers with pictures of terrified, hysterical office workers, many of them Catholics. The reaction against the Provisionals became even more bitter when, on 2 September, a stray Provisional bullet killed eighteen-month-old Angela Gallagher – from a Catholic family – during an ambush in Belfast. The Provisionals' tactics were fiercely denounced by the senior bishops of the Catholic church and by the more courageous Civil Rights campaigners.

The most worrying effect on the Ardoyne Provisionals was to deprive them of many formerly 'safe' houses in the area. Until then, gunmen could frequently avoid the Army by passing freely from one house to another in the maze of tightly-packed terraced homes: it is part of IRA legend that there was always a flask of tea and a plate of sandwiches waiting on the kitchen table. Now more and more front doors were being locked at night.

By contrast, the Army claimed to be benefiting from a greatly increased flow of information about IRA activities from disenchanted Catholics. From mid-September, it intensified its swoops on houses suspected of harbouring IRA men. How true the Army's claims really were is hard to assess: the identities of those they arrested in this particular incident in the Ardoyne suggests they were ready to act on decidedly flimsy grounds.

At 67 Northwick Drive, for instance, James McCann and his son, Seamus, were taken. McCann was in his fifties and had for several years suffered from a serious heart complaint

which had kept him off work: he had to be helped into the
vehicle. Seamus was mentally handicapped, although it was
not always apparent from his appearance. Hugh Martin was
arrested at 7 Eskdale Gardens: he was a former British Army
regular and was a prisoner-of-war in Germany for four
years. His wife had had several nervous breakdowns since
the troubles began. She was screaming after the troops left
with her husband.

Dermot McCarthy and two brothers, Daniel and Joseph
McStravick, were taken from adjacent houses in Holmdene
Gardens. The McStravicks' mother fainted from shock
when her sons were arrested. She fell against the front door
from inside and neighbours had to clamber in through a
window to calm her.

The six 'fall guys' had been carefully chosen. They were
all well-known in the area and, in a tight-knit community
like this, family circumstances like the McCanns' retarded
son and Mrs Martin's breakdowns were common knowledge. Equally, most Ardoyne Catholics had a shrewd idea
who the local IRA men were. They were adamant that none
of the six men were in any way involved. Insight's own in-
vestigators confirmed this. So apparently, did the Army's:
all six were released within a couple of hours.

By then, though, it was too late. Anger and bitterness had
returned, and people were once again out on the streets.
Lurid rumours about the decrepit condition of the lifted
men were already doing the rounds. One man, on local hear-
say, described the arrests as 'like a bloody procession to
Lourdes'.

A Green Howards spokesman later offered an interesting
interpretation of the incident. 'We acted on information
given by a resident of the Ardoyne ... When the men were
identified and we discovered they were not who we wanted,
they were released. In this case our information was wrong,

but it came from a single source, so we haven't made three mistakes.'

Three weeks after the incident, on 11 October, Tom Conaty, chairman of the Central Citizens' Defence Committee, and Father Padraig Murphy, one of the most influential Catholic priests in Belfast, complained to the Army about the clumsiness of the operation. At a stormy, four-and-a-half-hour meeting with General Tuzo, General Robert Ford and Howard Smith, the latest British representative in Ulster, they pointed out that the IRA could and would exploit this sort of situation with great enthusiasm. 'Would it interest you to know,' Father Murphy asked, 'that I have been reliably told that the phone call was a bum Provisional tip-off?' Neither General replied.

Without happenings like this, the Provisionals' own disregard of civilian life – Catholic as well as Protestant – might have been more noticed, and have done them more harm in Catholic areas. There is evidence that the Provisional high command was not merely prepared to see innocent civilians arrested and interrogated for its own ends: it was also prepared to see them shot. In at least one attested incident, gunmen appear to have used local citizens who had absolutely no connection with them as human cover for an attack on the troops.

Late in October, a young Belfast Catholic called Peter McAnespie was driving down the Falls Road with his wife and their three small children. As they approached the junction with Grosvenor Road, McAnespie saw that a hijacked bus had been set on fire, and that troops were attempting to disperse the crowd. Deciding to by-pass the trouble, he turned right up Clonard Gardens, a small side street. As he did so, a cherry-coloured Austin 1100 stopped in front of him: he overtook it and pulled into O'Neill Street, which runs parallel to the Falls Road. As he approached the Lshaped junction of O'Neill and Waterford Street, he noticed two men standing on either side of the road; they had a clear view down to the Falls Road where the troops were standing.

At the precise moment when McAnespie's car was neatly framed in the crossing, one of the men stepped forward, produced an automatic rifle and fired a burst of five shots at the troops 100 yards away at the end of Waterford Street. One soldier from the Royal Scots Guards was hit in the leg. The gunman then walked to the 1100 – which had slowly followed McAnespie along – threw the rifle in the back seat and climbed into the car. It reversed to the corner of Clonard Street, where the gunman got out and walked casually down towards the Falls Road. The 1100 drove off in the opposite direction with the rifle. The incident took less than thirty seconds.

It was a brilliantly executed operation. Had the Scots Guards returned the fire, they would almost certainly have hit the McAnespies' car, stranded in the middle of the road only 100 yards away. In a tiny Fiat containing five people – three of them young children – the results could have been catastrophic, both in terms of immediate casualties and Army public relations. Meanwhile the gunman, having disposed of his weapon in a fashion strikingly similar to that used by Algerian guerrillas in the film 'Battle of Algiers', could confidently expect to get clear of the area without trouble.

If these brief passages of arms had been better understood at the time, the Provisionals' standing in the community might have suffered. As it was, the real safeguard of their reputation as the Catholics' shield and buckler was the regularity with which the Army continued to give Catholics real or fancied offence. This was not merely a matter of questionable arrests: it was also a matter – or so the Catholics suspected – of allowing terrorists (and therefore by implication the surrounding Catholic community) to take the blame for the Army's own mistakes.

Mrs Sarah Worthington, a fifty-year-old widow with nine children, was the first woman to be shot dead in the Ulster crisis. She died on the night of 10 August during the vicious street fighting that erupted in Belfast following the announcement of internment. On the night she died, the RUC put out a terse statement that Mrs Worthington had been taken to hospital and was dead on arrival from a gun-shot wound. But subsequently Belfast papers described her as being killed by 'a terrorist sniper'. She was one of the few Protestants living in that particular area – the Valsheda Park Estate, on the fringe of the Ardoyne.

At the time, local residents insisted that a Protestant gunman had been firing down into the street from Berwick Gardens: there was, however, at least one IRA sniper operating in the area as well. As far as could be ascertained, neither the police nor the Army added anything at the time to the first short statement about Mrs Worthington's death.

So it was disconcerting when, almost exactly three months after Mrs Worthington died, the Army announced that – far from dying at the hands of an unknown sniper – she had been killed by a soldier in the Green Howards. At the inquest on 4 November, Private 'A' (his name was withheld for his own protection) told how he had gone into the Worthingtons' house looking for snipers. He had shouted to see if anyone was there, but received no reply. Then as he warily moved through the house he was startled by a sudden movement behind him. 'His military instinct took over, and he fired from the hip,' the inquest was told: on examining the body, he discovered it was a woman's.

Mrs Worthington's son, Cecil, alleges that he went back

to the house to see if his mother was all right: a soldier there refused to let him in, but through a broken window he saw her body lying near the kitchen door.

There is no question that Mrs Worthington's death was a genuine and tragic accident: the Green Howards had been under continuous sniper fire and must have been understandably edgy. But it is also beyond question that the Army must have known within a few hours, if not sooner, that she was shot by a soldier. It is inconceivable that Private 'A' did not immediately report the incident to a superior.

The Army's motives in concealing the true facts for three months are uncertain. It is quite conceivable that the authorities decided that a potentially controversial accident like this was the last thing they wanted in the bitter aftermath of the post-internment fighting. In three months' time, it could be argued, the matter could be dealt with in a far less emotive atmosphere. Yet precisely because the Army did not come clean straight away, there were plenty of Catholics in Belfast who believed – probably wrongly – that the authorities had really hoped to hush the whole thing up and leave Mrs Worthington as the victim of an unidentified gunman. And in Belfast, a belief of that kind becomes itself a fact to be reckoned with.

Chapter 17
Death of the State

By the end of 1971 the most sensitive single issue raised by British military involvement in Ulster had emerged: that of the Army's conduct there. Most British newspapers, indeed, found the mounting allegations so incendiary that they ignored them, or confined their concern to the events over the forty-eight hours of 9–10 August 1971, following the introduction of internment. Even the most formal of those inquiries was, as we shall see, in many respects inadequate. Yet it was undeniable that any research among the Catholics of Belfast in 1971 quickly revealed that their growing hostility throughout that year towards the Army was – they themselves felt, at any rate – influenced in large measure by the Army's own behaviour. It was surely necessary, therefore, to examine this.

Certain points were immediately apparent. The Army was behaving with incomparably greater restraint than, say, the French in Algeria or the Americans in Vietnam. Ulster had no My Lai nor yet, to summon ghosts from Britain's past, an Amritsar incident. That, of course, was irrelevant to the people of Ulster. Yet it had also to be recognized that this restraint was the more remarkable because the troops were under a strain inconceivable to those who had not experienced urban guerrilla warfare. In August 1971 the medical officer of the First Battalion, the Duke of Wellington's, analysed the effects of this tension: 'You can either become an over-the-trenches-and-straight-at-them, suicide-type thing. That's one way. The other way is to just sit there completely quiet – not aware of anything, not responding.' He spoke of a trooper actually paralysed by anxiety, of another who broke into 'very fearful screaming – terrified ...' Cases like those were rare. But anyone talking to soldiers on the streets could sense their strain and, frequently, their sheer exhaustion. (The mental damage among the populace was little explored.)

It was equally apparent that, by 1971, the Army resented and was bewildered by what it saw as an irrational change in the Catholics' attitude. 'When we came here,' a corporal brooded a few days before internment, 'I suppose eighty per cent of us were in favour of the Catholics. But now ...' A considerably more senior officer made the same point: 'The reason for the trouble is that the Catholics have been perfectly bloody. If they had been nice quiet people, the Army would have been nice quiet people.' But this purest expression of notional military quietism ignored the facts, also significant in assessing the Army's conduct, that throughout 1971 a lot of soldiers were injured in riots, and that the shooting of troops from February onwards understandably incensed the dead men's comrades.

Having said all that, however, a good deal of inquiry produced the tentative conclusions, first, that the Army had through 1971 increasingly used physical violence in circumstances which did not warrant it; and second, that the Catholics' awareness of this – and their inevitable exaggeration of its frequency and severity – was a major factor in securing a popular base for the Provisionals. Perhaps the Army did no more than behave like an Army, and a more disciplined

281

one than most. But the questions which then arose were those posed by Sir Arthur Young; they went to the heart of the Ulster crisis. Should the Army ever have been asked to play the role it now occupied? Was the United Kingdom seeking a military solution to the crisis at a moral price too high to be acceptable?

The two main sources on which conclusions about the Army's conduct might reliably be based were medical reports, and evidence accepted or proven in court.

There was also the testimony of lawyers. It was hard to dismiss merely as propagandists, for instance, the four solicitors who in August 1971 claimed to have watched a tall blond lieutenant of about twenty-five force an ageing Pakistani (in no way involved in trouble, they said) to spreadeagle himself against a wall in the street for so long – almost forty minutes, they said – that the old man collapsed a couple of times.

Nor was it possible to ignore the opinion of a consultant at one Belfast hospital who, asked by a lawyer to examine an accused man – and knowing from past experience, he said, that the Army explanation for injuries visible on a suspect in court was commonly that the man must have fallen – looked at this suspect's battered feet and remarked: 'I suppose this man fell ... into a mincing machine.'

The pattern which the available evidence suggested was not one of systematic brutality. It was, rather, of an angry soldiery venting its frustrations upon those it suspected of causing trouble – and, as the year progressed on its bloody path, drawing this category of supposed 'trouble-makers' wider and wider.

One of the earliest cases of 1971, that of Samuel Howell, was typical. Howell, a Protestant, was arrested on 23 January during trouble on the Shankill in which two policemen were hurt. He later claimed that he had been kicked, beaten and batoned while in the Army depot after arrest. He said that he had been forced to lie on the floor and, while one soldier had stood on his hands, another had kicked his face. A doctor, Desmond Hall, testified in court that when Howell was released from Army custody his nose was so broken, bruised and bleeding that Howell had to spend five days in hospital for an operation to relieve his breathing. He also had cuts or bruises on his skull, neck, back, thighs and testicles. Hall said that at least sixteen to seventeen blows would have been needed to inflict these – 'consistent with having been beaten up', he concluded. The riotous behaviour charge against Howell was dismissed.

The apparent manhandling of Howell came in the aftermath of a riot. The case of Patrick Higgins could similarly be explained in terms of over-wrought soldiers doling out summary justice – except that Higgins appeared to be innocent of anything save the error of not running when faced with a squad of Highland Fusiliers around 5.20 p.m. on 20 May.

There had been trouble around the New Lodge Road that day. But when Higgins – a quiet, slight, ex-seaman of thirty-eight, then just out of hospital after ten months' treatment for tuberculosis – left his home to visit his mother, there were still crowds about, but little unrest. According to Higgins and several witnesses, a squad of soldiers suddenly jumped him and beat him to the ground. When Higgins was taken to the Mater Hospital a couple of hours later, he was detained for six days. The consultant's report mentioned five stitches in his forehead, two in a scalp cut, severe bruising of his forearm, and abrasions and bruising around the spine. The doctor commented that had Higgins been in work, he would have been off for a month. (At the end of 1971, Higgins still had headaches, a stiff back and blurring in his right eye.)

The oddest feature of the case was that Higgins was charged with disorderly behaviour only six weeks later – after he had filed a civil claim for damages. The magistrate dismissed the criminal charge even before Higgins had called any witnesses.

Outside of riot situations, however, fear seemed still to motivate much of the Army's behaviour. The cases of James Goodman and Robert Elliman demonstrated the point. On the night of 13 June the Army raided a Republican drinking club in east Belfast. The troops were tense after a day of hand-to-hand fighting with Protestants who, in the course of an illegal parade, had tried to storm an Army barricade in Derry. (The three Protestants arrested were later released.)

Explaining the raid in Belfast, the Army said that it followed an explosion: they suspected that a bomb-thrower had taken refuge in the club. But there were twenty-seven men there and only a handful of troops. The soldiers took no chances: the men were made to squat for about an hour on the pavement. Goodman refused a command to do press-ups, and later claimed that he was then beaten up. Elliman also refused, and said afterwards that a soldier had taken him into the club toilet and beaten his head against a tap. The doctors' reports on both men were a detailed catalogue of cuts and bruises, in one case 'consistent with blows from a blunt instrument', in the other 'consistent with beating'.

By July 1971, though, Belfast doctors – by now concerned at the state of some of their patients – claimed to detect a more sweeping attitude among the police and military towards 'trouble-makers' deserving summary punishment. The doctors' evidence for this view does not need reciting in detail. But there was, for example, the eighteen-year-old apprentice baker out with his girl-friend in the Falls Road, pulled in by an Army patrol when he refused to tell them

Death of the State

what he was laughing at. On his release from Springfield
Road police station, he had a black eye, a swelling over his
right temple and large bruises on his left cheek-bone and
over his right kidneys – consistent, his doctor said, with the
youth's story of having been batoned.

There was the twenty-one-year-old patient of the same
doctor who, witnesses agreed, went out of his way to avoid
an area of trouble one day in the Lower Falls. He too was
picked up – and left Springfield Road station with bruises on
his buttocks and genitals.

Other cases could be cited: Fleming, McCogan, Murphy,
McLaughlin, McKavanagh, Rooney, McClean. In the case
of nineteen-year-old Raymond McLaughlin a doctor actually saw the beating, since it happened outside his front
window. In the others, the only reliable evidence remained
the medical reports, consistent in each case with the men's
stories of beatings at the hands of the military.

The case of Arthur Murphy was unusual in that he was
examined by a doctor – called in by the local MP, Paddy
Devlin – *before* he was released from Springfield Road
station. Murphy had been the passenger in a van which
backfired outside the police station on 7 August. A soldier
on sentry duty there thought he heard a shot, fired at the
driver, Harry Thornton, and blew half his head away.
Murphy, in a state of shock, was taken into the station. He
emerged from interrogation with severe bruises all over his
face, a bad black eye, a cut over his left eye which an Army
doctor had had to stitch, and a fractured cheek-bone.
Murphy claimed that, with a soldier grasping each arm, he
had been pulled face-first into a concrete pillar.

Those cases mostly arose in what could have been called
'action situations'. But the soldiers' everyday hostility
seemed in the main reserved for Catholic teenagers – who
were in other contexts, of course, the most ardent rioters.

One Belfast GP told us in August, and his comment was
echoed by six other doctors with him:

The soldiers seem to go for these young fellows and beat
them round the legs. That would be the main thing, and the odd
bruise around the face.

But he added:

One has seen many of these young lads who have been beaten
up. If they are lifted at all, they get a hammering. You take that
for granted. In recent weeks, at any rate, I have yet to see
anyone who was lifted who didn't get a hammering – even
fellows who haven't been charged.

It was possible, of course, that this somewhat casuistic
approach placed too much reliance upon doctors and medical evidence. One anecdote illustrates the futility of any
other method.

On the evening of internment day, 9 August, a prolonged
gun-battle took place on the Ballymurphy estate between
paratroopers sandbagged into the Henry Taggart Memorial
Hall and snipers in various hiding places around it. The
most famous casualty was a Catholic priest, Father Mullan.
But three other people were killed, and half a dozen
wounded – among them an eleven-year-old boy, castrated
by a high-velocity bullet.

At the time, reporters from Insight investigated that
shooting match in some detail. But how many snipers there
had been, and how many deaths had been caused by them
and how many by the Army's response, could not be determined. The attack did appear to have been less coordinated
than the Army believed at the time. On the other hand, certain bullet tracks visible round the Henry Taggart Hall suggested that at least one sniper must have been behind a
hedge only a few yards from the home of the man later most

286

vociferous in his complaints of Army shooting. The castrated child had been caught in the cross-fire: when he ran by the hedge for cover, the Army pardonably mistook him for a gunman.

But among those caught in that same cross-fire was David Callaghan, a fifty-nine-year-old retired postal engineer with chronic asthma. Crouching on open ground between the Army and that hedge-bound sniper, he was winged by a bullet. During a lull in the firing, the paratroopers sent an armoured personnel carrier to bring Callaghan and other casualties into the Henry Taggart Hall.

Callaghan's subsequent description of his treatment inside the hall – part savage, part kind – was convincing. He said that he was beaten behind the ear with a rifle butt as he was dragged in; yet he was also given tea and had his wound dressed. He related one chilling incident, however. While two soldiers held his legs apart, he said, a third had kicked him carefully and hard in the testicles.

We approached the major commanding the paratroopers in the battle. He was intelligent, sympathetic, highly professional, and clearly genuinely shocked by Callaghan's allegations. Callaghan, he said, had blessed them for bringing him in – which Callaghan agreed. 'We didn't have to risk our necks for him,' the major said. 'God, you can do nothing for these people.' The story, in fact, seemed merely to have confirmed yet another soldier in his dislike of Catholics.

In perplexity, we approached Callaghan's doctor, Damien Beirne. Callaghan had been taken by the Army directly from the Henry Taggart Hall to hospital, where he was examined. Dr Beirne told us his injuries, mainly cuts – 'And, of course,' he said, 'his testicles are still in a sling after two weeks. They were swollen to twice normal size. Didn't he tell you?'

Those who chose not to give weight to such evidence fre-

quently asked why, if their cases were so strong, those allegedly beaten did not file suit for damages. The answer was
that several of them did just that. But by August 1971 the
courts and the Army were so enmeshed that it was understandable when many Catholics assumed such matters were
better not pursued – an assumption fortified by the experience of Higgins and others, charged with criminal offences
only after they had opened civil proceedings. It was not
merely that the magistrates' courts were so clogged with
cases hingeing upon military testimony that the court-
building in Chichester Street looked daily more like a
barracks than a hall of justice. Nor was it merely that, however numerous a defendant's witnesses, one soldier's unsup-
ported evidence was commonly accepted in preference to
theirs. The interlocking of the Army and the courts went
deeper than this – as an incident at Ballymurphy illustrated.

In the small hours of 11 August, just forty-eight hours
after internment began, troops descended upon two roads
on the estate, Glenalina Road and Glenalina Park, and arrested thirty-one men – the bulk of their adult male population. They were taken to Girdwood Barracks, one of the
three 'holding centres' in the internment sweep, and there
they were questioned. Their subsequent allegations about
their treatment corresponded to the complaints of those detained on 9 August; but that was not the most significant
feature of those thirty-one cases.

Next day, Thursday 12 August, the thirty-one appeared in
court charged with riotous behaviour. The magistrates, at
the request of the prosecution, refused bail. The circumstances of these cases were so strange, however – precisely
when the riotous behaviour was supposed to have occurred
was in some doubt, for instance – that the solicitors at the
courts issued a formal warning that unless bail were granted
they would walk out as a body and refuse to practise in the

courts again. At this, the prosecution retreated: bail would be opposed only in eight 'particularly serious' cases.

In the succeeding days and weeks, all thirty-one cases went through the courts. The prosecution dropped *every single case*, even the eight 'particularly serious' ones. All defendants were awarded costs.

It seemed a baffling affair, until a senior Army officer explained to us: 'We just wanted to pick up these fellows to question them, and run a bit of a check on the successes and failures of the internment sweep,' he said. The charges were a necessary legal formality. To this the courts of Ulster had come.

*

The grievances against the Army which most inflamed the Catholic population of the whole province were the ones which arose from the growing belief that the men in detention or internment were being ill-treated. Within a few days of the 9 August internment sweep, charges to this effect began to filter out of Crumlin Road jail and Long Kesh camp – the two main centres where the men were held – through the agency of lawyers and priests who had been able to visit them.

By mid-August the charges, properly sanitized with quotation marks, began to appear in the British press. They were more fully reported in parts of the Irish press – several Dublin papers, notably the *Irish Times*, and specifically Catholic papers in the north. The *Tyrone Democrat*, for example, a weekly paper published in Dungannon and Coalisland, carried in its 19 August issue – with a page one heading which read 'Warning! Don't Read This If You Have A Weak Stomach ...' – an eight-page pullout filled with statements by men who had been arrested, and with reports of resulting local agitation. (The same issue of the paper had on its back page a lavishly illustrated report of the unveiling

289

of a memorial to an IRA volunteer who had been killed in 1921.)

The statements spoke of rough arrests in the small hours ('I was pulled by the hair onto the street, batoned on the head and kicked on the leg'), sectarian abuse on the ensuing journey ('Your Virgin Mary was the biggest whore in Bethlehem'), and various forms of maltreatment between bouts of questioning at their destinations (which were in fact holding centres at Magilligan in County Derry, Ballykinler in County Down or Girdwood Park in Belfast). Men who went to Ballykinler complained of exhausting exercises harshly enforced. At Girdwood, related Henry Bennett, a twenty-five-year-old Belfast man:

I was forced to run over broken glass and rough stones to a helicopter without shoes. I spent only fifteen seconds in the helicopter and I was then pushed out into the hands of military policemen. I was forced to crawl between these policemen back to the building. They kicked me on the hands, legs, ribs and kidney area . . .

Although at Westminster Parliament was not sitting, and repeated Labour pleas were not enough to get it recalled until several weeks later, a growing uneasiness about these charges finally persuaded Reginald Maudling, as Home Secretary, to appoint a committee of inquiry to look into them. Its chairman was Sir Edmund Compton, a man well used to the investigation of complaints and malpractices. A Treasury civil servant by training, he had been successively appointed Comptroller and Auditor-General, Ombudsman for Britain, and Ombudsman for Northern Ireland, a post he held till the end of 1971. His two colleagues on the committee were Edgar Fay, a QC who was also Recorder of Plymouth, and Dr Ronald Gibson, who had until recently been chairman of the BMA Council.

The committee was appointed on 31 August. Its terms of reference were:

To investigate allegations by those arrested on 9 August under the Civil Authorities (Special Powers) Act (Northern Ireland) 1922 of physical brutality while in the custody of the security forces prior to either their subsequent release, the preferring of a criminal charge or their being lodged in a place specified in a detention order.

The three men, with a Home Office official and a Whitehall lawyer to help them, went at once to Northern Ireland, where they made their headquarters for eight weeks at the Conway Hotel outside Belfast. But on 17 October, nine days before they returned to London, a report in the *Sunday Times* greatly enlarged the significance of the whole inquiry. The paper reported statements smuggled out of prison from eleven named men who claimed to have been interrogated for up to six days by methods calculated to drive them, at least temporarily, out of their minds.
'During the period of their interrogation,' the report ran,

they were continuously hooded, barefoot, dressed only in an over-large boiler suit, and spread-eagled against a wall – leaning on their fingertips like the hypotenuse of a right-angled triangle. The only sound that filled the room was a high-pitched throb, which the detainees usually liken to an air compressor.

The paper's report claimed that these 'disorientation techniques' were taught at the Joint Services Interrogation Centre ('whose location is an official secret'), and that the place where they were practised in Northern Ireland was Palace Barracks, Holywood – a little way down Belfast Lough from the city.

The Compton committee was confined, by its terms of

reference, to the cases of men who had been arrested on 9 August. The eleven had indeed been arrested on that date. But the *Sunday Times* report also carried statements from one man arrested on 17 September – Bernard McGeary – and another arrested on 11 October, both later released. The second man, a Queen's University student called Tony Rosato, also mentioned a third who was being interrogated at the same time as him: William Shannon.

Despite a submission by Brian Faulkner, on the telephone to Edward Heath, that the new charges were 'substantially without foundation', British ministers treated them with due gravity. Heath, Maudling and Carrington saw Wilson and Callaghan about them on the day after publication; and Maudling, eighteen days later, wrote to Compton to ask him

... to make inquiries within the security authorities operating in Northern Ireland in order to report to the Home Secretary on the interrogation of the three names mentioned in the *Sunday Times* issue of 17 September who were arrested at dates later than the 9 August arrest operation.

By that time the main body of the report was already being prepared for the printers; and when it was published twelve days later, on 17 November, the report of the second inquiry was produced as a separate addendum to the first.

The addendum, signed by Compton alone, found that the system in operation at the Police Holding Centre at Palace Barracks, Holywood, did not include any form of physical ill-treatment, and that there was no deviation from the general system in the cases of McGeary and Rosato. But Shannon had been ill-treated in the same way as the group of eleven men also mentioned in the *Sunday Times* piece. The substantive report, signed by Compton and his two colleagues, found that the main charges made about the treatment of the eleven – the posture on the wall (which one man had undergone for a total of forty-three and a half hours), the hooding, the continuous and monotonous noise, together with deprivation of sleep and of food and water – these were indeed true, and did constitute ill-treatment.

It will be noted [the report went on], that while we are asked to investigate allegations of physical brutality, our conclusions are in terms of physical ill-treatment. Where we have concluded that physical ill-treatment took place, we are not making a finding of brutality on the part of those who handled these complainants. We consider that brutality is an inhuman or savage form of cruelty, and that cruelty implies a disposition to inflict suffering, coupled with indifference to, or pleasure in, the victim's pain. We do not think that happened here.

The report did not say where *here* was. The addendum said that the interrogation centre was not the same place as the Police Holding Centre at Palace Barracks, but left open the possibility that it was in another part of the same barracks.

Compton had operated under difficulties. Of all the people arrested on 9 August, only one appeared before the committee. All the others rejected its invitations on the grounds that it sat in private and that there would be no opportunity for cross-examination of official witnesses. This prevented the committee from hearing any counter-argument to the evidence of the 139 Army and police witnesses who did appear.

It must nevertheless be said that, even within those limits, the report was not a wholly reassuring document. Perhaps because of excisions on security grounds, the report did not answer all the questions which might legitimately have been asked. It did not say how many others besides the eleven, if any, were subjected to 'deep interrogation'. It did not say who ran the interrogation centre – soldiers or policemen. It

Ulster

mentioned 'general rules governing the custody of detainees'; but it did not give those rules in full, nor did it say whose business it was to see that the rules were kept.

It was also a credulous report: credulous, at any rate, of official witnesses. It reported, without comment or apparent scepticism, the official submission that the fingertip posture on the wall 'provides security for detainees and guards against physical violence during the reception and search period and whenever detainees are ... awaiting interrogation'; that hooding, by preventing identification, 'provides security both for the detainee and for his guards'; that the continuous noise 'prevents their overhearing or being overheard by each other and is thus a further security measure'; and that a diet of bread and water 'may form part of the atmosphere of discipline'. (No official justification seems to have been put forward for depriving the men of sleep.) Of exercises at Ballykinler which were complained of as cruel, 'we prefer to take the view,' said the commissioners, 'that the exercises were devised to counteract the cold and the stiffness of which the arrested persons complained.'

The committee was disposed to believe that because a rule existed, it was therefore kept. Tony Rosato, the Queen's student, had spoken with great emphasis of an occasion at Palace Barracks when 'a blank cartridge out of something like a starting pistol' was fired just behind his head. 'My head seemed to jump three feet in front of me and leave the rest of my body stationary.' Compton had this evidence in writing (his second terms of reference did not require him to interview Rosato). He wrote in his subsidiary report:

This has been denied by all interviewers, who have pointed to the rule that all officers entering the Holding Centre must park their firearms at a central point for the duration of their stay, so that no firearms are carried by police during their duties at the Holding Centre.

He therefore concluded: 'I think the allegation improbable.'

Further, the main report reproduced – without seeking to refute it – the following official justification for the interrogation methods in general:

These methods have been used in support of the interrogation of a small number of persons arrested in Northern Ireland who were believed to possess information of a kind which it was operationally necessary to obtain as rapidly as possible in the interests of saving lives.

Yet if any such information was elicited, it does not seem to have invariably led the forces of order to the people they wanted: of the more than 1,500 people arrested within four months of the internment sweep, well over half were released again fairly quickly without charge. And Ministry of Defence figures show that arms, ammunition and explosive finds were at a scarcely higher level after than before internment, until there was a sharp rise in November – three months after the only acknowledged instances of 'deep interrogation'.

It is impossible to know whether these methods of interrogation continued after August. Compton's terms of reference were very restricted in point of date. By the time Maudling, on 5 November, had issued his subsidiary instruction to Compton to consider the allegations published in the *Sunday Times* on 17 October, the paper's issue of October 24 had already carried further sworn allegations of cruelty made by detainees: one of them was described by a psychiatrist who saw him after his release as still 'almost frozen with fear'. But Maudling made no direction that these should be looked at, and they were not. On 28 November in a report by Lewis Chester, the *Sunday Times* published still further allegations of cruelty by ten men whose

295

doctors said that their injuries were consistent with their stories. Eight of them had been arrested between 16 October and 2 November and the other two on 13 November and 18 November.

Another respect in which Compton's terms of reference were unhelpful is that they confined him to the investigation of *physical* brutality. The committee did not therefore consider the psychological effects of the 'deep interrogation' treatment, which some psychiatrists believe may be permanent and damaging (and may also be so severe at the time as to prevent the prisoner giving accurate answers even if he is disposed to). The 'rules' which the report published (they were said to have been issued in 1965, and revised in 1967 in the light of experience in Aden) prohibited 'outrages upon personal dignity, in particular humiliating and degrading treatment'; but the commissioners seem to have held that their terms of reference precluded their considering whether any such treatment had been meted out to the Ulster detainees, although several of them complained of something very like it.

Compton's only excursion into psychoanalysis was his insistence that brutality is in the mind of the perpetrator. Brutality was cruelty, he said, in effect, and cruelty must be deliberate, if not actually gloating. That element had not been present in the cases before him. ('A fat lot of comfort,' John Hume remarked, 'to the man at the receiving end.')

Still less did the three commissioners address themselves to the question of whether the State, as the guardian of law and civilized dealing, was justified or wise in subjecting to the routine described – a punishing routine, by any standards – men who were not proven criminals, and who were not even provenly in possession of the knowledge sought from them. Carrington publicly described the detainees as 'murderers'. In fact very few of them were ever charged with

296

any offence at all. They were not even confronted with a statement of the reasons for their detention. One of those given the 'hood treatment' was actually released afterwards, so little could the authorities find against him.

In sum, the Compton report left a number of questions unanswered and a number of anxieties unstilled. It nevertheless confirmed that citizens of the United Kingdom – innocent citizens, because not proved guilty – who were also Northern Ireland Catholics had been made to prop themselves against a wall by their fingertips, and to wear black hoods, and to hear frightening and deafening sounds, and to go without food and sleep, all for long periods. Whatever that meant for the moral health of the United Kingdom, its meaning for Northern Ireland Catholics was clear. Internment had been a grave injury: this was an irredeemable outrage. There could be no forgiveness for a state which did these things to their people. Its rulers could never be trusted again. For the great majority of Ulster Catholics, the State of Northern Ireland was dead.

Chapter 18
Outlook for Change

By the end of 1971 the signs of Catholic alienation from the régime were everywhere. Opposition MPs were not at Stormont. Most non-Unionist members of local councils and public bodies – even of the Derry Commission – had withdrawn from public work. An alternative assembly had met twice at Dungiven: it was not quite a parallel with the separatist beginnings of the Dail in 1919, but it was a deliberate sign from Catholic leaders that they saw no prospect of their community being governed from Stormont again. Over 20,000 Catholics, many of them members of the growing Catholic middle class, were taking part in a civil disobedience campaign: it mainly meant not paying rent and rates. The Stormont Government felt obliged to pass a Payments for Debt (Emergency Provisions) Act, which allowed sixteen different kinds of social security benefit to be withheld and set against the rent debt.

No appeal was possible. There was a certain justice in the measure, but families which had not saved the money they had withheld now found themselves grindingly poor. Again, the effect was widespread Catholic resentment.

Some reshuffling of the cards seemed indispensable – some redistribution of power which could make non-Unionists feel that their lives were not wholly in the hands of the Unionists and provide them with governing authorities whom they could respect, or at least tolerate.

The Unionist answer was that it had been done: the re-distribution of power had been contained in the reforms begun in 1968 and 1969, and now coming to completion. Nine days after the August internment moves, stung by sug-gestions from Dublin that the whole reform programme had been a sham, the Stormont Government reviewed and re-asserted its achievement in a white paper which it called 'A Record of Constructive Change'.

How much had in fact been done since those extra-ordinarily distant and different days when the first Civil Rights marchers took to the roads more than three years before?

The police, for a start, had been civilianized and removed from political control – during Young's year of office, which had ended in November 1970. It had been painful for the Unionists. 'What really sticks in their craw,' a very senior RUC man had said at that time, 'is that they know the Unionist Government can no longer give us orders. We are no longer the military arm of the Unionist party – the machinery for keeping Protestants on top.' This had been done by putting the RUC under the control of a Police Authority 'representative of the community as a whole'. The force had been disarmed, and the B Specials disbanded.

But Young had gone, and with him the independence which came from his having (as a personal Callaghan ap-pointment) a direct line to the Home Office in London. The Police Authority was largely staffed by the Home Affairs civil servants from Stormont who had administered the RUC before, and it had few powers to sack policemen. It was little heard from. During the 1971 disorders the RUC was progressively and inevitably re-armed.

The B men had gone. But numbers of them had kept their weapons: at least eight private gun clubs were known to have a membership made up entirely of old B men, and at least 100,000 firearms still remained lawfully in private Protestant hands. John Taylor, at the Home Affairs ministry, had virtually demanded the B men's reinstatement. Brian Faulkner himself, just before Christmas 1971, had given a measure of encouragement to the Protestant vigilantes – many of them old B men – who were appearing in ever increasing numbers on the streets of Belfast. They were to get official acceptance if they met certain conditions. They would not be armed; but many of them had guns at home anyway.

Two other notable reform commitments in the area of law enforcement were still un met. One was the appointment of a public prosecutor: while this duty lay with the police, they chose what charges to bring, what act to bring them under, whether to oppose bail, and what evidence to present; and the Catholic accusation was that they used this power to discriminate against Catholics. In the communiqué which Stormont ministers had issued in October 1969 while Callaghan stood over them, they had undertaken to appoint an independent public prosecutor. Fourteen months were then consumed by a working party; it made the same recommendation. Another five months went by – to May 1971: the Government confirmed the decision. Seven months after that, a little before Christmas 1971, a Prosecution of Offences Bill had its formal first reading at Stormont. But it would still be many months before a public prosecutor was established in his functions.

The other unredeemed pledge concerned the Special Powers Act. So far from having withdrawn the parts which conflicted with international obligations, the Stormont Government had deployed the power most offensive to international opinion – internment – on a bigger scale than ever before.

Besides a look at the Special Powers Act, the original O'Neill five-point plan of November 1968 had promised machinery for the investigation of grievances. This had been set up. Two acts passed during 1969 had established two separate offices: Parliamentary Commissioner for Administration, or Ombudsman, to examine grievances against central government; and Commissioner for Complaints, to do the same for local government.

In fact work in the two jobs had proved so light that from the beginning of 1972 it was found possible to combine them in a single man, John Benn, who had been Permanent Secretary to the Northern Ireland Ministry of Education before he became the first Commissioner for Complaints. But this could not be taken to show that there had been little to complain about. The basic trouble was that Acts required specific complaints; and it was always easy enough for a local council to produce reasons why it had not, for example, employed a particular Catholic as a clerk. What it might have had more difficulty in demonstrating was why it employed no Catholics as clerks, or very few; but the Commissioner for Complaints could not accept complaints of that general kind, and anyway – as Benn himself pointed out in his second report in that office – he had no power to make councils tell him what their employment ratios were, and often found them actively unhelpful.

Another O'Neill promise had been fair electoral representation for Catholics, which meant a wider local government franchise and more logical boundaries. The franchise was now put right. There could be no complaint about that. But council and ward boundaries were still unreconstructed; and for as long as they were, Catholics in Armagh and Omagh and Dungannon Urban Districts, and Dungannon Rural

301

District, and Fermanagh County, were still heavily under-represented. Yet while reconstruction was a prospect, there seemed no point in using the new franchise for elections (except a few by-elections) on the old boundaries.

Local government reform had been under desultory discussion in Northern Ireland since March 1966. By the end of June 1970 no fewer than three reports on the question had been published. Yet it was not till November 1971 that a bill was on its way through Stormont, providing for the number of councils to be reduced by more than half, and their functions rearranged. Work on redrawing ward boundaries within the new council boundaries was already in hand. The aim was to hold elections for the new councils in the autumn of 1972 (under the new franchise) and to install the new councils in the spring of 1973. Only then could reform begin to become a reality. The time-table was tight; and the disturbed state of the province made it tighter.

Stormont had also committed itself to a whole range of measures designed to make it as easy for Catholics to get jobs in the public service as Protestants. Many of these measures had been carried out. Employment in the Civil Service was open to the Ombudsman's inquiries. All or nearly all local councils and public bodies in the province had made a declaration that their aim was to have 'equality of employment opportunity without regard to religious or political considerations', and had adopted 'acceptable codes of employment procedure'. A permanent Local Government Staff Commission was written into the local government reform bill. From June 1971, an anti-discrimination clause formed part of all government contracts.

The powers to enforce these measures, though, were not there. The Ombudsman had the weakness already noticed: only particular complaints would do. The declaration and the codes were unenforceable. The Staff Commission's powers were to be advisory. To comply with the anti-discrimination clause, a contractor had to do no more than fill in an undertaking: if he then rejected a Catholic for being a Catholic, the only recourse against him would be a complaint from the rejected man, filtered through the man's MP, the Ombudsman and the department concerned – and the only sanction the possibility that the firm might not get another contract from that department.

In practical terms, the changes had not borne much fruit. Late in 1971 there were still no Catholics in senior posts in the establishment (i.e. personnel) divisions of any ministry, no Catholics in any minister's private office, no Catholics in the upper levels of the Ministry of Finance. Nearly every senior officer of the larger local authorities was a Protestant.

On the other hand, it has to be remembered that even if the fair recruitment of Catholics had begun as soon as Callaghan went back to London in October 1969, very few of them would yet have climbed to these levels in the service. It is also true that Catholics had sometimes been slow to put themselves forward for posts where they might have been welcomed. In the present mood of the Catholic community, that difficulty seemed likely to remain.

The much larger problem of unfair hiring by private firms was still untouched. A firm which kept the rules on its Government contracts could still discriminate against Catholics in the rest of its work. In certain industries, notably ship-building and printing, the senior trades were still regarded as Protestant preserves.

Things looked more hopeful in housing. True, the points scheme which Faulkner had imposed as Development Minister was still being operated, at the end of 1971, by unreconstructed councils. Some of them had found loopholes. Dungannon Rural District was one of a number of councils which had been allowed to divide its district into five areas: it was sometimes possible for a housing applicant in a Protestant area to be housed sooner than an applicant with many more points in a Catholic area. But in the course of 1972 all local councils were to lose their housing powers to the new Central Housing Executive, which had started work in May 1971.

The Executive had been slow in coming to birth, and its membership was clumsily chosen: Opposition MPs had been asked for names, but the Catholics on the Executive were not the ones they picked. Nevertheless, with new houses going up at a commendable rate, housing was an area where reform had a good chance of becoming a reality.

Finally, community relations. The Community Relations Commission had been active, said Stormont, 'in establishing a Community Development team, in convening conferences and in sponsoring research'. This could hardly have been harmful. The Community Relations Ministry had had one or two advisory tasks to discharge, and a little money to spend on social amenities in depressed urban areas. But bodies of this kind are only useful when they have perceptible reforms to build on, and the evident support of the authorities. The first Community Relations minister left the job in something like despair; the second was allowed to leave when no seat could be found for him in either House at Stormont.

One attempt at reform which had done nothing for community relations was the Prevention of Incitement to Hatred (Northern Ireland) Act. It became law in July 1970. The first prosecution under it was not brought until December 1971, when three men – among them John McKeague of the Shankill Defence League – were charged with publishing a song, 'I was born under the Union Jack', with intent to stir up hatred against Catholics. They were acquitted. Their counsel was Desmond Boal, who sits for the Shankill at Stormont. The job could probably have been done with equal success by a less able man than Boal. The Attorney-General had already acknowledged at Stormont in February that 'intent' was almost impossible to prove. Whether or not by mistake, the Bill had been so drafted as to be virtually useless.

That was broadly the extent of the reforms brought in by Stormont up to the end of 1971. A good deal of work had been got through. Not all of it, however, had been well done. Many of the measures lacked force and precision. An air of half-heartedness persisted. And aside from the appointment of a few Catholics (by Protestant choice) to public bodies, the problem of providing a sustained and significant Catholic voice in government was left untouched.

Faulkner's offer of committee chairmanships to the Opposition, in June 1971, had been a first stab at this problem. The offer had been rejected. The second was the 'Green Paper' produced, after many hiccups, at the end of October. It put forward three ideas: proportional representation (with a preference for a system known as the single transferable vote), a larger Stormont Commons, and a larger Senate (the upper House). All would probably result, if they were adopted, in more Catholic MPs at Stormont.

But they were only ideas. They were offered for discussion: there was no commitment. And one crucial idea was excluded even from discussion. There could be no question of having anyone in the Cabinet itself who had any other guiding belief except the indissoluble unity of Northern Ireland with Britain. Otherwise, Faulkner said, you would simply have 'a bedlam Cabinet – a kind of fragmentation bomb virtually certain to fly apart at the first meeting'. (It was an intriguing acknowledgement that any Cabinet discussion – whether about the economy, or agri-

305

culture, or tourism – was certain to come back to 'the constitutional question'. That was what Irish politics were really about.)

The day after the Green Paper was published, Faulkner – the compulsive balancer – put a Catholic into his Cabinet: Dr Gerard Newe. It had not happened in fifty years. But the Faulkner principle was maintained. Newe was that rare thing, a Catholic Unionist.

All these moves – the reform programme, the Green Paper, the Newe appointment – were based on the same premise: that the State of Northern Ireland could survive. The notion common to them all was that as long as adjustments were made, as long as the Catholics were admitted to the status of a substantial as distinct from a negligible minority, then things could go on much as before: Northern Ireland would remain to all intents and purposes a separate state, the British connection would endure, the south would thereby be kept at arm's length, and the blessed traditions of Westminster democracy would see to it that majority rule continued to mean uncontaminated Protestant rule.

Such calculations ignored the fact that the State was historically vitiated. The border was itself the first and biggest gerrymander: the six counties it enclosed, the new province of Ulster, had no point or meaning except as the largest area which the Protestant tribe could hold against the Catholic. Protestant supremacy was the only reason why the State existed. As such, the State itself was an immoral concept. It therefore had to be maintained from the first by immoral means – the fiddling of internal boundaries too, the steady pressure on Catholics to emigrate by making it hard for them to live and work, the police bullying ... And in the end the Army on the streets, internment, 'deep interrogation'. For the British, the tragedy was that – through historical obligation, and then through sloth and lack of perception – they became involved in the defence of a morally indefensible entity. For the Northern Ireland Catholics, the tragedy was that the British defence prolonged that entity's existence a few more, painful years. Nothing was more certain than that Catholics would continue to struggle against the State. They knew the evil in which it had been born and reared. And since evil begets evil, they were prepared to see their own struggle carried on by evil means.

A still more important point also followed. Since Protestant supremacy was the reason why the State was there at all, there was an essential philosophical contradiction about the notion of reform. Dismantle the apparatus of Protestant supremacy, and you have destroyed Northern Ireland's only justifications for being a State on its own. It might just as well not exist. That, in the end, although neither side may have formulated it in so many words, is why reform was half-heartedly proffered and mistrustfully received. It made no sense. It was out of character.

That, too, may have been part of the reason why late in 1971 Paisley himself, chaplain to the forces of no-surrender Protestantism and yet one of the most perceptive men in the north, began to make tentative sounds about the reunification of Ireland. Scrap the 1937 Constitution, he said in interviews with the *Irish Times* and Radio Telefís Eireann, and do away with the special position of the Roman Church, and we might look with different eyes on the Republic. Desmond Boal – the lawyer whom Paisley had first come to know twelve years before when Boal got him off with a £5 fine after he had thrown a bible at the ecumenical Methodist divine, Donald Soper, at Ballymena horse fair – began softly singing the same tune.

Faulkner, sure of his ground, attacked Paisley as 'the darling of the Republican press, wooed by Messrs Lynch and

Colley' (Lynch's Finance Minister). At least, that was what
the advance text of his speech said Faulkner would say. But
the speech was to be made to the Shankill Unionist Association; and on the platform in front of them, not quite so sure
of his ground, he left the line out. Paisley later backed off a
few steps. But Faulkner, by that little omission, had acknowledged that Paisley was a man who had a powerful
hold over his followers, and might lead them to strange
places.

The reunification dream depended to some extent on
Lynch, of course; and he – preoccupied with gaining entry
to the rich agricultural markets of the EEC, bruised by a
couple of encounters with an unyielding Heath at Chequers
in September, not certain in the last analysis that he would
find a million embattled Protestants digestible – preferred
the idea that the two factions in the north should kiss and be
friends among themselves before they came and asked to
join him. It earned him little credit with the hard men of his
own party, Fianna Fail; but it was at least a recognition that
there was very little positive reunifying influence which
Dublin could exert.

The steam behind the reunification idea had come most
recently from Harold Wilson, who was behaving at the end
of 1971 like a man who believed that an end of Britain's
Ulster problem was near. When he reshuffled his Shadow
Cabinet before Christmas, he took the Northern Ireland
portfolio himself – not the action of a politician who foresaw a further slow slide into the morass. After a quick visit
to Belfast and Dublin in November he had made a
Commons speech in which he had said:

I believe that the situation has now gone so far that it is
impossible to conceive of an effective long-term solution in
which the agenda at least does not include consideration of, and
which is not in some way directed to finding a means of achiev-

ing, the aspirations envisaged half a century ago of progress towards a united Ireland.

It was well wrapped up, but it was there. And Wilson also referred to a Guildhall speech of Edward Heath's at the beginning of the month, in which Heath had taken the first few hesitant steps along the same paths. Unification was not what the majority in Northern Ireland wanted today; but if they ever did, 'I do not believe any British Government would stand in the way,' said Heath.

Even that palpable truism could not have been safely enunciated by a British minister as little as three months before. The Protestant backlash had somehow begun to look less fearsome. The change of mood among Protestant hard-liners may only have been temporary, but it was perceptible. In September, before he spoke in Omagh on the same platform as Enoch Powell, Bill Craig had privately predicted that Faulkner would very soon publicly revert to being a right-winger in order to fight a General Election at the head of a united Unionist party and get a mandate to govern in the old pre-1969 ways. 'If Faulkner doesn't switch,' Craig said then, 'he'll be out by Christmas.' By Christmas, at any rate, Faulkner had not significantly altered his position; and he was still there.

It almost appeared, in December 1971, as if the thrust of British policy – more cunning than had hitherto been supposed – was to increase this new apathy in militant Protestant minds by increasing their bewilderment. On 15 December, leaving Belfast after a quick visit, Reginald Maudling told reporters that he could foresee a situation in which the IRA would 'not be defeated, not completely eliminated, but have their violence reduced to an acceptable level'.

The following day, after the predictable row at Stormont (in which Paisley and Boal had joined with gusto), Maudling

309

said that of course *previous* IRA violence had not been totally eliminated, but this time 'we must establish a situation in which no such campaign will occur again'.

An unintentional mistake, or an intentional attempt to reduce Protestants to such uncertainty about their own future that in the end they would be prepared to agree to anything?

These manoeuvrings could be construed as signs of hope. Yet the future was not hopeful. For the past three hundred years and more, there had been sectarian strife in Northern Ireland. For the past sixty years, the chosen remedy of successive British Governments had been to buy a partial peace by meeting at any rate the minimum demands of the sect which seemed prepared to make the most trouble, the Protestants. In the past three years this policy had been complicated by the threat of even greater trouble from the other side. In the past year, 1971, that threat had become a fierce reality. In the face of it, British policy had remained essentially the same: to embrace whatever expedient seemed at the time to offer the prospect of least pain. It was a search for soft options. Until that search was called off, the agony would continue.

Acknowledgements

Most of those who helped us asked not to be named. We can only express our gratitude for their anonymous patience and frankness. We also owe a debt to many of our professional colleagues; these we can name. On the *Sunday Times*, John Whale has directly aided us in the writing of parts of this book. Any present Insight team must also owe much to the professionalism of a previous editor, Bruce Page. We have benefited from the information and assessments of Tony Geraghty and Muriel Bowen of the news staff, and Murray Sayle and Peter Lennon of our features staff.

Among colleagues elsewhere, we must thank Vincent Browne, the able northern editor of the *Irish Press*, whose forthcoming history of the Provisionals should answer a lot of questions we have not been able to. Henry Kelly and his colleagues in the Belfast office of the *Irish Times* were unflaggingly helpful and hospitable. Dick Walsh of the *Irish Times* in Dublin can surely lay claim to know more about the byways of Irish politics than anyone except the participants.

We also owe much to the industry and ingenuity of Walter Macauley, chief librarian of the *Belfast Telegraph*. Arthur Green, secretary to the Scarman Tribunal, kindly made available to us volumes of useful evidence. Above all, we must thank the Army for its unfailing cooperation, particularly Colonel Tony Yarnold of the Lisburn press office who, within the limits of his orders, gave us every assistance – even when he knew he was likely to disagree with our conclusions.

None of these, of course, should be held responsible for any errors of selection, fact or judgement.

THE INSIGHT TEAM

31 December 1971

Index

Index

314

Index